Walking!

Walking!

by John T. Davis

ANDREWS AND McMEEL, INC.
A Universal Press Syndicate Company
KANSAS CITY

Line illustrations by Mark Weber

Library of Congress Cataloging in Publication Data

Davis, John T   1948 -
    Walking!
    Bibliography: p.
    1. Walking.   2. Physical fitness.   I. Title
GV199.5.D38   796.5'1   79-14354
ISBN 0-8362-2403-5
ISBN: 0-8362-2404-3 pbk.

To Alice Hartmann Davis

ACKNOWLEDGMENTS

I wish to thank my editor at Andrews and McMeel, Tom Drape, for his kind encouragement and astute editorial guidance; my researchers, John LaRoe and John Drape, for their substantial contributions to the book; Jean Lowe for her helpful editing; and the many walkers and walking organizations across the country that offered advice and information on the state of the art of walking in America.

Contents

1

Walking: The Natural Way to Fitness

If someone told you there was a way to improve your health, your mind, your appreciation of nature, and your perspective on life—almost effortlessly—and then added that the best medical authorities, some of the world's most famous people, and millions of ordinary men and women across the ages have sworn by it, what would your reaction be? I know what mine would be. I'd be skeptical. Like a Missourian, I'd say: "Show me."

Well, I'm talking about walking and I'm going to show you and, I hope, convince you that walking is worthy of consideration. It's sometimes overlooked because it's so simple, so obvious. Some people even say it's a lost art. I don't believe that. It may have been misplaced temporarily but it's never been lost. It's impossible to lose. Walking is what makes us human, separates us from our primate ancestors. The miraculous device known as the human stride is truly unique. It can do things for us that nothing else can.

Consider these facts.

Walking is the most popular form of exercise among adult Americans. Roughly 46 million of us walk regularly to keep in shape. That's somewhat astounding when you consider that only 66 million of us take any regular exercise at all. So nearly two out of three Americans who exercise do so by walking.

Walking is a proven method of strengthening your heart and lungs. When you walk on a regular basis, your heart becomes more efficient. Your circulation improves. Your ability to process oxygen is enhanced. Many authorities believe this conditioning of the cardiopulmonary system is a key tool in the fight against heart disease.

Walking has been shown in some studies to be more effective than running in producing physical fitness because walking results in fewer injuries which can either interrupt a training regimen or end it altogether.

Walking is believed to be the safest form of exercise because it is progressive. You can begin by walking slowly for short periods of time and gradually increase your speed and distance. It's hard to hurt yourself while walking. For this reason, walking is often recommended for people who are suffering from heart disease or are recovering from heart attacks.

Walking is the most natural form of locomotion. Human beings are the most prodigious walkers of all the creatures on earth. Babies are born with a walking·reflex. It's the first motor skill we want to do and the last one we want to give up.

Walking produces a tranquilizing state that is more effective than drugs for relieving insomnia, anxiety, and other nervous disorders. Furthermore, it relaxes us without producing the side effects that often accompany the use of drugs which can be as incapacitating as the anxiety itself.

Walking is a good way of warding off the lower back problems that are the bane of our sedentary way of life. Experts believe most back problems are caused by poor muscle tone which results from lack of exercise.

Walking will enhance your appearance by improving posture and circulation. It strengthens virtually every muscle in the body, giving you a youthful, athletic look and a new bounce of confidence in your step.

Walking is believed to lower the level of cholesterol and other fatty substances in the blood that have been linked to the occurrence of heart disease.

Walking will help you get a good night's sleep by relieving the tensions of daily living that interfere with your rest.

Walking is an effective way of losing weight. It works even without dieting, but combined with a moderate reduction in caloric intake, it's even more effective. What's more, it's easier and safer for overweight people to burn off calories by walking than by taking part in other, more strenuous forms of exercise.

Walking offers something to those of us who love to compete. Race walking is becoming an increasingly popular sport in this country and because of the relatively low level of stress it places on the heart and lungs, people of all ages can excel at it. Important records have been set by people in their sixties.

Walking enhances creativity and the ability to think clearly. Many writers, poets, philosophers, and scientists have been avid walkers and many have told of its beneficial effects on their work.

Walking opens up a whole new world of nature study and learning. Even in an urban area the walker can learn plenty about the natural world and walking is virtually the only way you can learn it.

Walking is the best way to explore the city or town where you live. It reveals a million details that are invisible to the traveler encased in steel and glass.

But how can something as simple as walking be so rich in benefits? First let's look at the apparatus from the bottom up. "Nature produced a magnificent architectural and functional design in the foot, which is designed to work efficiently under excessive loads of unnatural conditions," Dr. Harry F. Hlavac wrote in *The Foot Book*. "Throughout the 26 bones, the multitude of muscles, tendons, ligaments, nerves and vessels in each foot, each tissue and structure has a specific function. Each tissue performs this function within its genetic structural ability. Each tissue has a protective mechanism, a warning mechanism, a healing mechanism and the ability to strengthen itself under stress." This intricate instrument is attached to the ankle by a joint that allows for great flexibility in moving the foot up, down, and sideways; and at the same time, it works with the strong muscles of the calf well enough to allow dancers to stand on the tips of their toes. The knee does its job perfectly. It's a hinge that allows the leg to swing freely backward from a vertical position, but prevents the leg from buckling when it bears our full weight. The sturdy thighbone is crowned by a smooth, rounded surface that fits neatly into a cavity in the pelvis where it's held in place by suction.

And then there's the motion itself. It's been described as a con-

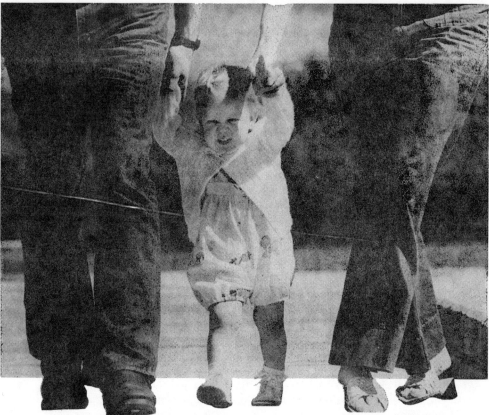

Photo by Ginzy Schaefer

tinual process of falling forward and righting ourselves just before we land flat on our faces. The potential for a catastrophic fall exists because the first thing we do when taking a step is to lean forward and move our center of gravity forward. Unless one of the legs is then advanced to compensate for this change in our center of gravity, we then fall. But when the advancing leg finally touches the ground, our center of gravity is then divided between the forward leg and the rear leg and we regain our balance. Once the first step has been taken, the rear leg drives the body forward by pressing down on the ball of the foot and then the big toe. When that foot leaves the ground, however, we are in trouble again.

Although most of us are endowed with the same essential apparatus and walking motion, there are individual differences that are as unique as our fingerprints and signatures. Take, for instance, men and women. Some authorities believe that differences in the structure of the male pelvis and the female pelvis require women to move their hips in a wider arc than men to attain any given stride length. On the other hand, an expert in the study of body motion has contended that the characteristic differences in the way men and women walk are matters of choice. She argues that we all must swing some part of our bodies from side to side as we walk and that we choose which part to swing. Ordinarily, women choose to swing their hips while men swing their arms and heads, she contends. In other words, the differences are learned rather than genetic. Other researchers have compared the walking habits of big-city residents to those of people from small towns. As you might expect, residents of such urban areas as Brooklyn, Prague, and Munich were found to walk twice as fast as the small-town folk.

Another study, conducted at Wesleyan University in Middletown, Connecticut, indicated our manner of walking can be so distinctive that it alone is sufficient to identify us. The researchers in Connecticut attached reflecting material to the joints, hips, and shoulders of six students and then filmed them as they walked. Through the use of photographic techniques, clues to the identity of the students were obliterated, except spots of light from the reflecting material. With nothing more than that to go on, the six students, and another observer who knew the students, were able to identify the walkers 38 percent of the time.

In a less conscious manner, we are all students of the body language of walking. We read people by the way they walk into a room. We judge their confidence, their age, their weight, their general attitude.

Finally, walking is just plain fun. It is the cheapest, simplest form of fun we have left in an increasingly complicated and gadget-filled world.

Yet facts tell only half the story. Experience tells the rest. The facts may persuade you to get out and walk but the experience is going to keep you coming back for more.

2

The Tortoise and the Hare:
I'll Walk . . . You Run

The story of participatory sports in America has been one of fad after fad sweeping the country, involving millions of people at their peak and then slowly fading into the hard-core devout. The rest of us are deposited where we began—in front of our television sets, cheering on our favorites.

If you don't believe me, take a look at your neighborhood tennis courts. Remember the lines a few years ago. Or talk to your friends about jogging. A lot of them have at least tried it. Have they kept it up? Why not? Perhaps they ran religiously for a few weeks or even months until cold weather or hot weather or a vacation or a muscle pull or a knee injury made them stop and they never could get back into it. Oh sure, they say, "I'm going to start again when . . . " But both of you are skeptical.

I was once a runner myself. I ran off and on for years, even before the sidewalks began to fill up with huffing, puffing joggers. I didn't begin thinking and reading about walking until I realized I wasn't cut out to be a runner.

The experts kept telling me that I had to "run through the pain." I could understand that. I accepted the fact that sports are a combination of agony and ecstasy and one is impossible without the other. But I couldn't accept the injuries that plagued me for hours and days after I had tossed my running shoes into the closet. The ailments were

7

bewildering. Why did moving my legs back and forth make my shoulder hurt for a month? I lay awake at night wondering and suffering. I never found out, because I couldn't see spending my hard-earned money for a diagnosis and then parting with even more cash for the treatments that physicians are likely to recommend.

C. Carson Conrad, executive director of the President's Council on Physical Fitness and Sports, told me that the council, which had been active in the promotion of running as a method of attaining physical fitness, is now trying to convince Americans that they don't have to run, that they can walk at a brisk pace and still achieve the cardiorespiratory fitness that is so important in the prevention of heart disease. "Our research shows that whether you run three miles, jog three miles, run and walk three miles or just walk three miles doesn't make any difference as long as you do it at a pace of under 15 minutes per mile," Conrad said, "but it's hard to get it across to people that walking is important. A lot of people are into running but they're experiencing back injuries, knee injuries and other injuries and we've got to get them into something else. That's why we're pushing walking."

Walking is the easiest, most natural form of exercise. Actually, it shouldn't even be called exercise. It's just something we do to a greater or lesser extent all of our lives. We make a big deal out of the first few steps we take, but after that, we take it for granted. Who contemplates the nature of walking while taking a moonlight stroll with a cherished companion? We may walk for miles along a beach, searching for shells, but the walking—the movement of the legs—is unconscious.

But because I had done some running, I was intrigued by the differences and similarities between the two pastimes—running and walking. I was also convinced that some people might feel compelled to choose between them, such is the popularity of running these days. So I began to ask the question: How are walkers and runners different?

For one, the runner is a lean machine. Experts on the sport say that a good long-distance runner should weigh only two pounds for every inch of height. In other words, if you are six-feet tall, you should weigh only 144 pounds—and many top runners are even leaner than that. Either running or walking will help you lose weight, but people that lean are born ectomorphs, a body-type characterized by thin bones and muscles. Those of us who are either mesomorphic (muscular) or endomorphic (fat) hold little hope of ever weighing only two pounds per inch, no matter how much we exercise. As a result, our chances of ever being good at running long distances, which is what mass running is all about, are somewhat limited.

"Only 10 to 15 percent of people are natural runners who will stick to it," Dr. George Sheehan writes in *Dr. Sheehan on Running*. "Others who are more athletic and muscular will run only as part of another sport. Those who tend to be more broad than long will not run at all." So one important difference between running and walking is that running is a suitable exercise for a rather small group of people; walking, however, is recommended for nearly everyone.

And there is a difference in mental intensity as well. Walking is an easy, very natural exercise, which really doesn't require much thought. All you have to do is watch where you're going. Your mind is free to wander wherever you wish—and it usually does. The walker thinks about something else besides walking: people, nature, or some inner puzzle. But running is a more complicated pastime (with the exception of backpacking which can be incredibly complicated). "The runner is still concerned with space and time," Dr. Sheehan writes. "He logs miles the way lesser men build their savings accounts . . . He runs with a goal and a purpose, training himself with gradually increasing loads, preparing himself for the ultimate effort, trying to reach his own perfection. All of this calls for constant attention—attention to breathing, to arm movement, to the rhythm of the thighs, to the acceleration of the straightened leg."

The walker is one of the few athletes who can be unconcerned about what his body is doing because the body works naturally, providing us with good health and physical fitness free of charge, so to speak. "Where all other athletes must be in attention to the way they move, the walker can find his inner world (and outer world, too) no more than a short stroll from home," Dr. Sheehan writes. "He steps out his front door, views the universe and knows it is good. The walker has found the peace that the runner still seeks."

A key question for anyone considering an exercise program of either running or walking is the degree of cardiorespiratory fitness it provides. How do the two stack up?

Running, without question, is the best exercise for attaining a high degree of physical fitness. Runners who stick with it and run hundreds of miles every year are in superb condition. And because running is a competitive sport, its benefits as a tool of cardiorespiratory fitness have been well documented. As a result, several researchers have commented on how walking compares to running in producing physical fitness. One of the primary ways physiologists determine if an exercise is resulting in greater cardiorespiratory fitness is by measuring the training heart rate. Everyone has a maximum heart rate, which is roughly 220 beats a minute minus your age. Physiologists consider it necessary to have a rate of around 60 percent of the maximum to produce a training effect or an improvement in physical fitness. In a study at Wake Forest University, Dr. Michael L. Pollock and other researchers found that some men who walked faster than four miles an hour had a training heart rate from 80 to 90 percent of their maximum, while the heart rate for others in the study was from 60 to 70 percent of their maximum. The researchers reported in the *Journal of Applied Physiology* that the results of the walking study compared favorably with eleven other studies conducted on men from forty to sixty-years old who had been trained by running and swimming. As a matter of fact, the researchers found that the improvement in the subjects' physical fitness was *three times as great as the improvement in some running programs.* They also found that walking faster than four miles an hour burned up more calories than jogging at slower speeds. Then the researchers made a statement that should probably be inscribed in bronze and put in a "walkers' hall of fame," if anyone ever opens one. The researchers wrote that the success of the walking study "may be partially explained in that the lower training heart rate values for walkers, compared to values found with joggers, was offset by an increased duration and frequency of participation." In other words, you can become just as fit by walking as you can by running—you just have to spend a little more time at it.

Yet, even with the other variables considered, the additional amount of time walking takes is less of a disadvantage than the time spent maintaining a running program. "It's a lot harder to keep running than it is to start running," Tony and Robbie Fanning wrote in 1978 in their book, *Keep Running.* "Ten million runners are on the road, but we know that next month it won't be the same 10 mil-

lion. . . . The fact is, most runners quit because it becomes a negative experience for them." The editors of *Consumer Guide* suggested
in their book, *Rating the Exercises,* that part of the problem might be
that many people are jogging who shouldn't be. "Jogging is very
popular these days, and some people who have no real interest in the
sport get involved just because all their neighbors are doing it (it's
fashionable). The point is that you probably needn't do anything that's
going to be a chore or a bore. If you loathe a particular activity, stay
away from it. If jogging is not your thing, or getting to the tennis courts
is a hassle, don't bother." In the study at Wake Forest, the researchers found that the drop-out rate (25 percent) in the walking
program was smaller than the 30 to 40 percent drop-out rate experienced in more strenuous exercise programs. They attributed the difference to greater group solidarity developed during the walking
periods, fewer knee and leg problems, and a "more tolerable working
rate." Two Cleveland researchers also found that the drop-out rate
was higher (42 percent) in a jogging program than in a walking program (28 percent). "Although the physical conditioning effects of a
brisk walk are less predictable, jogging by comparison is more
strenuous, may lead to physical injuries and is perhaps more boring,"
the researchers reported in the *Journal of Sports Medicine and Physical Fitness.*

One of the most prevalent criticisms of jogging is that it's boring. A
former official of the President's Council on Physical Fitness and
Sports once reported: "If jogging isn't the most boring thing around, it
is right there in second place." Researchers who have studied walking
believe the drop-out rate is lower in walking programs partly because
the participants can easily carry on conversations as they exercise. As
a result, greater group solidarity develops. A colorful distance walker,
Chris Clegg of Beverly Hills, California, is an outspoken critic of
jogging. Clegg, the only person in the world who in official amateur
race-walks has completed one hundred miles in less than 24 hours in
three different continents, says "while you walk you can easily talk,"
but many runners also carry on conversations during workouts. Some
running authorities even warn beginners that a safe pace is one that
allows for conversation.

Ordinary walking, however, certainly requires less concentration
on the body than running. Consequently, walkers can focus their

thoughts or conversations on other subjects. Many runners, however, find nothing more interesting than running, so they're thinking about what they want to think about. I personally don't find either sport boring so I suspect it depends on your personal taste and temperament, and perhaps, as I mentioned earlier, your body-type.

If there is any area where walking scores a ringing victory over running (although I don't really see it as a contest), it's in terms of injuries. Runners themselves acknowledge this and much of their literature is directed toward avoiding or repairing various common injuries. Some nonrunning physicians take it a step further and claim the sport is downright dangerous to your health.

Another one of Clegg's antijogging zingers describes the cause of most jogging injuries pretty well. "Jogging jars joints," Clegg says, and that's about the size of it. According to the editors of *Consumer Guide*, physicians reported that typical injuries include shin splints (pain along the inside of the shin), stress fractures to the bones of the lower leg and foot, Achilles tendinitis (tearing and inflammation of the tendon of the calf), plantar fasciitis (tearing of tissue near or bruising of the heel bone), and chondromalacia (a knee ailment).

A survey taken by *Runner's World* magazine showed that six out of ten runners were disabled at least part of the year by injuries. Most runners' injuries aren't serious or permanently disabling, but they tend, at least, to make this sport much more complicated than walking, which is practically injury-free. These complications may mean a lot of medical expense and worrying about present or potential injuries. Many people who have tried running have encountered these complications and given up the sport. The experts contend that these injuries can be avoided by proper medical attention, equipment, and training techniques, but there's something about running that seems to drive people to excess. One New York physician said: "Runners are fanatics. You can't tell a runner to cut back." Two other critics of running, Drs. Meyer Friedman and Ray H. Rosenman, have commented on the tendency of runners to increase their distance every day. "Jogging is a form of exercise in which man transforms himself into a machine," the two doctors wrote in *Type A Behavior and Your Heart*. "Chug-chug-chugging along, looking neither to the right nor left, the 'man machine' chugs along. And what is 'its' goal? To see if 'it' can chug-chug faster today than yesterday. And what is 'its' only

Photo by Ginzy Schaefer

joy? The soothing miraculous feeling of relief when the chug-chugging is finished." So despite the contention of running experts that injuries can be avoided through moderation, I'm not convinced that running is a sport which fosters moderation. In fact, I believe that the goal of most runners is to run more and more miles in less and less time and that many of them suffer from the delusion of running a marathon in less than three hours. As a result, injuries resulting from overused feet and legs are nearly unavoidable.

Walking, on the other hand, is virtually injury-free. The ordinary walker needs only to worry about the proper care of his feet to avoid blisters and other surface disorders that can slow him down for a few days. Even race walking, which is much more strenuous than ordinary walking, is relatively injury-free when compared with running. "It's no coincidence that a race-walker, not a runner, now holds the record for crossing the United States on foot," Dr. Sheehan writes. "Such a venture demands daily pain-free, uninterrupted mileage. And this is where race walking excels."

Much of the jolt of running results from one of the basic characteristics of the sport. When you run, you actually jump from one foot to the other, with only one foot on the ground at a time. This means that each time you put your foot down, it is supporting your entire weight. If you take 1,000 steps in a mile and weigh 175 pounds, then that's 175,000 pounds of pressure you put on your feet over the course of a one-mile run. Of course, your feet and legs must support the same amount of weight when you walk a mile, but there are important differences in the way the weight is carried. Walking is not a jumping motion. It's a smooth progression of steps in which the rear foot does not leave the ground until the advancing foot has touched down. Consequently, there is no quick transfer of weight from one foot to another that might result in the "jolt" of jogging. The motion of walking is horizontal and lateral. You're moving forward as your body shifts from side to side with each step. The runner is also moving forward but his lateral motion is less pronounced and the vertical motion more emphatic. The runner is literally "falling" onto each foot from a higher point above the ground than is the walker, and consequently, the runner's foot is hitting the ground with more force.

The injury-free nature of walking has persuaded many injured runners to turn to the sport of race walking. "It's not as hard on the cardiovascular system," one veteran race-walker told me. "You're not likely to hurt yourself very much. People are now swinging over from jogging to walking." One of those who made the switch was Art Fleming, a thirty-five-year-old dog trainer. "I broke my foot and after that I couldn't run," Fleming told me, "but it didn't hurt when I was race walking." Fleming now both runs and walks competitively and has an appreciation for both sports. He considers race walking the most difficult, even though it produces less injuries. "People see you walking down the street and they laugh," he told me. "But then when they get out and try it, they stop laughing. They realize it's a heck of a lot harder than running. Walkers are a breed apart."

Another question that inevitably arises when you compare two exercise programs is the danger of heart attack. "What are these severe or strenuous exercises which we are cautioning every Ameri-

can past thirty-five years of age to avoid as if they were a plague?"
wrote Drs. Friedman and Rosenman. "First on our blacklist is jogging. This miserable postcollegiate athletic travesty has already killed
at least scores, possibly hundreds, of Americans." And the supporters
of running have been equally forceful in denying this criticism. Some
have even claimed that running a marathon provides immunity to
heart attack by training the cardiovascular system. I have no desire to
be caught in the middle of this fray. People die of heart attacks doing
all sorts of things—shoveling snow, making love, playing tennis,
running and, alas, even walking. I only know that walking is recommended by physicians for almost anyone and in many cases when
running is not.

Dr. Kris Berg of the University of Nebraska, has reported on a
three-step exercise program in *The Physician and Sportsmedicine.*
Although the program eventually includes jogging, the first step is
walking. "Patients are assigned to this category if they have had no
regular aerobic exercise in the past several years, are obese (greater
than 20 percent fat composition for men and greater than 25 percent
for women), or have medical limitations, such as heart or lung disease, backache, or asthma," he reports. "Walking reduces the likelihood of joint irritation and muscle soreness, and also introduces
minimal risk to the heart and blood vessels as the oxygen cost is fairly
low." Even advocates of running routinely recommend that the beginner does a lot of walking mingled with running. The reason is
clear—walking is safer.

But what of the future of these two sister sports?

Since the famous New Zealand track coach Arthur Lydiard devised
jogging more than twenty years ago, as a way of keeping retiring
runners in shape, it has become an immensely popular sport in this
country. Although it originated as a mixture of running and walking,
the term "jogging" has fallen into disuse in recent years and the great
popularizers of the sport have used the word "running" to describe
everything from an amble to a one-hundred-yard dash. James F. Fixx
dismisses this apparent semantic discrepancy in no more than a foot-
note in *The Complete Book of Running:* "Although some would argue
the point, there is no particular speed at which jogging turns into
running. If you feel that you're running, no matter how slow you're
going, no one can say you're not."

Yet, I suspect the running evangelists have brought about more than a semantical change. They have eliminated the "walking" part of "jogging" for many of their followers. One gets the definite impression from much of the current literature on running that the authors are really talking about competitive running. It would be ironic if an athletic movement, which began with a gentle mixture of walking and running to help *former* competitive runners keep in shape, has itself become competitive. Fixx, himself, wonders about the future of the sport. "Perhaps there will always be a place in running for those of us who are more interested simply in doing it than in comparing ourselves with others. But perhaps not," he wrote. "If running ever becomes trendy, as tennis has during the past decade, might it not become just another activity for the display of machismo? I hope not. Whatever eventually happens, it remains for the moment wondrously free of the irrational, brain-numbing competitiveness that has soured so many people on Little League baseball. But as the mass media give increasing attention to running, who can predict what eventually may happen?"

Yet, despite the trend toward greater competitiveness in running and the abandonment of walking as a part of the "jogging" formula, it's undeniable that the slow, distance training practiced by most runners is a sort of compromise between running and walking. As a result, it's inevitable that a greater appreciation of walking will be one outgrowth of the running movement.

An indication that runners are coming full circle to an understanding of the importance of walking is a book by a former national champion distance-runner, Tom Osler. In the *Serious Runner's Handbook*, Osler mentions walking no less than thirty times. "In the past, walking was considered to be an integral part of the runner's training program," Osler reports. "This is no longer true for most runners, and they suffer because of it. . . . Brisk walking is probably the most natural exercise for man. As a tool for promoting good circulation and overall robust health, it is unmatched. Yes, it is even better than running. . . ."

And, I must admit, the sport of running has influenced the practice of walking. Many people run during the week and hike on weekends. Running is a widely recommended way of training for strenuous backpacking trips. Running, apparently, has even had some influence on

the pace used by many walkers and on the way walkers regard themselves. Edgar B. Heylum, president of the Southern Arizona Hiking
Club, wrote me that "here in the West, I think you'll find that the
English – New England term 'walking' has fallen into disuse. Whereas
we do, indeed, walk when we go hiking, the topography is so rough,
and the going is often so difficult, that 'walking' is hardly an appropriate term. 'Walking,' to most of us, implies an easy saunter on a
well-worn trail through the woods, perhaps topped off by a spot of tea
or a bit of ale. Not that we don't top off our hikes, but sometimes we
are too exhausted to do anything but collapse. . . . Every weekend,
summer and winter, we have between six and eight organized, guided
hikes, ranging from twenty-five-mile-marathon affairs to easy four-or
five-mile rambles. However, in almost all cases, an effort is made to
climb a mountain, or in some way gain elevation so that a physical
workout is achieved. We are more an athletic club than a social club.
. . . A recent fad in the club has been peak-bagging, seeing how
many different mountain peaks can be climbed in one day. Those that
attempt such hikes do so on a half-run, so it's far from 'walking.' "
The evolution of walking into "peak-bagging" is no more strange than
the progression of jogging into running. And at least in one respect
running and walking are identical—they both seem to spur people on
to seek greater and greater challenges.

3

Walking for the Health of It

Walking is the most popular form of exercise among adult Americans. According to a national survey by the President's Council on Physical Fitness and Sports, 45.9 million adult Americans walk for exercise. That's about 34 percent of the adult population.

This figure doesn't seem very impressive at first glance; but when compared to the total number of Americans who exercise—66 million or about 49 percent of the adult population—it takes on greater significance. It means that nearly two out of every three adults who practice any form of exercise believe in the importance of walking.

In recent years, especially since the running craze swept the country, many people have come to believe that exercise must be violent before it can provide benefits or enhance physical fitness. If you're one of those people, you're wrong. There is a gentle, natural way of exercising that's virtually injury-free.

Avid walkers, of course, have long known of, and written about, the healing characteristics of their favorite pastime. The prominent English historian, George Macaulay Trevelyan, who died in 1962 at the age of eighty-six, was a prodigious walker who intuitively understood what researchers in the field of exercise physiology are still trying to prove.

"I have two doctors, my left leg and my right," Trevelyan wrote in *Clio, a Muse.* "When body and mind are out of gear (and those twin

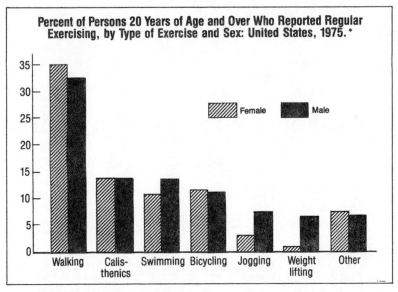

Percent of Persons 20 Years of Age and Over Who Reported Regular Exercising, by Type of Exercise and Sex: United States, 1975. *

*Source: National Center for Health Statistics

parts of me live at such close quarters that the one always catches melancholy from the other) I know that I shall have only to call in my doctors and I shall be well again."

Another prodigious walker, the late John Finley, who as editor of the *New York Times* assessed the condition of his city by taking a yearly walk around the perimeter of Manhattan, agreed with Trevelyan in an essay in *The Art of Walking.* "Sometimes the long walk is the only medicine," Finley wrote. "Once when suffering from one of the few colds of my life (incurred in California) I walked from the rim of the Grand Canyon of the Colorado down to the river and back (a distance of 14 miles, with a descent of 5,000 feet and a like ascent), and found myself entirely cured of the malady which had clung to me for days."

Veteran walkers and other athletes intuitively know the feeling of being physically fit. When you're fit, you feel good. Your body runs smoothly like an engine in tune.

Your fitness will manifest itself in a variety of ways. Your arms and legs (especially your legs if you're a walker) seem stronger and more flexible. You move about with greater ease. You can lift objects more easily. Your abdominal muscles hold your stomach flat against your body, giving you a clear view of the ground beneath you.

Yet researchers in recent years have found that the most important area of physical fitness is found in our cardiorespiratory system, that intricate complex of functions that provides oxygen to the cells of our body.

The term "aerobics" was coined in the 1960s by Dr. Kenneth Cooper, a former aerospace physician, to describe those exercises which improve the functioning of the oxygen-processing system in the human body.

Aerobics begins with the lungs, which draw in fresh air and remove used air from our bodies. In the lungs, oxygen is transferred to the blood where it is picked up and carried along by hemoglobin. Pushed along by the pumping of the heart, the oxygen is then distributed via the arteries and capillaries to the tissue of the body.

Once this oxygen reaches the cells, its utilization depends on the efficiency of tiny structures called mitochondria and the presence of certain enzymes. Energy is then produced when the oxygen is combined with food.

When you walk, the movements of your legs and arms put a strain on this system. It taxes the ability of the lungs to process a sufficient amount of oxygen into the blood stream. It forces the heart to pump harder to deliver more oxygen-carrying blood to the tissues. The same strain is placed on the arteries and capillaries for they too are being asked to provide more oxygen-ladened blood to the cells. And finally, the cells themselves, are pressed to provide energy at a faster rate.

It all sounds a little scary. You are huffing and puffing. Your heart is beating faster. Your arteries are dilating to allow the blood to move more efficiently to cells crying for more oxygen. And it would indeed be scary and, as a matter of fact, suicidal if the body didn't adapt. But it does.

If you walk regularly, your heart becomes stronger and better able to provide for the increasing blood needs of the body. The ability of the arteries and capillaries to force blood into the muscles improves and the ability of the muscles to process oxygen is enhanced by an increase in the number of mitochondria and the production of enzymes. These result in an improvement in your physical condition.

Walking has been prescribed by physicians for thousands of years. Indian doctors are known to have recommended it as an antidote for a variety of ailments over five thousand years ago. Hippocrates, the Greek physician who is generally regarded as the father of western medicine, prescribed walking for his patients around 400 B.C. He suggested an early morning walk for patients with mental problems and fast walking for weight loss.

It wasn't until recently, however, that physicians and other researchers actually set out to determine what effects walking has on the body and especially the crucial oxygen-processing functions.

Two Cleveland physicians, Drs. Myron H. Luria and Keith R. Koepke, noted in a report in the *Journal of Sports Medicine and Physical Fitness:* "Walking is a popular form of exercise which is highly recommended by physicians. However, there is a paucity of information documenting not only its conditioning effects but also the feasibility of a walking program in relation to other forms of exercise."

To carry out their experiment, the physicians selected nine men and nine women between the ages of twenty-two and fifty-five and began a ten-week program in which the subjects walked two miles within thirty minutes, five days a week. Five of the participants dropped out of the program for various reasons, but the other thirteen walked their prescribed distances on a course on hospital grounds or on a measured course near their homes.

At the end of the study, the researchers found that the participants had increased the work-load ability of their hearts and their pulse rates had declined steadily.

"Although the minimal level of physical conditioning necessary for maintenance of good health remains to be demonstrated, walking may provide sufficient exertion for selected individuals to reach and maintain an improved level of physical conditioning," the physicians concluded, cautiously.

What the researchers discovered, in plain language, was that each beat of the subjects' hearts was more productive and fed more blood to the body. The result was a drop in the number of heart beats necessary to supply the tissues with an adequate amount of blood.

The cumulative effect over a lifetime of a drop in the number of heart beats is awesome. If your pulse rate is eighty beats a minute, your heart will beat roughly 42 million times a year. Reduce that pulse rate to seventy beats a minute and you save about 5 million beats a year or 350 million beats over a lifetime. That's quite a bit of strain on your heart that can be avoided simply by participating in a regular walking program.

Researchers in England in the 1950s were looking for a quick way of getting troops into better physical condition when they began a study of forty-four members of the Royal Air Force, only three of whom were already in good shape. Eight of the servicemen were asked to walk only about three kilometers (1.9 miles) a day.

The remainder were broken up into three groups of twelve. One group was asked to walk ten kilometers (6.2 miles) a day; the second, twenty kilometers (12.4 miles) a day; and the third, thirty kilometers (18.6 miles) a day.

The researchers reported in the *Journal of Applied Physiology* that all three of the groups walking ten kilometers or more showed a "highly significant" improvement in their heart rate.

If 6.2 miles seems like a long distance to you, just consider the fact that the average housewife walks about eight miles a day just around the house. You could take a thirty-minute walk on your way to work every morning, a thirty-minute walk on your way home, and another half-hour walk during your lunch break or with your family in the evening and easily cover 6.2 miles a day.

That's the beauty of walking. You can do it in the course of your daily life without too much of a special effort, equipment, or expenditure of time.

The landmark study on the conditioning effects of walking was performed in 1970 at the Physical Fitness Research Laboratory at Wake Forest University under the direction of Dr. Michael L. Pollock, one of the premier researchers in the area of exercise physiology.

Dr. Pollock and his fellow researchers reported in the *Journal of Applied Physiology* that they too were curious about walking because, although it has long been recommended by physicians for cardiovascular conditioning, little proof on its benefits was available.

They picked sixteen sedentary men between the ages of forty- and fifty-six-years old, who were in good health, to participate in the study. The training program was twenty weeks of walking, for about forty minutes a day, four times a week. The researchers noted a marked improvement in all the indicators of physical conditioning measured in the study. Maximum oxygen intake, for instance—an indicator of the body's ability to process oxygen—improved by 28 percent in the twenty-week period. Heart rate, both during and after exercise, improved significantly.

In addition to the aerobic conditioning improvements which, despite their importance, don't show up in a business suit, the participants in the study showed other benefits. They lost weight and body fat; they lost inches around the waist and buttocks; and their ability to puff out their chests, military-style, was improved. The distances walked in the forty-minute period increased from 2.5 miles to 3.2 miles, the speed from 4.26 to 4.74 miles an hour, and the number of calories burned from 241 to 357.

What more could you ask from an exercise program? After only twenty weeks, the men in this study had improved the performance of their lungs, their cardiovascular systems, and other oxygen-processing functions. And perhaps it is even more important to those of us who need visible rewards from an exercise program, that they were thinner and more muscular.

All these benefits are obtainable from the simple act of walking that we learn in our infancy. No expensive lessons are necessary. No special equipment, other than a pair of gym shorts and jogging shoes, need be purchased.

In fact, one of the real advantages of walking for exercise is that you don't even have to wear gym shorts and jogging shoes. Comfortable, loose-fitting clothing and a good pair of shoes will do.

In *Aerobics for Women* by Mildred Cooper and Dr. Kenneth Cooper, both leading experts on exercise programs noted this advantage of walking: "I'm sure many women will prefer this less vigorous method of conditioning. It does consume more time per session, but it has the overwhelming advantage of being feasible for anyone, anytime, anyplace. It doesn't even have to look like exercise. For those of you who are self-conscious, the latter can make a decisive difference. . . . You can make it part of your routine (by walking to the store, the office, the kids' school) without its ever seeming like a routine."

Since the publication of *Aerobics* in the 1960s and the establishment of his Institute for Aerobics Research in Dallas, Dr. Cooper has had an unparalleled opportunity to gather information about the benefits of walking and other aerobic exercises. Several of these benefits are discussed in *Aerobics for Women*.

For instance, the number of headaches are reduced. The Coopers offer no explanation for it, but they have received numerous letters from people who have been cured of migraine headaches through regular exercise programs. One correspondent wrote that she was not only cured of headaches, but her problem with varicose veins was substantially reduced after participating in a walking program for four months.

Others reported better eyesight. "A lot of people have claimed they've had to get prescription changes in their glasses once they started to exercise because their vision improved," the Coopers write. They go on to explain that exercise seems to reduce pressure in the eyeball, one cause of a type of glaucoma.

The Coopers noted that an improved physical condition sometimes shows up in the mouth where the gums are healthier due to improved circulation. Also they reported that complexions were improved. Here again improved circulation leads to a rosy glow of good health and sweating tends to cleanse the skin of excessive oil that leads to many complexion problems.

Dr. Cooper, Dr. Pollock, and other researchers at the Cooper complex in Dallas studied about three-thousand men over a period of three years in an effort to establish some link between heart disease risk factors and physical condition. They found significant differences between those men in good condition and those in only fair condition, and somewhat slighter differences between men in fair condition and poor condition or very poor condition. The men in better condition showed safer levels of serum cholesterol in their blood, lower blood pressures, and less body fat. All three of these areas are listed as risk factors by the American Heart Association.

The effects of walking and jogging on high blood pressure, which physicians say is the most common cardiovascular malady, were measured by two San Diego researchers, Drs. John L. Boyer and Fred W. Kasch. Studies have shown that of men in their forties, 10 percent have high blood pressure, and 25 percent of men in their sixties suffer from this disorder. So this is an area in which walking could have a significant impact on our health.

The researchers selected twenty-three men with high blood pressure, and twenty-two men with normal blood pressure levels, to participate in the experiment. All of the men were between the ages of thirty-five and sixty-one. The men either walked or jogged for thirty or thirty-five minutes twice a week. The exercise sessions were preceded by fifteen to twenty minutes of warm-up exercises. The training program lasted for six months. At the end of the study a drop in blood pressure was recorded for all of the men with a blood pressure prob-

Photo by Ginzy Schaefer

lem. This occurred after only one hour of exercise, two days a week—a moderate conditioning program, indeed. The researchers concluded in their report in the *Journal of the American Medical Association* that "interval exercise was of supplemental value in the therapy of this group of hypertensive middle-age men."

Another study found a group of people whose life-style requires a great amount of daily walking, indicating a link between their levels of physical activity and the serum cholesterol found in their blood. In an effort to pin down the link between diet, physical activity, and serum cholesterol, researchers Dr. Daniela Gsell and Dr. Jean Mayer, studied residents of the mountain town of Blatten, Switzerland, and compared them to a group of relatively sedentary working-class people in the Swiss city of Basel.

Here's the researchers' description of the life-style of the residents of Blatten from a report in the *American Journal of Clinical Nutrition:*

"They support themselves by farming performed under extremely difficult conditions. Up to 1955 the village was separated by several miles from the next road fit for automobiles, trucks or carts. Farming areas are spread on steep slopes varying in altitude from 4,000 to 8,000 feet. All distances have to be walked. Mules are rare and expensive; hay, wood, dung, building material, food and milk are usually carried on the back. . . . During the summer, the greater part of each family, including all school-age children, walk daily up the high pastures of the 'Alps' situated at an altitude 1,500 to 2,500 feet higher, where cows and goats are kept, and carry the milk back down to the village."

The way of life of these Swiss villagers compares to that of American farm families more than one-hundred years ago. Walking is an integral and necessary part of their lives. The researchers found that despite a diet that included high levels of fat, which has been linked to high levels of cholesterol in the blood, the cholesterol levels of village residents were comparable to or lower than that of city dwellers, who had a level of physical activity typical in western, industrialized countries.

"It seems reasonable to ascribe the lower serum cholesterol levels observed in Blatten . . . to the intense physical activity of this population," the researchers concluded. "This does not mean that variables such as the fat content of the diet or the proportion of saturated fat are unimportant. It may mean, however, that they are less important than the activity factor or that they manifest their importance only in physically inactive populations."

We obviously can't return to the way of life we abandoned one-hundred years ago, but the evidence I've reviewed in these three studies indicates that we should be heading in that direction, during our leisure time, at least. If the activity gap between a rural life-style and our present sedentary existence seems insurmountable to you now, it won't seem so after you've become a serious walker and developed the deep affection for walking that comes with time. You'll find that you might walk all day, one day a week, without even leaving town and this is the kind of exercise that rapidly closes the gap between a sedentary and an active life-style.

Walking is a progressive exercise. You can begin doing it no matter what your level of physical fitness (with a few exceptions), and gradually develop speed, endurance, and interest. Sometimes I see walking as a trail beginning at my front door and ever so gradually leading into a neighborhood park, then the countryside, and finally the wild mountain country. And that's how it can be for you, too. With a little patience and perseverance, you can follow the walking trail with greater skill, endurance, and knowledge until you've opened up a vast new vista of living that didn't seem possible to you before you became a student of the art of walking.

Elizabeth Young, a Cedar Rapids, Iowa, woman walks more than thirty miles a week and took her late husband and two children on many long walking trips which lasted a month or more. "We never owned a car," she wrote in *Family Afoot*. "We always walked a lot, and for the first thirty-four years of our married life, virtually the only medical expenses we had for ourselves were those of child-bearing and check-ups."

Dr. Albert A. Kattus, a cardiologist at the University of California at Los Angeles, recently told *House and Garden* magazine: " . . . The problem with many people is that they do not walk nearly enough in their daily lives. At Los Angeles airport, there are even mobile sidewalks so you do not have to walk at all! We recommend that normal people who lead sedentary lives should walk regularly each day, as fast as possible, for anywhere from twenty minutes to an hour. The fastest most people can walk is 4½ miles per hour, and that is not making a high demand. But two or three miles like that every day will counteract the dangers of a sedentary life."

Dr. Hans Kraus, one of the nation's leading experts on back and neck pain, has written extensively about the "dangers of a sedentary life."

In 1961, this New York physician and an associate, Dr. Wilhelm Raab, published a book called *Hypokinetic Disease*, a term coined to describe those maladies which they believe are caused by our sedentary way of life. Essentially, they espouse the theory that because our society produces few opportunities for physical action, our anxieties and frustrations are turned inward, doing physical damage to our own bodies.

"In our civilized cities we lead the lives of caged animals, with little opportunity to respond, without inhibition, to outside ired for release. Since our civilization does not permit the natural response through fight or flight, and since we do not have vicarious outlets through heavy exercise, tension is stored up in our muscles. This constant tension shortens muscles and deprives them of elasticity. Once the muscle tightness has reached a sufficiently high level, and lack of physical activity has weakened the tense muscles, the stage is set for the first episode of back pain. Even so small an act as picking up a paper or pencil may precipiritations," Dr. Kraus wrote in the *Clinical Treatment of Back and Neck Pain.* "There is often the added burden of emotional problems, which increase the need for release. Since our civilization does not permit the natural response through fight or flight, and since we do not have vicarious outlets through heavy exercise, tension is stored up in our muscles. This constant tension shortens muscles and deprives them of elasticity. Once the muscle tightness has reached a sufficiently high level, and lack of physical activity has weakened the tense muscles, the stage is set for the first episode of back pain. Even so small an act as picking up a paper or pencil may precipitate the first attack, which leaves the muscles weakened and more stiffened—ready for the next episode of pain which in turn will compound the symptoms."

Dr. Kraus cites study after study, showing a close relationship between lack of physical activity and back and neck pain. Some studies even show that lack of physical fitness in children makes them potential victims of backache later in life.

Though this disease isn't fatal like heart disease, it's incredibly common in our society. Just stop for a minute and think about the number of times it's mentioned on television commercials for aspirin and other remedies. Think about the people you know who are either plagued or even debilitated by it.

Dr. Kraus writes that only about 20 percent, and probably fewer, of the cases of low back pain are actually caused by mechanical problems in the structure of the back. Most of the cases, he writes, result from muscle problems related to inactivity.

"Exercise has a 'protective value' in prevention of back pain, directly by keeping posture muscles flexible and strong and indirectly by serving as an outlet for nervous irritations," he writes.

The tranquilizing effects of walking have been certified in a study by Dr. Herbert A. de Vries in California. He reported that a fifteen-minute walk at a moderate pace produced a tranquilizing effect in nine men and women over fifty-two-years old that lasted for at least an hour afterward.

But we don't need scientists to tell us that a brief walk is relaxing. You can feel the layers of tension peel away on a short walk. You may perceive it as a psychological relaxation and certainly it is, but your muscles are relaxing too. Their flexibility is increasing and they're growing longer and more efficient. When you return home, you're more in tune with your body, more comfortable with it. And you've reduced the potential for back problems.

Most of us, sometime in our lives, have experienced the devastating effects of insomnia. Problems or pain seem conquerable when we have the option of forgetting them for a while through long, satisfying sleep. But take away this option and we only look forward to hours of tossing and turning, as we struggle to free ourselves from whatever is bothering us.

Sometimes the best medicine is a good, long walk. You not only tire yourself physically, but often you can find answers to the problems that are bothering you. Clearly, regular walking produces a deeper and more satisfying level of sleep.

A New York psychiatrist, Dr. Frederick Baekeland, set out several years ago to test the popular belief that "exercise promotes sound or deep sleep" and reached some interesting conclusions. He selected fourteen college students who were accustomed to regular exercise and asked them to refrain from exercising for an entire month. Dr. Baekeland discovered during that experiment that a "significant increase" had occurred in the amount of wakefulness and the number of bodily movements during the night. The students reported that they were not sleeping as deeply as they were before the test began. "As judged by its effects on their sleep and subjective reports, the last month of the experiment was a psychologically stressful experience for the [students], not just a period of exercise deprivation," Dr. Baekeland wrote in the *Archives of General Psychiatry*.

The benefits of walking are numerous: You'll reduce your chances of having a heart attack, low back pain, complexion problems, insomnia, and headaches. But what about weight problems? Can you walk those away too? Many authorities believe you can and it's been proven by many an avid walker.

4

The Great Walking Experience

One crisp, clear autumn day I found myself following a winding road along the bluffs of the Missouri River. It was an unlikely place, really, for me to be feeling the way I was. Only a few miles away, several thousand men and women were sweating out their days in the complex of federal, state, and military prisons situated in the twin cities of Leavenworth and Lansing, Kansas. Yet even these reminders of the shortcomings of the human race couldn't dampen my spirits.

I was soaring. Somehow, my walk had produced a sense of great clarity. The changing leaves, the river shimmering below me, the people occasionally passing by on foot or on horseback, all seemed part of a benevolent order of the universe. I felt strong and healthy, of course, but there was something happening to me that I couldn't define. It was, perhaps, produced by the easy, rhythmic motion of my legs and arms, but yet it was more mental than physical.

I've talked to many people who have had similar feelings while walking and I've found references to it in dozens of books and periodicals. For some people, it's the ability to think more clearly or to enjoy the company of family and friends. For others, it's a deeper experience, profound at the most and intensely memorable at the least. Even a brochure from the American Medical Association says walking is "a stimulating exercise that is a tonic to both body and mind." If I were a more religious person, I would tend to call these walking

33

feelings "revelations" or "religious experiences." One psychiatrist has coined the phrase "positive addiction" to describe similar experiences. But I'm not a preacher, a doctor, or a psychologist, I'm just a walker. So I'm going to call these feelings the *Walking Experience.*"

Clearly, the *Walking Experience* must satisfy some great inner need in human beings or it would not produce this feeling of well-being and it would not be so popular. So what are those needs that walking seems to fulfill? *The need for relaxation!*

Not long ago I spent a pleasant afternoon walking in a "Volksmarsch" (a people's walk). Now, to Americans that sounds faintly military, but it isn't. A Volksmarsch is nothing more than an organized walk over a measured distance—they are extremely popular in Germany and equally as rare in the U.S.

Every weekend Germans by the thousands walk distances of ten kilometers or twenty kilometers with their families and friends. Just about every German town has a Volksmarsch organization which sponsors the walks and rewards the finishers with little medals or other awards after they return from the woods. Time is not a factor. The walkers can take all day to complete the Volksmarsch or they can finish it in a few hours, drive to the next town, and walk again. Some families spend all weekend going from Volksmarsch to Volksmarsch, collecting medals and memories. In even a small German town, as many as twenty-thousand people might turn out for one of these weekend walks.

I talked to a German military officer about the Volksmarsch system and I quickly concluded that exercise was a secondary consideration for the walkers. "It's announced in the newspaper and people come from miles away," Major Gerd Stamm told me. "They give very nice medals of iron or bronze or pictures of the landscape or the town hall with the date on them. For many people like me, it's a very good memory—the landscape, a lot of medals on the wall." Some of the walkers try to rack-up as many miles as they can, but most of them are just there to have fun. Stamm said, "It's just bringing together family and friends for a nice walk in a nice area."

As I progressed along the course of my American Volksmarsch, I tried to look at my fellow Americans through the eyes of my German friend—to imagine millions of Americans strolling around the woods with their friends and families. As I passed each group of walkers, I talked with them and watched them closely. Their behavior seemed so unlike Americans. They were having fun in a simple way. That pained, driven look of the golfer, the tennis player, the runner, was totally absent. Instead, there was a look of calm relaxation. They pushed their babies along in strollers, while the older children raced playfully ahead. The families were getting to know each other in a way that is only possible when you're relaxed and time is no object. Their everyday worries didn't seem so important.

Henry David Thoreau, who did more walking than anyone would care to tabulate, wrote that walking is priceless. "No wealth can buy the requisite leisure, freedom and independence which are the capital in this profession. It comes only by the grace of God. It requires direct dispensation from Heaven to become a Walker. You must be born into the family of Walkers." I suspect this is even more true now than in Thoreau's day. Over the years, the promise of material success in America has spurred us to a hectic pace that is reflected in our pursuit of leisure time. We tend to choose sports that are fast moving, hectic, and violent when what we really need is a pleasant, afternoon walk with the family. That's the kind of recreation that produces lasting relaxation because, in the course of a walk, we can get comfortable with ourselves, our families, and our friends, making it easier for us to relax with them even when the surroundings aren't so pleasant and conditions aren't so ideal.

When I was in college, I spent my summers as a dock-hand at a large marina. During the week, the lake was as smooth as glass, the calm broken only by an occasional passing fishing boat. On weekends, all hell broke loose. Thousands of families would drive out from the cities with their boats in tow and one of my jobs was to make sure they got their boats in the water, their outboard motors started, and the whole clan in the boat without mishap.

It was a tough job. Typically, the men in the group had been drinking all the way out from the city, so they were in no mood to handle all the important little details that make for successful boating. Soon, they were yelling at their wives and children and sometimes me. Even if we managed to get the boat in the water without mishap, we had to deal with one of the most unreliable and cantankerous of the gasoline-powered phylum—the outboard motor. Invariably, they needed new spark plugs or more expensive repairs, which the slightly tipsy captains insisted on correcting themselves, fearful of the additional expense of a mechanic. The result was almost always disastrous. If an expensive tool, motor part, or pair of eyeglasses didn't forever lose itself at the bottom of the lake, then the captain himself took a plunge. It was amazing, too, how many of these boaters couldn't swim. I could never understand what motivated these people to torture themselves all weekend, only to return home with a hangover, an inflamed nervous system, irritable children, and a depleted bank account. And a surprising number of them keeled over and died of heart attacks on our campground. Yet, one of my friends in the retail business tells me that boating is still considered one of the most popular outdoor sports.

It makes so much more sense, from a mental and physical standpoint, just to take the family on a walk around town, to a local park, or to a wooded area. Some cardiologists believe that your very life may depend on it. Drs. Friedman and Rosenman reported in their controversial book *Type A Behavior and Your Heart* that heart attacks are caused by a behavior pattern of excessive competitiveness, aggression, impatience, and urgency. "Individuals displaying this pattern seem to be engaged in a chronic, ceaseless, and often fruitless struggle—with themselves, with others, with circumstances, with time, sometimes with life itself," the cardiologists wrote. They couldn't have described better those weekend boaters I grappled with in my college days. "In the absence of Type A Behavior Pattern, coronary heart disease almost never occurs before seventy years of age, regardless of the fatty foods eaten, the cigarettes smoked, or the lack of exercise," they wrote. "But when this behavior pattern is present, coronary heart disease can easily erupt in one's thirties and forties. We are convinced that the spread of Type A Behavior explains why death by heart disease, once confined mainly to the elderly, is increasingly common among younger people."

If you're the type of person who is addicted to deadlines, more interested in piling up large sums of money in your bank account than spending it, feel driven by time, and are unsure or insecure about your own personal worth, then you probably fit into the Type A category. And walking may be one of the best ways for you to relax a little bit. Friedman and Rosenman wrote about one bank president, who spent his lunch hour strolling around a city park wondering what the flowers were thinking. Needless to say, they didn't believe this man was Type A. Yet, he was as successful as many people who seem to be more driven and competitive. He had just found a simple way to relax.

The authors of *Type A Behavior and Your Heart* recommend moderate exercises, such as walking, instead of the more violent ones. "Certainly, at least one hour a day and preferably more time, should be spent in moving your legs and arms," they wrote.

What these doctors are really talking about is the American way of life—the intense striving for more and more in less and less time. And they have only confirmed in their research what common sense has been telling us for a long time—that kind of behavior is deadly.

That's why walking is so important. It offers the kind of brief interlude that is relaxing both physically and mentally. It helps us keep our ambitions and ourselves in perspective. Thoreau once wrote that it took less time for him to walk somewhere than for someone else to take public transportation. The reasoning behind his little riddle is that the person who has to pay for transportation has to earn the money for the fare first. You can't buy time. You have to seize it.

In the study by Dr. Herbert A. de Vries, the researcher found that only fifteen minutes of walking resulted in a state of relaxation that lasted for an hour or more. The study was conducted to determine if exercise could be used instead of tranquilizing drugs to reduce tension in extremely anxious people. The subjects selected for the study were suffering from headaches, insomnia, excessive fatigue, nervous tension, and an inability to relax. The researchers concluded that for those ten men and women between the ages of fifty-two and seventy, walking was more effective in producing relaxation than a tranquilizer. An additional advantage, according to the report, was that exercise induced no undesirable side effects such as "impaired motor coordination and reaction time and driving performance," which result from even small doses of the tranquilizing drug "meprobamate."

In most businesses today, the fifteen-minute break, twice a day, is standard procedure. The de Vries study proves that we shouldn't be using that break for a cup of coffee and a cigarette. We ought to be walking, if only around in a circle for fifteen minutes. By combining two fifteen-minute walks with a half-hour walk during your lunch break, you rack-up an hour of walking a day without eating up any of your leisure time. The research shows that you feel better when you return to your desk after only a fifteen-minute walking break.

And if you walk during the week, you'll be in shape for the longer walks on weekends—the kind of recreation that is truly relaxing.

That's how Harold Diamond of Brooklyn, New York, spends his weekends. Diamond and his friends in the New York Hiking Club head for the hills and parks of New York and New Jersey for their recreation. And hectic isn't the word for it.

"Hiking is beneficial to all participants and satisfies many wants and needs," Harold says. "It is good for all ages and is an excellent means of tapering off for athletes as they mature. Some people plan months ahead for a picnic. Hikers do that every weekend.

"Only our hike leaders obligate themselves to show up. Therefore it is exciting to see just who comes out.

"Trails look different each season of the year, in fact, at different times of the day, and in the directions one walks them. Eating on a mountaintop or at lakeside is very pleasant, especially to city dwellers.

"When walking singly, Indian-style, on narrow trails is a good time to clear the cobwebs from one's mind. And as you walk over twigs and rocks you seem to forget the world you left behind. And as you walk with others on wider trails, you often find things of material interest to talk about.

"The usual one-hour drive to and from the hike is often an enjoyable interlude in itself. After a full day outdoors one comes home rejuvenated spiritually and people do not mind a day or two of rain during the week.

"Many go for the exercise alone; while just as many enjoy and appreciate the plants and wildflowers or the social aspects. A light pack, a thermos bottle, and good walking shoes are all you need to start you off."

It's taken me a long time to realize it, but people like Harold and the families in the Volksmarsch I mentioned, have reached a level of pleasure and relaxation that is rather uncommon in our fast-paced society. Once you get a taste of this aspect of the *Walking Experience*, you won't ever go back to the kind of hectic, murderous recreation that is just an extension of your normal murderous, hectic life-style.

Yet, the power of walking extends beyond the field of recreation into the intricate relationship between the mind and the body.

Dr. Oliver Wendell Holmes wrote that in every form of exercise three forces are at work—"the will, the muscles, and the intellect." In different types of exercise, one or the other of these forces will exert control. "In walking," he wrote in *The Autocrat of the Breakfast Table*, "the will and muscles are so accustomed to work together and perform their task with so little expenditure of force, that the intellect is left comparatively free. The mental pleasure in walking, as such, is in the sense of power over all our moving machinery."

Whatever the source of its mysterious power, walking definitely satisfies a *Need for Mental Pleasure* and satisfies it so well that veteran walkers are addicted to the pleasure. "If it weren't for walking, I'd be a raving lunatic," one walker told me. "I had better admit right away that walking can in the end become an addiction, and that is then as deadly in its fashion as heroin or television or the stock exchange," wrote Colin Fletcher in *The New Complete Walker,* a book about backpacking. "But even in this final stage it remains a delectable madness, very good for sanity, and I recommend it with a passion.

"A redeeming feature of the condition is that no matter how heavily you have been hooked you can still get your kicks from very small doses."

Addictions have fascinated me ever since I wrote a series of newspaper articles on the heroin trade. To those addicted to it, the pursuit of heroin becomes an all-consuming drive that provides meaning and structure to their lives. Every waking hour is committed to obtaining the money and then the drugs to satisfy their craving for a "high."

Yet, people in the Western nations seem to be peculiarly susceptible to this kind of addiction. In Turkey, where the opium poppies that eventually become heroin are grown, addiction is uncommon. The poor, Turkish peasants don't seem to have a need for the kind of "high" heroin produces. Their struggle to survive in a harsh environment and their deep belief in the Greek Orthodox faith seem to satisfy their spiritual needs or perhaps, more likely, faith gives them the strength to refrain from using the drug. Here in America, where the struggle to survive is more psychological than physical, and the underpinnings of faith have been eroded for many people, heroin and other drugs, such as alcohol, are in great demand.

One authority, Dr. William Glasser, has suggested that we counteract this susceptibility to become addicted to destructive forces by seeking out forms of "positive addiction." In his book by that name, Dr. Glasser lists hiking as one of the possible ways of attaining "positive addiction."

I think Dr. Glasser's ideas are important enough to walkers and prospective walkers to be explained here at some length. Even if you come to the end of this book and decide walking isn't for you, at least you will take with you an interesting theory of what recreation can do for you and some tips on how to pick a form of recreation that suits you. I, of course, contend that walking is one of the best ways to obtain a "positive addiction."

"Very few of us realize how much we choose the misery in our lives," Dr. Glasser writes. "Even when we do, we still go ahead with the disastrous choice because we are convinced that we don't have the strength to choose better. A child doesn't give up in school or a wife on her marriage, because each believes it's a good move. They give up because they no longer have the strength to keep up the struggle."

Dr. Glasser recommends "positive addiction" as a way of gaining the mental strength to make the choices that are best for you. "The positive addict enjoys his addiction but it does not dominate his life," Dr. Glasser writes. "From it he gains mental strength which he uses to help himself accomplish whatever he tries to do more successfully. Unlike a negative addict, who is satisfied completely to live for his addiction, to the exclusion of everything else, a positive addict uses his extra strength to gain more love and more worth, more pleasure, more meaning, more zest for life in general. Positive addiction is especially valuable because it is a way in which anyone can increase his strength."

Dr. Glasser lists six criteria for selecting an activity for your "positive addiction."

1. It must be something noncompetitive that you like to do and can spend an hour at every day.

2. It should be easy.

3. You should be able to do it alone without help from others.

4. You must believe it is valuable. (Walking, for instance, is good exercise.)

5. You must believe that your ability to do it will improve with time.

6. You must be able to do it without criticizing yourself.

For most people, walking fits these criteria perfectly and many walkers, like Colin Fletcher and Dr. Oliver Wendell Holmes, have described its pleasantly addictive effects. One young woman told me that "90 percent" of her "ego development" came from a race-walking program she participated in during junior high school. "It was so easy for me," she said.

The prolific journalist, James Michener, became committed to walking while a student in Scotland. "On one heroic effort, which gained me some credit in my university crowd, I hiked across Scotland in one unbroken trip," Michener writes in *Sports in America*. ". . . It was a journey I have never forgotten, the kind of thing a man should do when young, and one of the most rewarding things about it was that I did it alone, so that the full force of nature could impress me and give me strength as I hiked through the dark hours.

" . . . It was this long walk that committed me to constant hiking, and for the past twenty-five years, whenever I have been at home, I have left my desk almost every afternoon to walk with our dogs through the woods that surround the small plot of ground on which we live."

Michener writes that his walking affects his ability to work. "When my writing goes poorly it is always because I have not walked enough, for it is on these uneventful and repititious walks that I do my best thinking."

The carryover effects of such walks and other forms of exercise have been well documented by the scientific community. One study, carried out at the University of Minnesota, the University of Wisconsin, and Pennsylvania State University, examined the influences of exercise programs on behavior and attitudes. The researchers found that exercise programs produce a wide range of beneficial changes in the lives of the participants in addition to improving their physical condition.

According to *Public Health Reports*, 60 percent of those who commented on their work performance said they had noticed a significant improvement. Fred Heinzelmann and Richard W. Bagley wrote that participants typically commented: "I have a greater capacity to work harder, both mentally and physically" or "I have improved my power of decision and concentration."

The same beneficial changes were found in the participants' attitudes toward their work. About 40 percent of the men said that they had a more positive attitude. "I feel more energetic and more productive; I enjoy my work more because I get more done; my normal work routine seems less boring now," the participants told the researchers.

Changes in eating behavior also were noted by the researchers. "The majority of the participants who reported changes in this area indicated they were eating less and avoiding snacks between meals when possible," Heinzelmann and Bagley wrote. " . . . In general, participants appeared to be more interested in, and more aware of, the importance of weight control than members of the control group."

The researchers found that participants in the study were taking part in more recreational activities with their families and friends, were walking more, and were walking up stairs rather than taking elevators when they had the opportunity. "In short, physical activity had become a pervasive habit in the life-style of many of these men," the researchers wrote.

Substitute the word "addiction" for "habit," and these researchers are saying virtually the same thing as Dr. Glasser and the walkers I've quoted. There is something about certain kinds of exercise that produces these lasting and wide-ranging effects on our lives. I wouldn't say walking is the *only* way to obtain the strength you need to live honestly, but it is one proven way. I'm sure sewing, transcendental meditation, running, and a myriad of other activities provide the same kind of experience for some people, but it's at least one more plus for walking.

Even Shakespeare, centuries ago, knew what walking could do for your life when he wrote "Jog on, Jog on, the footpath way." Another great literary walker, Leslie Stephen, wrote in *Studies of a Biographer*, that Shakespeare "divined the connection between walking and a 'merry heart'; that is, of course, a cheerful acceptance of our position in the universe, founded upon the deepest moral and philosophical principles."

Trevelyan goes about as far as anyone in recommending walking as a means of getting control of ourselves and summoning up the strength to manage our lives. This dramatic passage from Trevelyan's essay on walking in *Clio, a Muse*, is worth quoting because most of us have had similar experiences at one time or another.

"Once in every man's youth there comes the hour when he must learn, what no one ever yet believed save on the authority of his own experience, that the world was not created to make him happy. . . . Every man must once at least in life have the great vision of Earth as Hell. Then while his soul within him is molten lava that will take some lifelong shape of good or bad when it cools, let him set out and walk, whatever the weather, wherever he is, be it in the depths of London, and let him walk grimly. . . . Let him walk until his flesh curses his spirit for driving it on, and his spirit spend its rage on his flesh in forcing it still pitilessly to sway the legs. Then the fire within him will not turn to soot and choke him, as it chokes those who linger at home within their grief, motionless, between four mean, lifeless walls."

Everyone has known a person who has used walking to grind away their disillusionment. I knew a young man who was studying to be a doctor and had the habit of crashing through the woods every time he began to despair of the long road ahead of him. He always took off at night and he seldom followed any path. He preferred to work out his misery on the underbrush and low-hanging limbs that tore at him as he walked. He'd return from these walks early in the morning with bruises and scrapes and torn clothing, but he was always wearing a smile.

I suspect the claim that "the Marine Corps builds men," if true at all, is based on the amount of walking young people are forced to do in basic training. My observation has been that people in the service react rather badly to the harassment that is part and parcel of basic training, but the continual, daily marching of long distances gives them a great deal of confidence in themselves. Many people who have been through the experience say they enjoyed the long marches led by veteran drill sergeants who knew how to set a good pace and keep to it.

Somehow people instinctively turn to walking when, as Trevelyan says, they "have the great vision of Earth as Hell." When I was in journalism school, I lived in a dormitory with many young men who had just completed their military service and were having difficulty adjusting to civilian life. Oddly, almost all of them used walking to keep their mental balance. One of them, a graduate student in chemistry, walked miles every afternoon along an abandoned railroad track. He knew every stream, weed, tree, and wildflower along the tracks like the back of his hand. And he always returned refreshed.

I did my walking at night, after studying. Whenever I couldn't sleep, I would roam the streets of that college town until the problems of maladjustment that were plaguing me didn't seem so important anymore. Then I could sleep. My body was exhausted and my mind relaxed.

I didn't know it then, but as a young person trying to learn how to be a writer, I was following in hallowed footsteps on my nightly walks. Charles Dickens, the author of *David Copperfield*, *Oliver Twist*, and many other great works of literature, used a similar method of vanquishing his devils and getting to sleep.

Dickens wrote in *The Uncommercial Traveller*: "Some years ago, a temporary inability to sleep, referable to a distressing impression, caused me to walk about the streets all night, for a series of several nights. The disorder might have taken a long time to conquer, if it had been faintly experimented on in bed; but it was soon defeated by the brisk treatment of getting up directly, after lying down, and going out, and coming home tired at sunrise."

Mental pleasure is certainly an important aspect of walking that helps the walkers. There's nothing really mysterious about the way walking eases your mind. Dr. Glasser writes that "there is no disease known to man that cannot be imitated so well by a psychosomatic condition that even a good doctor will be unable to tell whether the symptoms come from within or without." These diseases are called psychosomatic because they result from a mental, rather than a physical condition. Yet, on the other side of the coin, the body can influence the workings of the mind. As you walk, the rhythmic motion of the arms and legs and the stretching and smoothing of the long muscles send signals through the central nervous system to the brain, saying in effect, "calm down, everything's going to be all right."

I mentioned in the last chapter that Dr. Hans Kraus and others believe that the prevalence of hypokinetic disease in our society is due to the fact that modern life produces tension without providing an acceptable means of releasing those pent-up tensions. It's here that walking satisfies another fundamental human requirement—*The Need to Escape.*

There aren't many places where you can escape from the telephone, the television, the newspapers, a disgruntled boss, noisy children, your work, whatever produces tension in your life. This is especially true during the work week when tension is more pronounced. Many popular forms of escape, such as golf, are hectic affairs. You rush out to the course; you play as fast as possible so you can get in your eighteen holes before dark; then you rush home for dinner. If you play badly, you're unhappy with yourself and vow to take some lessons. And even on the golf course, you can be traced by a boss who wants to squeeze just a little bit extra out of you that day.

The walker can escape through his front door. Every night, I put on a pair of old pants and a cap and walk for at least an hour. I live in an ordinary neighborhood so my walks don't take me through quiet woods or past famous historical sites. For the first fifteen minutes after leaving my house, I'm a little stiff and my mind is still clogged by the frustrations of the day. But soon my legs begin to loosen up and flow smoothly and the tensions of the day begin to loosen their grip on my mind. By the time my walk ends, I've obtained a new perspective on my life. I haven't solved anything, but I've escaped it long enough to realize that I'm capable of handling just about anything that comes along.

There's something about human nature that doesn't like to be cooped-up. That's why we like houses with big windows; why we sometimes dream of retiring in the country. The human race lived outdoors for at least a half-million years before it became sophisticated enough to build the structures of modern civilization. So the pull of history is strong. If we were meant to be cooped-up inside, why did we develop confinement as a means of punishment? Even a small child who committed some no-no around the house is sent to his room for a period of confinement.

Mrs. Larsh Young of Cedar Rapids, Iowa, has written an entertaining book called *Family Afoot*, about four long walking tours she took with her husband and children. "Before the first trip," she wrote, "I was in a deep despairing rut of housewifely routine. I felt ready to burst." She began urging her husband to go on a walking trip and eventually was successful. In walking, she found what she was looking for. "It's a magical moment—that first stepping out; that severing of the last tie with the machine age; that renunciation of wheel, piston and gear; that splendid gesture of independence. Your knapsack is on your back. You take a deep breath and simply start walking."

Yet the feeling of escape, that "splendid gesture of independence," can occur on any walk, no matter how brief. "Even when I walk to the office in the morning, I fancy I have achieved something more abiding than mere physical exercise," J. Brooks Atkinson wrote in *The Art of Walking*. "The first two blocks take me to the subway entrance. As soon as I have passed that, and have thus voluntarily chosen 30 minutes of walking instead of noisy riding, I feel myself reclaimed from civil activity. . . . In taking the first step I have done all that is really essential; I have lost identity in the city, and no one can tell what adventures lie ahead."

For some reason, our curiosity seems to grow with regular walking and any neighborhood or business district provides walkers with enough entertainment to prevent boredom. One businessman told me that he didn't really "see" the high-rise district he works in until he began walking during his lunch hour. Now, he's an authority on the architecture and people of the area. "I'm never bored," he said.

Stephen wrote in *Studies of a Biographer* that walking somehow jogs the memory as well. He wrote of one walking tour: "I kept no journal, but I could still give the narrative day by day—the sights which I dutifully admired and the very state of my bootlaces."

So walking not only provides a means of escape from our daily routines but it also gives us the ability to pursue new avenues of thought. Some psychiatrists believe that some mental illness is caused by recurring patterns of thought which etch themselves into the brain, causing what we perceive as mental pain or a headache. Walking seems to break through these patterns and frees our minds for original thought. That's one reason so many great thinkers, such as Einstein, Freud, and Thoreau, were also great walkers. Clearly, walking fulfills *The Need for Creative Thinking.*

Even people who don't really consider themselves walkers value its ability to produce original thought. I was talking to one young woman at a cocktail party recently and boring her to death, I am afraid, with facts and figures about the various health benefits of walking. But when I mentioned what it does to your mind, she lit up like a Christmas tree. "Oh yeh, I do my best thinking on my way to school in the morning," she said. "It's about a three-mile walk." Another woman told me she had preserved her marriage by going on regular walks with her husband. "Every time we walked, we found a new way of looking at a disagreement we'd had," she said.

And professional walkers like Colin Fletcher, who has written many books on his walking adventures, have talked extensively about this thought-producing quality of walking. "Yet 'think' does not seem to be quite the right word," Fletcher writes in *The New Complete Walker.* "Sometimes, when it is a matter of making a choice, I do not believe I decide what to do so much as discover what I have decided. It is as if my mind, set free by space and solitude and oiled by the body's easy rhythm, swings open and releases thoughts it has already formulated. Sometimes, when I have been straining too hard to impose order on an urgent press of ideas, it seems only as if my mind has slowly relaxed; and then, all at once, there is room for the ideas to fall into place in a meaningful pattern."

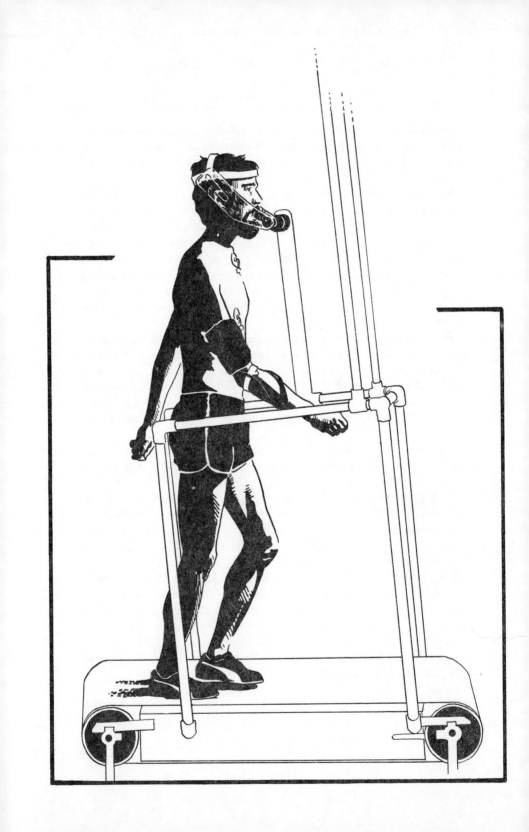

5

Walking and Your Heart

"Here you are perfectly normal and healthy and the next second it hits you for no apparent reason. After fourteen years I almost forgot about it. I was the most surprised man in the world when the second one hit me," Marvin Tucker remembers. The Kansas City attorney suffered his first heart attack in 1960 while sitting at home watching television. The second one struck fourteen years later while he was sitting by the swimming pool at his country club. "Hell, I wasn't doing anything. I couldn't have been doing anything less than lying around the pool or watching television."

After his first heart attack at the age of forty-five, Tucker wasn't told to walk, because it wasn't routinely prescribed by cardiologists in those days. But in 1974, when he had another attack, Tucker was told to start walking. Slowly, he built up speed and endurance until in 1978, when I talked with him, he was walking two-and-one-quarter miles, twice a day, as fast as he could go. He doesn't particularly like walking. "I'm not doing it for pleasure. I get up there and grind it out," he says. But he likes what walking does for him. "I feel good, so I'm afraid to stop. I feel great. I'm healthy."

For Tucker and the millions of heart-attack victims across the country, walking is therapy. * Their physicians tell them to walk be-

---

*If you have had a heart attack, or believe you are suffering from some form of heart disease, you should consult your doctor before you start walking.

cause it's a gentle, safe way of reconditioning the heart muscle and improving circulation. Many of these people enjoy walking, but whether they enjoy it or not, they all realize they're walking to stay alive, to avoid another attack that might be fatal. "You're buying time," Tucker continues. "You're doing the best you can. You watch your diet, walk, try to avoid stress, and do things in moderation. You can still have a heart attack, but these things are under your control. I know I'm doing my best."

Walking has become part of Tucker's daily routine. "I don't even think about it," he says. "I feel like I'm doing what I can. It's just like brushing my teeth. It's part of my life. Getting up and going out in the morning and the evening is just part of my life."

Tucker can never be sure of what walking is doing for him, but I know other walkers who feel it has saved their lives or at least prevented a heart attack or heart surgery.

One of the fastest walkers I've ever seen, race-walkers not included, is Bill Sight, the owner of a car dealership that covers most of a city block. Sight walks his two miles a day at more than four-and-one-quarter miles an hour, which is a fast pace when you take into consideration the fact that Sight is not a big man. Sight started walking in 1971 after suffering a heart attack at the age of forty-two. He believes that walking may have saved his life because it was while walking that he first began feeling angina, a stabbing pain in the chest area associated with heart problems. Realizing that something was wrong, he then underwent heart surgery. "If I hadn't felt that pain when walking, I probably would have had another attack," Sight says.

Don Brown and his wife, Flo, started walking in 1960 about the time Brown quit smoking and took up an interest in working with the Boy Scouts. "I thought if we were going to be keeping up with the kids, we'd better get in shape," he said. The Browns enjoy their two-mile daily walking regimen because it makes them feel good and provides a quiet interlude away from distractions. "You derive a feeling of better health," said Brown, vice-president of a prestigious clothing store. "But one side effect is that you get to talk to one another without being pressed by the tube. It's just a good time to talk." While walking, Brown was also able to construct the framework and compose the first chapter of a book about the retail clothing business. But the benefits—such as feeling good, having time to talk, and thinking clearly—pale when compared with something that happened to Brown in 1974, fourteen years after he began walking. It was then Brown discovered that he had a heart problem. A test showed that an artery to the heart was blocked, a diagnosis that normally would lead to heart surgery. But Brown was lucky. He was a walker. He had developed collateral circulation, which occurs when new vessels form around the blocked one and restore the flow of blood to the heart muscles. "Probably because I had been exercising, new vessels had developed," Brown said. "I have a natural bypass rather than an operative bypass and that prevented me from having a heart attack." After his heart problem was discovered, Brown's physician limited his activities, especially the hiking in high-altitude areas that he had been particularly fond of. But by 1978, even that restriction had been lifted and he was looking forward to a trip to Switzerland.

Although walking has effectively reconditioned many people who have had heart attacks, it is even more important as a method of preventing heart attacks altogether. Although in recent years, the death rate from heart disease has tapered off somewhat, it is still the number-one killer in America. The American Heart Association estimates that it will take nearly a million lives in 1979 and one-quarter

Leading Causes of Death United States: 1976
Number of Deaths (in Thousands) ■ Under age 65 □ Age 65 and over

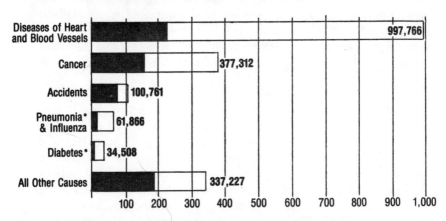

Diseases of Heart and Blood Vessels		997,766
Cancer		377,312
Accidents		100,761
Pneumonia* & Influenza		61,866
Diabetes*		34,508
All Other Causes		337,227

100 200 300 400 500 600 700 800 900 1,000

Source: National Center for Health Statistics, U.S. Public Health Service, DHEW
*Deaths from certain causes of mortality in early infancy, cirrhosis of the liver, suicide and homicide exceed those from pneumonia and influenza, and diabetes for persons under age 65.

of the people who die of heart attacks will be under the age of sixty-five.

Dr. Harry Julius Johnson, a longtime advocate of walking and an expert on longevity, wrote in 1968 in *Eat, Drink, Be Merry and Live Longer* that the rapid rise in the death rate from heart attacks between 1930 and 1960 was paralleled by an equivalent decrease in the amount of walking done by Americans. "It was during this same thirty years that Americans started to drive rather than walk—that suburban communities were laid out without sidewalks—that a man walking down the street became a subject of investigation by the police—that the exercise in golf was extracted by the invention of the electric golf cart," Johnson wrote. And the person, the middle-aged male, who has the best chance of having a heart attack, is the one who walks the least, Johnson continued. "Every morning he steps into a conveyance, his car, his cab, his limousine, or bus and drives or rides as close to his office, shop, or field as possible. At noon, depending on his economic status, he eats a sandwich in his shop, his office, or goes to the executive dining room, which he reaches by elevator. If he has to go out in the daytime he drives or takes a cab. And he returns home the same way he came."

There is a large body of research linking heart disease to a lack of physical activity. They are called epidemiological studies because they are based on observations of large environmental groups. They don't rank as high as other studies in the minds of many medical authorities because they aren't conducted under controlled laboratory conditions. But they are, nevertheless, highly regarded and they have led to a substantial change in the way the medical profession regards exercise.

A group of English researchers led by J. N. Morris has studied the heart attack rate for people in the same line of work, but with assignments calling for varying degrees of physical activity. In 1949 and 1950 they studied 31,000 men between the ages of thirty-five and sixty-four who worked for the London public transportation system. In reviewing the health records of the drivers and conductors of London's double-decker buses, they found considerably fewer instances of heart disease in the conductors than in the drivers. The researchers reported that the difference could be explained by the amount of physical activity required in their work. While the conductors were moving around the buses, climbing stairs, and taking tickets, the drivers were confined to their seats all day.

Morris found a similar relationship between heart disease and physical activity in a study of 110,000 English postal workers. The instances of heart disease were considerably lower for the postmen, who walked several hours a day with a light load delivering the mail, than for the telephone operators, clerks, executives, and other postal employees whose jobs required less physical activity.

In yet another study, the Englishmen looked at the leisure activities of 16,882 male office workers between the ages of forty and sixty-four. The office workers were interviewed about the amount of vigorous activity, including brisk walking, they took part in on a typical Friday and Saturday. The researchers found that only 11 percent of the men who later developed heart disease had taken part in any vigorous physical activity, while 26 percent of those who didn't have heart disease had exercised vigorously during the two-day period.

Several U.S. studies have also confirmed the connection between heart disease and inactivity. A classic study of San Francisco longshoremen, by Dr. Ralph S. Paffenberger and Wayne E. Hale, indicated that longshoremen who did only light and moderate work ran an 80 percent greater risk of suffering from heart disease than those doing heavy work. Their risk of dying suddenly from a heart attack was almost three times as great. The researchers reported in the prestigious *New England Journal of Medicine* that during the time period covered by the study, from 1951 to 1972, the number of longshoremen engaged in heavy work decreased from 40 to 5 percent because of automation. "On entering their industry, 6,351 longshoremen were all physically able and required to perform the heavy work of cargo handling which repeatedly called for bursts of high energy expenditure," the researchers reported. "Those who stayed in the heavy work brackets fared better than their fellow workers who moved into lighter jobs." Since automation in industry had eliminated the need for hard physical labor, the workers' leisure hours had become much more important. "If high energy output is protective, workers thus deprived of heavy work on the job may have to compensate by rigorous leisure time activities, lest they encounter increased risk of fatal coronary heart disease," the researchers suggested.

Another comprehensive study of heart disease was conducted by

the Health Insurance Plan of Greater New York, with the cooperation of the National Institutes of Health. The men participating in this study were questioned about the amount of exercise required in their work: The amount of time spent sitting and walking; the amount of walking back and forth from work; the frequency of lifting heavy objects; and the number of hours worked per week. In addition, they were asked about recreational walking, participation in sports, and gardening. Dr. Charles W. Frank reported in the *Bulletin of the New York Academy of Medicine* that the most active men appeared to run less risks of dying within a month after suffering a heart attack. Forty-four percent of the least active died within the first month, while 29 percent of those with intermediate activity and 21 percent of the most active men, died within that crucial period.

The epidemiological studies have yet to reveal what causes heart attacks, but they have established a statistical link between certain "risk factors" and the likelihood that someone will have a heart attack. The studies, especially a U.S. Public Health Service study of the inhabitants of Framingham, Massachusetts, have suggested that there are eleven such "risk factors." Four of them are totally beyond our control: heredity, sex, race, and age. The studies have shown that past family history plays some role in whether a person has heart problems. Young men run a greater risk of heart attacks than young women, but the difference levels off once women reach menopause. Blacks in America have a much higher incidence of high blood pressure than whites. And your chances of having a heart attack increase with age.

The remaining seven risk factors can be reduced through a change in personal habits or treatment under a doctor's supervision. The risks are: A high level of serum cholesterol, high blood pressure, diabetes, cigarette smoking, diet, stress, and exercise. All of these risk factors may also be affected by walking.

Serum cholesterol is one of several fatty substances normally found in the blood in moderate amounts and essential to our survival. Excessive quantities of cholesterol, however, can become deposited in the walls of the arteries and cause the blockage that leads to heart attacks. Studies have shown that groups of people who walk a great deal have lower levels of cholesterol despite a diet high in cholesterol. In at least one study, treadmill walking showed a reduction in the level of fatty substances in the blood.

High blood pressure is the most prevalent cardiovascular disease. One study indicated that walking or jogging for only one hour, two days a week, was sufficient to reduce blood pressure levels at the end of a six-month training program.

Some forms of diabetes seem to be hereditary, but the milder cases that sometimes develop in middle-aged people, can be greatly alleviated by exercise. A study in South Africa in which eight diabetics exercised thirty minutes, four times a day, for eight months, was so successful that all but one of the patients lost all symptoms.

Cigarette smoking, diet, and stress can be indirectly influenced by walking. It can't replace the self-discipline required to quit smoking, but it helps build your desire to stop by introducing you to the feeling of good health. It's also a good way to get out of the house and away from cigarettes. Diet is a concern because your weight and the kinds of foods you eat effect the likelihood of heart attacks. Walking can help you with your weight. It can't, however, tell you what to eat. As for stress, walking is a better relaxant than tranquilizers and it has no debilitating side effects.

Scientists need more than epidemiological studies before they can prove beyond a shadow of a doubt that exercise such as walking will lengthen your life by reducing the risk of heart attack. Scientists need the kind of proof that can be verified under laboratory conditions where all the variables can be controlled. Some laboratory studies have shown that exercised rats suffer less severe heart attacks than sedentary ones, but the researchers still weren't convinced that the differences were influenced by other factors besides exercise. Such experiments can't be carried out on people. For one reason, you could not control all the variables unless the volunteers were willing to spend their entire lives in a laboratory. Secondly, the ethics of science and medicine prevent researchers from deliberately withholding certain drugs and techniques from people in a way that might harm them. For example, asking a group of people to refrain from exercise for a period of many years would certainly endanger their lives, given what we know already about the link between inactivity and heart disease.

The closest scientists have come to studying the effects of inactivity under laboratory conditions is in the space program. After three astronauts spent twenty-eight days in Skylab I, where the lack of gravity produced an extreme state of inactivity, they were found to be extremely weak and disoriented and their heart rate and blood pressure were dangerously distorted. The astronauts recovered after a few weeks, but the effects of inactivity had been dramatically demonstrated and they were disastrous. Needless to say, exercise became an important part of the astronauts' routine on subsequent missions to the space laboratory. "This problem of weightless human bodies, serious enough to scare space physicians in the early days of orbital exploration, has relevance to everyday life here on earth," Clayton R. Myers writes in *The Official YMCA Physical Fitness Handbook.* "It gives us a concentrated example of the effects of a sedentary life—a lifetime in miniature—of what happens to the human body with no muscular activity or practically none to keep its juices flowing."

Even if conclusive evidence isn't available, a growing number of experts now believe that it is convincing enough to recommend some form of daily, planned, rigorous exercise to counteract the effects of inactivity.

"Possibly the health profession could best serve the population by somehow making us exercise more," Dr. Jean Mayer writes in *A Diet for Living*. "But I am convinced that U.S. medicine has yet to recognize fully the formidable health problem caused by the growing physical inactivity (now almost total) of our citizens. Doctors certainly have not come to grips with this problem in their personal lives: I don't know many who have their own daily regimen of exercising. And while they may prescribe more exercise for their patients, they do it without conviction. They almost never put their recommendations in the form of a detailed program similar, say, to the taking of a drug they might prescribe or even to the dietary schedule established by the dieticians to whom they may refer you."

But the responsibility for maintaining good health doesn't really lie with the medical profession; the enemy is us. Many of the problems of inactivity have been public knowledge for decades. Thousands of books, magazine stories, and newspaper articles have been written about them. Yet despite this media-pounding, we still don't get enough exercise.

Dr. Theodore Cooper, a former assistant secretary for health in the Department of Health, Education and Welfare, has suggested that we need a new concept of health and how it is obtained. He says we must adopt "the idea that individuals and communities have a major responsibility for their own health; that illness and injury usually represent a departure from the norm, the result of a failure of omission or commission; and that medicine is an art and science concerned as much with preserving health as with restoring it."

The experts are urging that a new emphasis be placed on "preventive medicine," especially in view of the growing realization that health care costs are bourne by the healthy as well as the sick. The adoption of Medicare and Medicaid has meant an increase in the government's share of health costs for all Americans from $4.4 billion in 1965 to $50 billion in 1977. And with the cost of medical services rising at about 9.5 percent a year, it's bound to go higher.

So if these studies linking lack of exercise with heart disease seem a little unreal to you, think about paying two-hundred dollars a day for hospital care. That's getting you where you know it hurts.

6

Walking and Your Weight

Several years ago, at the University of California, eleven desperate women began walking. Some of the women had been grossly overweight for many years. All of them had tried to lose weight by dieting and they had failed miserably. After enrolling in a program designed by Dr. Grant Gwinup, an expert on the problems of obesity, the women began walking for gradually longer periods every day, until some of them were exercising as much as two to three hours a day. They were told to ignore their eating habits, to forget about dieting. At the end of a year, these women, who had tried everything and failed, had lost an average of twenty-two pounds each, even though they were eating more than when the program began.

"It is often said that you can't actually lose weight by exercise alone," Dr. Gwinup reported in *Harper's Bazaar*. "Our walkers ate more than they had before, as a matter of fact, but they lost an average of twenty-two pounds a year—or close to half a pound a week. This is a relatively slow rate of loss, but it has its advantages. If you lose weight slowly, you have a better chance of keeping it off. And your skin will adapt more easily to your new weight as it shrinks." Furthermore, the weight loss didn't occur just around the arm and the leg muscles used in walking. "The reason for this is that whenever you use a muscle or a group of muscles they send out hormonal signals to every fat cell in your body. These cells release fat molecules into the blood stream, which takes them to the working muscles to be used as fuel. You don't draw only on the fat near the muscles being exercised; you draw evenly on your total reserves."

In a more detailed report on his work in the *Archives of Internal Medicine*, Dr. Gwinup revealed that thirty-four people, twenty-nine women and five men, initially entered the program but only eleven of them, all women, maintained an exercise regimen of a minimum of thirty minutes a day. Significantly, eleven of the people who dropped out had tried to fulfill their exercise requirement by jogging, swimming, or cycling. Only the walkers completed the program. "On the basis of this experience, walking would have to be recommended as the most practical form of exercise for obese subjects who wish to lose weight," Dr. Gwinup reported.

Dr. Gwinup's success was more astounding than it might seem. For years, the medical community has viewed the problems of overweight people, especially those who are grossly overweight, with something akin to anguish. As just about anyone with a weight problem knows, losing weight can be virtually impossible. At a conference at Cornell University in the 1950s, Dr. Albert Stunkard reported that of one-hundred persons who were treated at the nutrition clinic of New York Hospital, only twelve had succeeded in losing more than twenty pounds at any time during the year and four of those gained back most of the weight almost immediately. Dr. Stunkard concluded that "most obese persons will not stay on treatment for obesity. Of those who stay in treatment, most will not lose weight, of those who do lose weight, most will regain it." He suggested as well that the treatment of obesity could sometimes be dangerous to the patient because of the psychological problems that arise when they begin dieting.

This is no small problem. Experts estimate that roughly 35 percent of all Americans are overweight and 20 percent of us are so overweight that we should be classified as obese. At the same time, both medical advice and popular culture inform us that we need to be thin. Researchers have found that overweight people run a greater risk of having heart attacks and that extra body weight puts a heavy strain on the heart, liver, kidneys, and other organs that are intended to serve a leaner machine. And overweight people in America tend to suffer from social rejection and self-image problems because slimness, particularly for women, is valued highly in our society. In response to all this, dieting has become one of our great preoccupations.

As researchers delved more deeply into the causes of our ever-increasing national girth, many of them have concluded that the primary problem isn't food. It's inactivity. Dr. Jean Mayer wrote in *A Diet for Living:* "Although Americans generally have been getting fatter and fatter over the last seventy years, the surprising fact is that people today actually eat less food and get fewer calories than they did in 1900. The only possible explanation must be inactivity." A study of overweight high-school girls in Boston revealed that they ate no more food than their peers. They just moved around a lot less. Another study of two-hundred overweight people traced the beginning of their obesity to a period of sudden decreased activity. Upon closer examination, researchers have found that the appetite decreases with the level of activity only to a certain point, then it begins to increase. Dr. Mayer wrote: "We are learning more and more about the mechanism in the brain which regulates the sense of hunger and satiety and thus controls caloric intake. We have established that the mechanism just does not operate at very low levels of activity. Unfortunately, this is where more and more of us live!"

The good news in all of this for the person who wants to lose weight or maintain his present level is that he can do so by walking or by combining walking and dieting. Either method is less painful and more lasting than dieting alone. To compare and contrast dieting and exercise as a means of losing weight, Drs. W. B. Zuti, a physical education expert, and L. A. Golding, a physiology specialist, devised a study in 1975 in which twenty-five overweight women were placed in a diet group, an exercise group, and a combination group. The diet group reduced its food intake 500 calories a day; the exercise group walked for roughly two hours a day, five days a week; and the combination group cut 250 calories from their daily diet and walked one hour a day. At the end of a four-month period, the average weight loss for all three groups was more than ten pounds per person, but the differences between the groups were negligible, according to a report in *The Physician and Sportsmedicine.* The researchers did find, however, that the women who used dieting alone lost lean body tissue, while in the other two groups it actually increased slightly.

For the normal person, weight gain or loss is directly related to a unit of energy called the calorie. All foods and beverages, with the exception of water, contain calories. At the same time, our bodies are constantly using up those calories, Even while reading, watching television, or sitting at a desk, we're burning up about 80 to 100 calories an hour.

The number of calories each person needs every day varies with size, sex, age, and level of activity. Most men need more calories than women because they are larger and have a greater proportion of muscle tissue. Large people burn more calories than small people, much in the same way that a car with a large engine and greater weight burns more gasoline than a compact model. Children, who are still growing, need more calories than older people, who have stopped growing. Active people need more calories than inactive people.

Height (without shoes) MEN	Weight (without clothing)		
	Low Pounds	Average Pounds	High Pounds
5 feet 3 inches	118	129	141
5 feet 4 inches	122	133	145
5 feet 5 inches	126	137	149
5 feet 6 inches	130	142	155
5 feet 7 inches	134	147	161
5 feet 8 inches	139	151	166
5 feet 9 inches	143	155	170
5 feet 10 inches	147	159	174
5 feet 11 inches	150	163	178
6 feet	154	167	183
6 feet 1 inch	158	171	188
6 feet 2 inches	162	175	192
6 feet 3 inches	165	178	195
WOMEN			
5 feet	100	109	118
5 feet 1 inch	104	112	121
5 feet 2 inches	107	115	125
5 feet 3 inches	110	118	128
5 feet 4 inches	113	122	132
5 feet 5 inches	116	125	135
5 feet 6 inches	120	129	139
5 feet 7 inches	123	132	142
5 feet 8 inches	126	136	146
5 feet 9 inches	130	140	151
5 feet 10 inches	133	144	156
5 feet 11 inches	137	148	161
6 feet	141	152	166

Source: *Food and Your Weight*, U.S. Department of Agriculture, Home and Garden Bulletin, No. 74.

You can determine your desirable weight from the chart below. It shows the average weights of persons from twenty to thirty-years old. Experts believe that for most of us our weight during those years is "normal." If you have a small frame, your weight should fall between the weights in the "low" and "average" columns. The weight of some-one with a large frame should fall between the "average" and "high" columns. If you have an average-size frame, your weight should be about "average" on the chart.

You also can use this chart to determine the approximate number of calories you need to consume every day. Find the midpoint of your range of desirable weight. (If your weight should fall between 155 and 170, the midpoint would be about 162 pounds.) Multiply that figure by eighteen if you're a man and by sixteen if you're a woman. The result is the number of calories burned daily by someone with an average level of activity. For instance, an adult man with a large frame should weigh about 162 pounds. His daily caloric need is 18 x 162, or about 2,900 calories. If you are very active, your caloric need will be considerably higher than that indicated by this method of calculation. If you are quite inactive, it would be lower.

And despite what the apostles of bizarre dieting techniques claim in their advertisements, calories do count. You gain weight when you consume more calories than you burn up. It doesn't matter if the source of the calories is yogurt or chocolate cake. A calorie is a calorie.

I'm sure this sounds elementary to veteran weight-watchers, but many people don't understand that the calorie isn't associated with any particular food. It's a unit of energy. A friend of mine, for instance, returned recently from a vacation during which he walked a great deal and lost a noticeable amount of weight. Anxious to maintain his losses, he was concerned about what he should be eating. He kept asking, every time he sat down to eat: "Is this fattening?" And the answer was always "yes." I was concerned for a while that his confusion would lead him to fasting. So remember: Every food and beverage contains calories and any food or beverage can be "fattening" if the number of calories we consume is greater than the number of calories we burn up. Consequently, the three-hundred calories you use in an hour's walk have as much or even more effect on your weight as the piece of chocolate cake you don't eat for dessert.

You can be as technical or nontechnical as you please about losing weight the walker's way. Rather than count calories, some people would rather just go out and walk as much as possible and monitor their progress occasionally on the bathroom scale. Dr. Gwinup's study at the University of California indicates that even if you don't mess with your diet at all, the chances are good you will lose weight. But for those people who want to count calories and perhaps lose weight at a certain rate, much information is available on calorie counting the walker's way.

Every pound of stored fat in your body consists of about 3,500 calories. So every time, through exercise or dieting, you burn up 3,500 more calories than you consume, you lose one pound. If you walk an hour a day and keep your diet at its normal level, you could lose a pound in roughly twelve days. That's a relatively slow rate of loss. But if you cut your calorie intake by an equal amount, or roughly three-hundred calories a day, and continue to walk for an hour a day, you could lose a pound every six days. And that's about as fast as you should be losing weight without a doctor's supervision.

The number of calories you burn while walking varies with your speed, your weight, and the inclination and ruggedness of the terrain.

The Number of Days Required to Walk Off 1 to 20 Pounds With and Without Dieting *

Min. Per Day	Miles Per Day	Caloric Deficit	Days To Lose 1 Pound	Days To Lose 5 Pounds	Days To Lose 10 Pounds	Days To Lose 20 Pounds
30	1¾	0	23	117	233	467
30	1¾	200	10	50	100	200
30	1¾	400	6	32	64	127
30	1¾	600**	5	23	47	93
60	3½	0	12	58	117	233
60	3½	200	7	35	70	140
60	3½	400	5	25	50	100
60	3½	600	4	19	39	78
90	5¼	0	8	39	78	156
90	5¼	200	5	27	54	108
90	5¼	400	4	21	41	82
90	5¼	600	3	17	33	67

*Calorie expenditure is 5 calories per minute, about average for a 154-pound person walking 3.5 m.p.h.
**Your calorie intake should not go below 1500 calories a day.

The caloric loss while walking increases with body weight, simply because it requires more energy to move a heavier object any given distance. This is actually good news for overweight people because it reduces the amount of time needed to walk off the pounds. Unfortunately, as you lose weight, the amount of time it takes increases. Researchers also have found that a backpack, worn properly, effects energy cost in the same way an equivalent amount of body weight would. So you can use the chart below to calculate the number of calories you burn while backpacking. Just add the weight of the pack to your body weight. For instance, a 160-pound person, carrying a 40-pound pack, would burn as many calories as a 200-pound person, carrying no pack—or 5.3 calories per minute.

Number of Calories Burned by People of Various Weights at a Walking Speed of 3 M.P.H. *

	Weight of Walker in Pounds									
	120	140	160	180	200	220	240	260	280	300
Calories Per Minute	3.6	4	4.4	4.9	5.3	5.7	6.1	6.6	7	7.4
Calories Per Mile	72	80	89	97	106	114	123	131	140	149
Calories Per Hour	216	240	264	294	318	342	366	396	420	444

*Calculated from a formula suggested by Roy J. Shephard, M.D., Ph.D., in *Alive Man: The Physiology of Physical Activity*, (Charles C. Thomas, Springfield, Ill., 1972).

Speed effects the caloric cost of walking in much the same way as weight. The faster you go, the more calories you're burning per minute, simply because you're covering a greater distance. Researchers also have found that at speeds greater than four miles an hour, the energy cost of walking rises steeply because we walk less efficiently at higher speeds. A race-walker, for instance, traveling at eight miles an hour is burning 18.9 calories a minute or 142 calories by the end of his seven-and-one-half minute mile.

The figures provided in the charts in this chapter are only approximations, but they should give you some idea of how you can use walking to lose weight. Essentially, your weight loss will depend on the amount of time you spend walking, your walking speed, your

Calories Burned by a Person Weighing 154 Pounds *

Speed in M.P.H.	Calories per Min.	Calories per Hour	Calories per Mile
2	3.1	184	92
2½	3.7	222	89
3	4.4	260	87
3½	5.0	299	85
4 **	5.6	337	84
4½	7.4	444	99
5 ***	8.7	519	104

*Calculated from formulae in *Alive Man: The Physiology of Physical Activity*.
**The same energy cost as walking at 2 m.p.h. on a 10 percent uphill grade.
***The same energy cost as walking 3 mp.h. on a 10 percent grade.

current weight, and your eating habits. If you are a good deal over-weight, you should drop pounds easily at first, without needing to pay much attention to the information in this chapter. But as your weight drops closer and closer to a "desirable" level, you'll find that it may be worth your while to study the figures carefully and to set some sort of daily caloric goal for yourself.

When you lose weight, you begin to expend fewer and fewer calories for each minute of walking at the same speed. You can somewhat compensate for this by increasing your walking speed and, if possible, the total amount of time you spend walking. Most people who walk for exercise find that their walking speed gradually increases with practice and that their tolerance for walking increases as well. Many people can walk for seven or eight hours without any discomfort. When you reach that point, weight will no longer be a problem.

I mentioned earlier in this book that most experts believe it's important to walk continuously for at least thirty minutes to produce an enhanced level of cardiorespiratory fitness. Fortunately, this is not true for people who are trying to lose weight. There is no need to walk continuously for a certain time period. You can burn off calories just by walking in brief interludes, whenever you have the opportunity. If you walked every time it was practical during the day, you soon would notice some weight loss. That's an advantage of walking to lose weight. You can do it secretly and surprise everyone with your newly earned slimness. Who's to know that you're walking to work to lose weight. Tell them your car broke down.

It's beyond the scope of this book to recommend a specific diet, but since I may have provoked some of you to begin worrying about your weight and consequently to begin dieting, I feel compelled to discuss some of the general principles involved in the art of proper eating. Perhaps some of you are also concerned about your walking performance and are looking for some miraculous concoctions that will help you walk longer and faster. Or maybe you're looking for verification of your belief that your secret concoction works wonders on the road. I'm afraid you'll be disappointed on both counts. For one, the race-walkers I interviewed (who should know) about what they eat didn't serve up any bizarre or intriguing recommendations and I, personally, am an unconscious eater who never paid much attention to the subject other than favoring an occasional meatless meal. Secondly, the leading authorities on nutrition offer a variation on what every parent must have harped on since the beginning of time: "Eat your vegetables, children!"

Yet even if the nutritionists tend to be rather conservative, it's safer to listen to them than to a clerk in a health-food store who has good intentions but is ignorant; or to the apostle of some "miraculous" diet, who's out to make a quick buck. The real experts on nutrition and diet, as opposed to the fly-by-night quacks, believe that moderation, common sense, and regular exercise are the essential elements of a sound weight-loss program. "If you need to lose weight do so under the direction of your physician," says the President's Council on Physical Fitness and Sports. "Don't lose more than two pounds per week without his knowledge and consent. Determine to reduce gradually and consistently. Determine to develop proper eating habits! A change in diet—perhaps a change as slight as taking a little less sugar or none in beverages—may be all that is necessary to bring your weight down and keep it down, especially if coupled with the essential exercise regimen." Dr. Mayer writes: "Good nutrition is not a matter of emphasizing the actual or supposed importance of one or more particular foods. Nor is it a pattern of eating whatever you please or whatever is put before you. The way to keep yourself properly nourished is to accustom yourself to a diet of great variety."

You can ensure the proper variety in your diet by choosing foods every day from each of the four food groups that you learned about in elementary school: Milk, meat, vegetable-fruit, and bread-cereal. Then you'll be getting all the vitamins, minerals, proteins, fats, and carbohydrates you need without taking diet supplements. You lose weight by watching the amount of each kind of food you eat and the caloric content of different foods within each group. You can get a calorie counter that will show you how many calories are contained in certain portions of foods and you'll see that how much you eat is equally as important as what you eat. You'll also notice that each food group has at least one item that is considerably lower in calories than the others. Skim milk, for instance, has only slightly more than half the calories of whole milk. Once you've studied the matter, it won't be absolutely necessary for you to count calories. You'll know what foods to avoid and you'll be able to control your weight and stay healthy simply by eating smaller portions of a wider variety of foods.

As simple as the nutritionists make dieting sound, eating well still escapes many people. In many cases, it's because we tend to focus our attention on one particular aspect of nutrition. The result is often expensive, almost always fruitless, and sometimes even dangerous. So use common sense and moderation in your dieting and walking.

THE WALKER'S CALORIE COUNTER

The number of minutes of walking required to burn up calories equal to those in various foods and beverages. *

Food or Beverage	Portion Size	Calories	Minutes of Walking
MILK PRODUCTS			
Whole Milk	1 cup	160	32
Skim Milk	1 cup	90	18
2% Skimmed Milk	1 cup	145	29
Cream	1 tablespoon	30	6

*The calculations are based on a 154-pound person walking at 3.5 miles an hour.

Food or Beverage	Portion Size	Calories	Minutes of Walking
Sour Cream	1 tablespoon	25	5
Blue Cheese	1 ounce	105	21
Cheddar Cheese	1 ounce	115	23
Cottage Cheese	1 cup	260	52
Swiss Cheese	1 ounce	105	21
Chocolate Milk	1 cup	240	48
Chocolate Shake	12 ounces	430	86
Ice Cream	1 cup	255	51
Yogurt	1 cup	150	30

MEAT AND OTHER HIGH-PROTEIN FOODS

Food or Beverage	Portion Size	Calories	Minutes of Walking
Roast Beef	3 ounces	375	75
Steak	3 ounces	330	66
Hamburger	3 ounces	345	49
Corned Beef	3 ounces	185	37
Beef Stew	½ cup	95	19
Veal Cutlet	3 ounces	185	37
Pork Chop	2⅔ ounces	305	61
Bacon	2 slices	60	12
Pork Sausage	2 patties	260	52
Liver	3 ounces	195	39·
Frankfurter	1	170	34
Broiled Chicken	3 ounces	115	23
Fish Sticks	3 ounces	150	30
Oysters	6 to 10	80	16
Shrimp	3 ounces	100	20
Tuna Fish	3 ounces	170	34
Fried Eggs	1 large	100	20
Boiled Eggs	1 large	80	16
Lima Beans	½ cup	130	26
Baked Beans	½ cup	155	31
Almonds	15 almonds	105	21
Peanuts	2 tablespoons	105	21
Peanut Butter	1 tablespoon	95	19

VEGETABLES AND FRUITS

Food or Beverage	Portion Size	Calories	Minutes of Walking
Asparagus	6 medium spears	20	4
Green Beans	½ cup	15	3
Beets	½ cup	30	6

Food or Beverage	Portion Size	Calories	Minutes of Walking
Broccoli	½ cup	25	5
Cabbage	½ cup	15	3
Coleslaw	½ cup	85	17
Carrots	1 carrot	30	6
Celery	3 stalks	10	2
Corn, plain	½ cup	70	14
Cucumbers	6 slices	5	1
Lettuce, raw	2 large leaves	5	1
Mushrooms, canned	½ cup	20	4
Onions	1 tablespoon, chopped	5	1
Potatoes, baked	1	145	29
Potatoes, boiled	1	90	18
French Fries	10 pieces	215	43
Sweet Potatoes	1 potato	160	32
Tomatoes, raw	1	20	4
Apples, raw	1 medium-sized	80	16
Avocados	8 ounces	205	41
Bananas	1	85	17
Blackberries	½ cup	40	8
Blueberries	½ cup	45	9
Strawberries	½ cup	30	6
Cherries, raw	½ cup	30	6
Fruit Cocktail	½ cup	95	19
Grapefruit Juice	½ cup	50	10
Grapes, raw	1 bunch (3½ ounces)	45	9
Grapejuice, frozen	½ cup	65	13
Oranges, raw	1	65	13
Orange Juice	½ cup	55	11
Peaches, raw	1 medium-sized	40	8
Pears, raw	1 pear	100	20
Watermelon	2 pounds	110	21

BREADS AND CEREALS

Food or Beverage	Portion Size	Calories	Minutes of Walking
Rye Bread	1 slice	60	12
White Bread	1 slice	70	14
Whole-Wheat Bread	1 slice	65	13
Saltine Crackers	4 crackers	50	10
Doughnuts	1 doughnut	165	33
Muffins	1 muffin	120	24
Pancakes	1 cake	60	12
Pizza	5⅓-inch slice	155	31

Food or Beverage	Portion Size	Calories	Minutes of Walking
Hamburger Bun	1	120	120
Waffles	1 waffle	210	42
Bran Flakes	1 ounce	85	17
Corn Flakes	1 ounce	110	22
Grits	¾ cup	95	19
Noodles	¾ cup	150	30
Oatmeal	¾ cup	100	20
Instant Rice	¾ cup	135	27
Spaghetti	¾ cup	115	23

FATS, OILS, AND SALAD DRESSINGS

Food or Beverage	Portion Size	Calories	Minutes of Walking
Butter	1 tablespoon	100	20
Margarine	1 tablespoon	100	20
Cooking Oils	1 tablespoon	120	24
French Dressing	1 tablespoon	65	13
Italian Dressing	1 tablespoon	85	17
Mayonnaise	1 tablespoon	100	20

SUGAR AND SWEETS

Food or Beverage	Portion Size	Calories	Minutes of Walking
Chocolate Mints	1 ounce	115	23
Fudge	1 ounce	115	23
Jellybeans	1 ounce	105	21
Chocolate Syrup	1 tablespoon	45	9
Honey	1 tablespoon	65	13
Table Syrup	1 tablespoon	55	11
Jam, Preserves	1 tablespoon	55	11
Sugar	1 teaspoon	15	3

SOUPS

Food or Beverage	Portion Size	Calories	Minutes of Walking
Bean with Pork	1 cup	170	34
Beef Noodle	1 cup	65	13
Chicken Noodle	1 cup	60	13
Mushroom, with water	1 cup	135	27
with milk	1 cup	215	43
Tomato, with water	1 cup	90	18
with milk	1 cup	170	34
Vegetable	1 cup	80	16

Food or Beverage	Portion Size	Calories	Minutes of Walking
DESSERTS			
Brownies	1 piece	90	18
Angelcake	2½-inch slice	135	27
Chocolate Cake	1¾ inch slice	235	47
Chocolate Chip Cookies	1 cookie	50	10
Apple Pie	3½-inch sector	300	60
Cherry Pie	3½-inch sector	310	62
Peach Pie	3½-inch sector	300	60
Pecan Pie	3½-inch sector	430	86
Chocolate Pudding	½ cup	160	32
OTHER BEVERAGES			
Ginger Ale	12-ounce can	115	23
Cola	12-ounce can	145	29
Beer	8-ounce glass	100	20
Liquors, 86 proof	1 jigger	105	21
Table Wines	1 wine glass	85	17
Dessert Wines	1 wine glass	140	28
Lemonade	½ cup	55	11

7

On Walking and Aging

Walking has long been regarded as a fountain of youth. Charles Dickens noted "certain ancients, far gone in years, who have staved off infirmities and dissolution by earnest walking—hale fellows, close upon ninety, but brisk as boys." Dr. Alexander Leaf, a professor at the Harvard Medical School, reached the same conclusion after studying groups of people around the world who live to be very old but retain their physical vitality. Dr. Leaf reported in *Executive Health* in 1977: "These men I have examined around the world who live in vigorous health to 100 or more years are great walkers. If you want to live a long, long time in sturdy health you can't go wrong in forming the habit of long vigorous walking every day . . . until it becomes a habit as important to you as eating and sleeping."

The saying "you're only as old as you feel" is, truly, the gospel. Research into the effects of aging has shown that many of the diseases commonly associated with old age are caused by the way we live, rather than how long we live. For that reason, it's difficult to choose examples of people who have retained their vitality in "old age" by walking. For what is "old age"? It's certainly not the kind of life-style these people, all over seventy, are living.

Every Wednesday morning a handful of "old men" gather at their "club house," a parking lot in Carmel, California, to begin a day of hiking. They meet at 8:30 a.m. sharp and pool their cars for the drive to whatever trail they've decided to follow that day. They may walk as many as twelve miles and they usually log many of those miles on a strenuous, uphill grade. "Last May, we climbed the trail to the top of Yosemite Falls," says William Bauer, a retired professor of electrical engineering. "This is a fairly strenuous and rocky trail giving us a climb of 3,000 feet in about three miles. All but two made it to the top. An eighty-year-old man took a census of those at the top and found that our average age was seventy-three."

Bill Lyons is one of several hundred people who walk every day in a Kansas City shopping mall. He's a wiry fellow with a spring in his step. He sparkles when you ask him his age, because he's proud of it. "I'm eighty but I look younger than a lot of sixty-year-old men I know," he says. And he's right. But Lyons wasn't always so spry. At seventy, he suffered a massive heart attack. "The doctors use me as an example because I wasn't supposed to make it," he says. After his attack, Lyons's doctor told him to start walking. At first, he could manage only a hundred yards at a time, but slowly he worked up to the doctor's prescription of two miles a day. In the spring and fall, he walks outdoors, but in the heat of summer and the cold of winter he takes to the smooth, level, temperature-controlled shopping mall, where he's become a sort of folk hero—a prime example of the curative powers of walking. Lyons walks two miles a day. In his "younger" days he walked the distance in thirty minutes. Now, he's slowed down to a three-mile-an-hour pace that is more in keeping with his status as the grand old man of the mall. In the ten years since his heart attack, Lyons figures he's walked the distance from New York to San Francisco and back. By my calculation, he's not far off the mark. He's walked 7,300 miles. In a sense, Lyons is a professional walker. He gets paid for what he does, not in dollars but in years. He drew a big dividend in 1976 when he was back in the hospital again with possible heart trouble. "I was supposed to have heart failure but they told me I'd cured myself. They told me I'd walked myself out of it," he says as he leans into a curve.

Another venerable walker over seventy-years old is Larry O'Neil, a lumber company executive in Kalispell, Montana. O'Neil set a national record for the one-hundred-mile walk in 1967 at the age of sixty. In fact, he was the first amateur to walk one-hundred miles in twenty-four hours in this country since the 1800s. I didn't meet O'Neil

until 1978, when he was seventy-one-years old. In the intervening years, he repeated his one-hundred-mile feat several times and was back in Columbia, Missouri, for the annual one-hundred-mile national championship walk. In 1978, no one thought O'Neil was going to actually try to do another hundred. They figured he was just there to do a quick fifty and call it a day. But after the long, cool night had passed and the sun was blazing down again on the high-school track, O'Neil was still steaming along with his characteristically fluid stride. He didn't do another hundred that day, but he did walk ninety-four miles in twenty-three hours and he made believers out of us all.

One of O'Neil's predecessors in the one-hundred-mile walk was the great apostle of pedestrianism, Edward Payson Weston. This remarkably gifted athlete did a great deal to set to rest the superstition that age equals infirmity, when he walked from New York to Chicago, from New York to San Francisco, and from New York to Minnesota, in the early 1900s. He made all the cross-country walks after he was seventy-years old and these feats of foot made him a national hero, probably the first athlete-hero in America.

We live a lot longer now than we did in Charles Dickens's day and the sight of ninety-year-old's who are as "brisk as boys" isn't really all that remarkable anymore. Yet our expanded life-spans do not always mean an equivalent improvement in the quality of life. "The years in later life—particularly those of the post-retirement period—should be happy years," says the President's Council on Physical Fitness and Sports. "But the full promise of this stage of life comes only to those who are healthy, alert, and active."

The best way to retain our vitality is to be habitually active throughout our lives. Studies of rats show that those who were exercised at an early age lived longer than those who were not exercised. Studies of rats who were first exercised at a later age showed no increase in longevity, however. In an effort to measure the effects of aging, researchers have tested the "physical working capacity" of people of various ages and have found that physical ability declines from 35 to 40 percent between the ages of thirty and seventy. Yet walking can effect this decline. In a study of 109 women between the ages of ten and sixty-eight, researchers at the University of California found that exercise was as important as age in determining their levels of physical deterioration. The researchers found that older women, who had exercised regularly, had a level of physical ability similar to that of nonactive women in their twenties. Another study of the effects of exercise on aging showed that middle-aged men, who exercised vigorously for as much as an hour, two to three times a week, could stop and even reverse the customary decline in their "physical working capacity," despite their increasing age.

A great advantage of walking as an exercise is that you can start young and keep at it throughout your life. It's noncompetitive, largely unskilled, and totally individual. Once people develop a taste for walking, they don't give it up easily. Wilbur C. (Doc) Batchelor has walked 2,278.5 miles on hikes sponsored by the Central Ohio Biking Club since he helped organize the club in 1936. In 1978, Batchelor was still hiking with the club at the age of eighty-eight. Harold Atkinson of San Francisco reports that he has been hiking on nearby Mount Tamalpais since 1915. "As a small lad I camped all over the area," he says. As trail maintenance director of the Tamalpais Conservation Club in 1978, Atkinson, age seventy-six, was still hiking all of the Mount Tamalpais trails twice a month. Another lifelong walker, the Rev. A. Rufus Morgan, an Episcopal priest from Franklin, North Carolina, says: "Strangely enough, my earliest recollections of hiking nearly ninety years ago, have not to do with pleasure hiking but trips into the mountains to look up cattle and sheep which had been taken into the mountains for the summer. Checks had to be made of these animals to see that they did not go too far astray and that they were faring well. . . . These trips had their bonuses. I can still remember when I was a small boy waking up in the early morning, in the log cabin far away from any habitation, to the wonderful chorus of songbirds."

Unfortunately, many people stop exercising during the middle years of their lives. The pressures of raising families and establishing careers are so strong during those years that, even though we know we should get some exercise, we don't do it. And many of us lead extremely sedentary lives during those years. We sit behind a desk all day, grinding away at the paperwork. We smoke. We drink too much, both to escape from the pressure and to reach the level of conviviality that we think is good for business. At the end of the day, we drive home to our television sets for another stint of sitting, smoking, and drinking. We grow tired and waddle into bed. On weekends, we wonder why our golf game has gone to hell. We try to make up for our lack of physical vitality by living vicariously through our heroes, the professional athletes. One day we reach the age of sixty-five and the corporation that's been the focus of our lives for forty years puts us out to pasture.

But just because we reach our retirement years in poor physical condition doesn't mean there's nothing we can do about it. As one expert told a White House Conference on Aging: "Man at any age, if he is reasonably healthy, can be physically conditioned. While we may not be masters of our destinies, we can affect the degradation of our bodies." And the President's Council again: "Fortunately, even if you have let too many years slip by when good intentions of keeping fit were sacrificed to other demands of life, you still can pick up at some level of physical performance and work yourself up several notches."

Walking can also help us retain or resurrect another aspect of life that we sometimes lose during the busy middle years: the ability to play. As we grow older, our opportunities for play seem to dwindle, or at least we think they do. We have a tendency to sit around and grumble about our infirmities as if we were in some sort of contest in which first prize goes to the one in the worst condition. This is especially true if we haven't developed or maintained the ability to participate in some lifetime sport, such as golf or tennis. It's possible to take up golf or tennis when you are over sixty, but it's not easy. You have to worry not only about getting in shape, but mastering a new skill as well. The frustration of trying to enjoy a game of golf when every other shot lands in a subdivision or a cow pasture is likely to add to our overall depression about being old. Many elderly people have told me that walking has turned their lives around. It's renewed their ability to play, to have fun.

Johan Huizinga, author of a classic study called *Homo Ludens: A Study of the Play Element in Culture,* argued that Homo Ludens (Man the Player) deserves as much attention as Homo sapiens (Man the Thinker) and Homo Faber (Man the Maker). It's clear that we all start out as players. Children play endlessly, even when technically they're working. Later on, our play is organized in the form of sports. In our early years, we're participants, but as we grow older we gradually become strictly observers. And watching other people play isn't the same as playing ourselves.

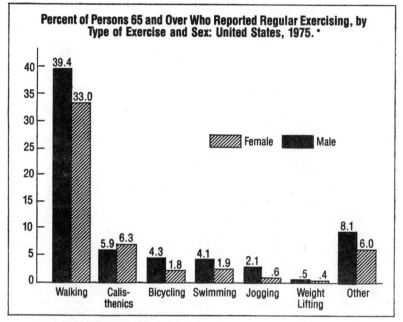

Percent of Persons 65 and Over Who Reported Regular Exercising, by Type of Exercise and Sex: United States, 1975.*

*Source: National Center for Health Statistics

Walking is a way of taking control again. Most authorities would argue that ordinary walking for exercise or pleasure is not a sport. After all, it's not competitive; you don't keep score; and it's not really an acquired skill. But I believe there are elements of sport involved in walking. I've sat for hours watching people walk a half-mile course in a shopping mall. I've watched them take the corners gracefully or clumsily; I've seen them pass other walkers with a gleam of victory in their eyes; I've seen the walkers pace themselves so they know exactly how fast they are walking without looking at a watch; and I think these people are playing. They're participating in a subtle kind of sport.

A national survey in 1975 showed that walking is virtually the only exercise taken regularly by men and women sixty-five and over. It's easy to see why. It's safe and effective. Herbert A. de Vries, who has

WALKING PROGRAMS FOR PERSONS OVER 60

1st and 2nd Weeks	3 sessions on alternate days. Emphasize good walking style, good breathing and posture.	¼ mile
3rd Week	3 sessions on alternate days. Use interval training* and lengthen stride. Practice deep breathing.	½ mile
4th Week	3 sessions on alternate days. Practice deep breathing.	¾ mile
5th Week	3 sessions on alternate days. Practice deep breathing. Lengthen stride. Use Interval training.	1 mile
6th Week**	5 sessions. Practice deep breathing. Emphasize posture. Use interval training.	1 mile
7th Week	5 sessions 3 m.p.h.	1 mile in 20 min.
8th Week	5 sessions 3 m.p.h.	1½ miles in 30 min.
9th Week	5 sessions 3 m.p.h.	2 miles in 40 min.
10th Week	5 sessions 3 m.p.h.	2 miles in 40 min.
11th Week	5 sessions 3 m.p.h.	2½ miles in 50 min.
12th Week	5 sessions 3 m.p.h.	3 miles in 60 min.
13th Week	5 sessions 3¼ m.p.h.	3 miles in 55 min.
14th Week	5 sessions 3½ m.p.h.	3 miles in 50 min.
15th Week	5 sessions 4 m.p.h.	3 miles in 45 min.

*Interval training simply means that you increase your speed until you feel uncomfortable and then slow down again.

**The first six weeks of training are intended to acclimate your body to walking. The President's Council suggests that if you don't feel comfortable increasing the distance weekly that you remain at a comfortable distance and increase the number of walking sessions.

studied extensively the effects of exercise on older people, reported in *Geriatrics* in 1971 that vigorous walking, thirty to sixty minutes a day, would bring about an improvement in physical fitness in all but the most highly conditioned men in that age group. Walking and other forms of exercise also have been shown in various studies to be particularly effective in curing or alleviating the afflictions most often associated with old age: brittle bones, emphysema and other lung disorders, diabetes, arthritis, and heart disease.

Although this book contains a walking program that should work for people of all ages, C. Carson Conrad, executive director of the President's Council on Physical Fitness and Sports, has developed a walking program especially for people over sixty, who have led a sedentary life for many years but still are in good health. The program takes into consideration the fact that some people who haven't exercised for many years may need a graded program for gradually working themselves into shape. *

---

*For further discussion of a walking program see Chapter 8.

8

Your Personal Walking Program

First things first. For the walker, physical fitness and health are the first essentials. So this chapter is devoted to the work aspect of walking rather than its pleasures. Its purpose is to show you how to become physically fit through walking and getting into shape is never easy, not even for walkers. Consider it a temporary phase, something you had to go through in order to more thoroughly enjoy the age-old institution of walking.

For those of you who are already veteran exercise walkers, this chapter may seem elementary, but I hope that even you veterans will find something of interest here, if only verification of your long-held conviction that walking makes you feel good. That's what physical fitness is all about. The immense amount of research on exercise has uncovered many interesting and important facts about the benefits of walking, but the real motivating factor for most of us is the continuing feeling of good health, both mental and physical, that we get from regular exercise.

And even if you're not at all interested in physical fitness, if all you want to do is get out into the woods to hike or backpack, you'll need some sort of regular conditioning program.

The first question anyone recommending a regular exercise program has to answer is, "How much exercise is necessary." Unfortunately, this is the one question upon which the experts often disagree.

In fact, there seems to be more agreement on the benefits of exercise than on the amount of exercise necessary to reap those benefits.

Although walking may be a good form of alternative training for competitive athletes, most people are only looking for a way of staying in shape, keeping their weight down, and avoiding health problems and these are things any regular exercise program should do. Yet the question still remains: How much exercise is necessary to achieve these goals?

There are six different existing programs for walkers. Some of them only differ slightly. Others differ significantly. Some experts have recommended specific exercise programs, there are others who have merely studied the effects of walking at various distances, speeds, and for various amounts of time, and have drawn certain conclusions from their tests. Since I believe that everyone who begins an exercise program should know why they're being asked to do certain things, I'm going to review several of these exercise programs and walking studies and state my reasons for approving or disapproving them. All of them should provide an adequate level of physical fitness, so you're welcome to adopt one of them if you prefer it over the one I'm going to suggest.

The YMCA Program.

Perhaps no organization has more experience with exercise programs than the Young Men's Christian Association. As explained in *The Official YMCA Physical Fitness Handbook,* the goal of their program is the ability to walk two miles in thirty minutes. As you work up to that pace, you vary your walking speed between the "endurance pace," which is four miles an hour, and the "alternating pace," which is a mixture of the endurance pace for "no more than four minutes" and "a period of slower, leisurely walking." On the first day, the walker is expected to go three-quarters of a mile in twelve minutes, using the alternating pace. At the end of ten weeks of exercising, three days per week, the walker is expected to be able to complete two miles at the endurance pace, which should give him a completion time of thirty minutes. As an alternative, the YMCA also explains the program in terms of time rather than distance, for your ease when distance is difficult to determine. Even so, the YMCA program calls for a precision that is difficult to attain.

Aerobics.

Probably the most widely used walking program is the one devised by Dr. Kenneth Cooper, who has made Aerobics into a household word. Dr. Cooper's program is based on the accumulation of Aerobic points per week. The points are earned by walking a specified distance in a specified amount of time. The requirements for obtaining points increase between the first week of training and the twelfth week and Dr. Cooper provides charts for different age levels. The requirements for obtaining Aerobic points become progressively easier as the participants grow older. He also has separate programs for men and for women. Dr. Cooper's program is less difficult to follow than the YMCA program because it doesn't involve an "alternating pace." The necessity for walking a measured distance still exists, however, and tends to limit the variety of walks you can take.

My main objection to the Aerobics program is that it's too scientific, too objective. As long as the effort to obtain Aerobic points reigns supreme, the walker seems to have little opportunity to develop his own subjective indicators of how he is doing and how he feels. Aerobics is sort of like painting by numbers. You don't really have a feel for what you're doing.

The Royal Air Force Study.

Earlier, we examined the results of research in Great Britain which found walking was one way of getting troops into good physical condition quickly. In their study, members of the Royal Air Force were divided into four groups. One of the groups walked less than two miles a day; the second, 6.2 miles a day; the third, 12.4 miles; and the fourth, 18.6 miles. The participants in this experiment, with the exception of the first group, showed significant improvements according to several indicators of physical fitness. One advantage of an exercise program built on this study would be its flexibility, because the participants did not do all of their daily walking at once. On the other hand, at the brisk pace of four miles an hour, it would take an hour-and-a-half to walk 6.2 miles and that's more time than many people can afford.

The Pollock Study.

Dr. Michael L. Pollock and other researchers studied the effects of walking on sixteen sedentary men, forty to fifty-six-years old, and reported that by walking forty minutes a day, four times a week, at a speed greater than 4.26 miles an hour, the men significantly improved their level of physical fitness.

My Walking Program.

It is based on Dr. Pollock's theories—but with an added dimension of simplicity. Basically, all you do is go out for a walk and take with you an understanding of the physiological research previously discussed.

But before you get started, there are some other matters you need to consider. The most important is your current state of health. Nearly every author who urges people to exercise includes some sort of warning about obtaining clearance from a physician. It always seems like a cop-out on the part of the author to tell you to see your doctor after many pages have been devoted to the glorification of exericse, but I, nevertheless, feel compelled to follow suit. *Go get a checkup before you start walking,* especially if you haven't been exercising regularly.

"If you're under thirty, you should have a complete medical history and physical examination within the preceding year before you start exercising," Dr. Cooper wrote in *The Aerobics Way.* "If you're between thirty and thirty-five, you should have the complete history and physical examination within six months before you start exercising, and the examination should include a resting electrocardiogram (ECG). If you're over thirty-five, you should have the complete history, physical examination and resting ECG within three months before you start. Additionally—and this is important—your physician should perform a stress ECG. . . ."

The stress ECG that Dr. Cooper is talking about is commonly known as a "stress test" and is the most widely used method of determining not only the condition of your heart, but your general level of physical fitness as well.

So even if you're convinced that you're not going to die of a heart attack while walking, you can learn a lot about your present physical condition by taking a stress test. Your family doctor can tell you where to get one or you can just call a hospital in your area and ask them about it.

If you decide against the more thorough physical examination that Dr. Cooper recommends, you should at least talk to your family doctor about what you are planning to do and get his opinion. People with certain illnesses should not exercise at all and others should exercise only in medically supervised programs. So if you're suffering from some serious illness you should definitely discuss it with a physician.

Just plain common sense is probably your best defense against hurting yourself in an exercise program. If you feel bad for several hours after exercising, you've either overdone it or there's something physically wrong with you. If these feelings persist, you should definitely see a physician.

Whatever you decide to do about seeing a physician it's important that you yourself take stock of your physical condition. The success of any unsupervised exercise program depends mainly on the participant's good sense. You won't win any medals for valor if you wear yourself out the first day. People who take up exercise programs and stick with them generally view them as long-term investments in good health. So take a realistic look at yourself. Here are some of the questions you should be asking:

1. Have you exercised regularly for the past several years?

2. Are you overweight and, if so, how much? (Take a look at the chart in the chapter on weight loss if you're in doubt.)

3. Do you have any habits such as smoking or excessive drinking, which tend to reduce your level of fitness?

If you haven't exercised regularly, if you're overweight, and if you either smoke or drink heavily, then I recommend that you spend at least a week acclimating yourself to walking before you try to walk for even fifteen minutes. Gradually during that week, try to walk a little more than you normally do. Take your dog for a walk around the block. Walk to the mailbox. Work in the yard a little more than usual.

In the meantime, start planning what you will wear.

SHOES—As you already know, you can walk in just about any pair of shoes, even high heels. But once you begin walking distances of several miles, you'll soon learn that a suitable pair of shoes is essential. High-heel shoes may not do that much damage if you're sitting down all day, but any substantial amount of walking in them will lead to a sore back, feet, and perhaps even injury. So do your walking in shoes with a low rubber heel, sturdy sole, and good support in the arch. If you need to buy a pair, jogging shoes with a wide, cushioned heel are the best bet for walking in urban areas because they provide good heel protection, arch support, and traction, yet they're light-weight. If you buy a new pair of shoes for walking, break them in gradually by wearing them around the house in the evenings.

SOCKS—What you put between your feet and the shoe depends largely on the weather and your personal taste. In hot weather I don't like to wear socks at all. When it's cold, I'd like to wear a ton of socks but, unfortunately, my shoes only allow room for a thin pair. Unless you're like me and you enjoy the feel of your foot against the surface of the shoe, I recommend that you buy your shoes large enough to accommodate heavy cotton socks in the summer and equally heavy wool socks (or even two pairs of socks) in the winter. That means you'll have to wear a heavy pair of socks when you try on a new pair of shoes and you'll want to be able to wriggle your toes freely even while wearing these heavy socks. In most cases, your walking shoes should be at least one-half size larger than you normally wear because your feet tend to spread out when you walk.

CLOTHES—As you progress through this walking program, you'll find that the amount of clothing you need is almost totally governed by the weather. Brisk walking generates more body heat than strolling or window shopping and you probably will work up at least a mild sweat on most days, but you won't generate enough heat to keep you warm in cold weather. You need to prepare yourself for the cold the way you always have. If you customarily wear gloves, put them on. If you wear a hat or stocking cap, put it on. The only way walker's garb differs from any other cold-weather attire is that it should be loose fitting and light-weight. Instead of wearing a heavy overcoat that would impede my arm motion and make me feel boxed in, I put on several layers of light clothing, starting with an undershirt, then a long-sleeved pajama top, then a turtleneck shirt, then a regular cotton shirt, and finally a light jacket to break the wind. I know this sounds a little silly, but I've found that my "layering" keeps me warmer than one or two items of heavier clothing and it's easier to match my apparel to the tempera-ture outside. You'll soon learn how many layers are needed to keep you warm at various temperatures. Another advantage of "layering" is that your body temperature increases as you walk and it's easy enough to take off one shirt and wad it up in your hand if you become too warm.

If your upper body is warm, your legs will almost take care of themselves, but when it gets really cold, you'll need to wear some long underwear or a pair of pajamas underneath your pants. Most women prefer to wear pants for warmth but some of the hardier ladies can manage with a skirt, stockings, and a pair of long socks.

Warm-weather attire is hardly worth mentioning. Just wear something cool and comfortable. Some of you will want to wear gym clothes or warm-up suits; others may prefer loose-fitting pants and shirts. There is no reason why women can't wear skirts in warm weather if they prefer them. I usually wear a baggy pair of cotton pants and a light cotton shirt. "Layering" is also useful on cool days in the spring and fall, when you're unsure of how much clothing you should wear.

I discuss clothing in greater detail in the chapters on hiking and backpacking; but for now you probably have enough information to begin walking. Yet there is another aspect of exercise that you still need to consider before striking out—that's the warm-up.

It may seem odd that you have to warm-up before walking, since you've been walking all your life and gotten by okay so far. But the kind of walking I'm suggesting is a little different from the ordinary stroll, saunter, or amble. I'm talking about what has been variously called brisk walking, fast walking, or striding. In other words, you'll be walking a little faster than normal and that requires a warm-up to acclimate your body to the pace.

There are two ways you can warm-up. The easiest way is to walk very slowly for the first five minutes or more until you can feel your arms and legs loosening up. Then pick up the pace. The second method involves doing some specific exercises that increase your body temperature, gently stretch the ligaments to avoid sprains, and stimulate the muscles that maintain good posture. Although every athlete has a favorite set of warm-up exercises (and you'll develop your own), I suggest starting with those recommended by the American Medical Association. All of the exercises should be performed while standing.

1. Head and Neck Exercises—Move the head gently forward and backward several times. Then turn your head to the right and left several times.

Photo by Ginzy Schaefer

2. Arm Exercises—With arms at your sides, swing them backward and forward and then outward. Then stretch them out at right angles to your body and move them in a circle, first forward, then backward, several times. With your arms at your sides again, reach overhead with each arm, one at a time.

3. Trunk Exercises—Gently bend sideways from the waist. Then with your arms extended outward, twist your upper body to the left and to the right. Then lean up against a wall and pull your knees, one at a time, toward your chest with both hands.

4. Leg Exercises—Standing on one leg, swing the other leg forward, backward, and to the side. (You may need to lean against a wall for this one.) Then lunge forward on alternate legs and then sideways.

5. Cardiopulmonary Exercises—Run or walk in place. Hop five times on each foot.

It should take you roughly five to ten minutes to complete these exercises. Perform each movement until your muscles and joints feel relaxed and loose. They should be done vigorously enough to work up a sweat but be gentle with yourself. Don't strain.

Equally as important as the warm-up is what's commonly called the "warm-down." When you walk, your leg muscles aid the heart in circulating blood through the body. If you stop suddenly after a vigorous walk, this circulatory help stops along with you, allowing the blood to pool in the legs and causing a strain on the heart. So you need to take a few minutes at the end of your walk to allow your body to adjust. The best way to do this is to slow your pace to a stroll as you near your destination, then slow down a little more, and then stop.

After the warm-up's, you're ready to begin. My program is designed to comply with what physiologists believe is the amount and intensity of exercise needed to improve physical fitness, while allowing for the variety and randomness that make walking a lot of fun. You might say I'm trying to combine business with pleasure.

The ultimate goal is to walk for forty-five minutes at a pace of four miles an hour, four days a week. You'll remember that in Dr. Pollock's walking study, the participants held to a similar regimen and the results were improved physical fitness and weight loss. My program is based on time rather than distance, as a specific goal limits the variety of your walks. Obviously, you would have to walk on a measured course, either on one you measured yourself or on an indoor or outdoor track. Since I believe variety is the spice of walking, I try to avoid this.

In my program, you can just head out the door of your home or office and walk in any direction you wish. Your main concern should be whether it is an area where your continuous pace will seldom be interrupted, because it is important to walk continuously. For most of us, the main obstacle is the street crossing, and if a car is coming, you've got to stop. When you reach that point, *don't stop and don't walk* into traffic either. Just stay on the sidewalk and keep moving by walking in place, changing directions, or backtracking until you can cross the street. If you stop moving, you tend to lose the training effect of your walk.

The main thing to keep in mind as you begin this exercise program is that a speed of four miles an hour for forty-five minutes is the ultimate goal, not the immediate goal. If you are out of shape, walking at that pace for three miles probably will be very difficult or even impossible. You might not be able to walk for forty-five minutes at any pace. So simply take it easy, walk until you begin to feel tired, and then turn around and go home. Gradually, you'll become accustomed to walking and you'll find that it's really pretty easy to walk for forty-five minutes.

That's when you need to pick up your pace. The normal pace for most people is somewhere between three and four miles an hour. Yet, it's obviously more difficult for someone five-feet-tall to walk four miles an hour than it is for someone six-feet-tall. This is equally true of weight differences. The heavier you are, the more energy is required to move your body a given distance. For that reason, you shouldn't begin thinking about your pace until you can easily walk for forty-five minutes.

When you're ready for a little more speed, the place to start is with the length of your stride. Get in the habit of stretching your advancing leg a little farther forward than is comfortable. Try to hold that pace until you become quite uncomfortable. Then slow down. Eventually, you'll become accustomed to that pace and can keep it up for the entire forty-five minutes. Then you may want to repeat the process until you reach the next plateau, and so forth. The trick is to do it gradually. I won't tell you how fast you should be progressing, because we are all different. Your ability to train varies with your weight, age, height, and innate capacity. Keep the old athlete's adage in mind: "Train, don't strain."

Another important determinant of speed is the way you walk. Much has been written about the proper way to walk and a great deal of research has been done in this area, most of it aimed at finding methods of rehabilitating people who have lost a leg or part of a leg. I believe the usefulness of this information to the average person is limited. If you have persistent pain in your feet and legs, I would suggest that you see a podiatrist or an orthopedic specialist, because the natural act of walking should not produce serious medical problems in the average person. On the other hand, if you do have a problem, it's likely that it can be corrected by something as simple as inserts for your shoes. Most physicians will probably advise you to simply cut back on your training program until the problem subsides.

There is one improper walking style that is so common, however, that it deserves comment—toeing-out. We're toeing-out, as the name implies, when we walk with our toes pointed to the sides rather than straight ahead. We all know someone who is an extreme example—someone who walks like a duck, wobbling from side to side. Yet many of us have this problem to some degree and this improper gait cuts down on our efficiency of motion. In the normal gait, the heel strikes the ground "just to the outside of the heel bone," podiatrist Dr. Harry F. Hlavac writes in *The Foot Book*. "This produces a normal wear pattern on the heels of the shoes about one-half inch to the outside of the middle of the shoe." As the weight shifts from the rear of the foot to the front, the line of stress runs from the outside of the heel, through the center of the foot, to the first and second toes where the "toeing-off" or propulsion phase occurs. To take full advantage of the natural motion of the foot, you should walk as much as possible with the toes pointed directly forward. But if you have a problem with toeing-out or even toeing-in, which is commonly known as a pigeon-toed walk, don't try to force your foot into the correct position. Usually these problems will correct themselves once you start walking on a regular basis.

A good walking style goes hand-in-hand with good posture and the American Medical Association in its booklet, *The ABC's of Perfect Posture*, suggested an excellent way of evaluating your walking style and learning what you're doing wrong. Although I recommend that you take their advice, I want to emphasize again that imperfections in your walking style work themselves out slowly. So don't expect to correct all your errors right away.

Here's what the AMA says about the right way to walk.

You can learn new habits of walking just as you can learn skills of standing and sitting correctly. Try this:

1. Facing a full-length mirror from eight to ten feet away, stand erect with toes straight ahead and feet about four inches apart.

2. Bend your right knee and swing your right leg forward from the hip.

3. Place your right heel on the floor as your weight is pushed over the right foot. Keep your toes straight ahead.

4. Push your weight over your right foot by straightening the right knee and pushing off the floor with your left toes. Your body is leaning forward slightly.

5. Bend the left knee. Carry the left foot through and place the left heel on the floor.

6. Push the weight over the left foot by straightening the right knee and push off with the right toes. Your body is leaning forward slightly. Don't push too forcefully or your body will fall forward. Correct walking is a combination of pushing yourself forward and using the pull of gravity. A common fault is leaning forward too much, using gravity alone. This causes the walker constantly to lose and regain his balance and results in a jarring walk.

As you walk toward the mirror stop at various points to check details. You can watch the foot roll from heel to toes as it strikes the floor. Place it carefully ahead. Consciously keep the weight from rolling to the inside of the foot as the back leg is carried forward. . . .

You can see the lack of grace when you walk toward the mirror with your feet turned out. You can also see when the weight is incorrectly centered over the arch of the foot, rather than over the heel, the outside of the sole and the front of the foot—the areas specially designed to support weight.

As you progress through this walking program, occasionally monitor your walking style in a mirror as the AMA suggests. You'll see steady improvement and this becomes another incentive for continuing.

Once you start working on speed, you'll need a way of measuring how far and how fast you're walking. There are several ways to do this and they range from the simple to the complicated. Some require that you walk on a measured course of some kind, and others do not. I've made clear my personal belief that it's more fun to seek variety in your walks; so I suggest that if you do use a measured course to determine your speed and distance, then walk it only occasionally to monitor yourself and get a feel for how fast you are walking. Some of you may wish to walk on a measured course every day. That's okay too. Here are some ways to find out how far and how fast you are going.

1. Walk on a measured course. You can use an indoor or outdoor track or you can measure your own course. The easiest way to do this is to drive along the course in your car and measure the distance on your odometer.

The length of your course depends on where you choose to walk and how far. You can measure a one-mile course and walk it three times to fulfill the requirement of walking forty-five minutes at four miles an hour. Or you can measure a course three miles long or longer. Some people mark segments of distance by painting slashes on the curb at various intervals or remembering a tree, house, or some other landmark that is a certain distance from the beginning of the course.

When you walk any measured course, your speed is simply a function of time and distance. To determine your speed, divide your time for a one-mile walk into 60 and you'll arrive at your miles per hour. For a three-mile walk, divide your time into 180. Or you can get your approximate speed from this chart.

WALKING TIME IN MINUTES

One Mile	30	27	24	22	20	18	17	16	15	13	12
Three Miles	90	80	72	65	60	55	51	48	45	40	36
Speed in M.P.H.	2	2¼	2½	2¾	3	3¼	3½	3¾	4	4½	5

2. Walk with a pedometer. A pedometer is a device that counts the number of steps you take. You adjust it to the length of your stride and

every time it feels a jolt, such as a foot hitting the ground, the pedometer ticks off a unit of distance equal to your stride. It adds them all up and shows you how far you've walked in miles or kilometers. Some models attach to your belt or a pants' pocket. Others can be attached to your feet. Since you know how far you've walked, you can use the chart above to determine your speed.

In theory, pedometers are perfect for keeping track of your progress because you can take them anywhere and still know how far you've walked. For that reason, many walkers use them. I personally don't. I did buy one for $15.95 at a sporting-goods store, but the device for adjusting it to my stride is so imprecise that the pedometer doesn't give a true reading. I suspect most of the less expensive models have this deficiency, so if you're concerned about accuracy you may have to pay more than I did. Another shortcoming of pedometers is that they register "jolts" caused by motions other than walking. If you stop to rest and squirm around for a few minutes to get comfortable, you'll find that your pedometer will tick off a few paces, free of charge. Unless you think you might walk off and forget it, take the pedometer off your body when you stop. Pedometers also do not work well on rough terrain that forces you to vary the length of your stride.

3. Use the foot and brain calculator. The human body has been used as a unit of measurement since the beginning of man. A "hand" is a unit of measure that is used to gauge the height of horses. The "foot" originally was a unit of measure equal to the length of the human foot. Now, of course, it's twelve inches. The "yard" apparently sprang from the Old English word, "gierd," meaning twig or measure, but a "yard" would be nothing without its three "feet." And in a pinch, the human step is a ready and willing substitute for the yardstick. The walker can take advantage of the body's capacity for measuring distances by knowing the length of his own stride. Technically, a stride is composed of two steps. It begins when you push off with one foot and it ends when that same foot hits the ground again. You can count the number of strides you've taken by counting the number of times either the right foot or the left foot (but not both) hits the ground. If the right foot hits the ground one-hundred times, that's one-hundred strides. To determine the length of your stride, you need to measure a distance of at least twenty-five feet. Then count the number of steps you take within that distance, divide that number into

twenty-five (or whatever distance you walk), and multiply by two. The result is your stride length. If you don't feel like measuring your stride, you can assume it's five-and-one-half-feet long, about average for an adult. Once you've settled on a stride length, you need only count the number of strides taken in one minute to determine your speed and distance. You can approximate your walking speed from this chart.

STRIDE LENGTH	STRIDES PER MINUTE						
	40	45	50	55	60	65	70
4 feet	1¾	2	2¼	2½	2¾	3	3¼
4½ feet	2	2¼	2½	2¾	3	3¼	3½
5 feet	2¼	2½	2¾	3	3½	3¾	4
5½ feet	2½	2¾	3	3½	3¾	4	4½
6 feet	2¾	3	3½	3¾	4	4½	4¾
6½ feet	3	3¼	3¾	4	4½	4¾	5¼
7 feet	3¼	3½	4	4¼	4¾	5¼	5½
SPEED IN M.P.H.							

After you've determined your approximate speed, it's easy to figure how far you've walked. You just multiply the time walked by your speed in miles per hour. Here's a formula you can use.

$$\frac{\text{TIME x SPEED}}{60} = \text{DISTANCE}$$

The walker who has a consistent stride is virtually a walking tape measure. Most of you will be satisfied, however, with an estimate of your speed and distance. It's seldom necessary, after all, to know these things exactly. But for those of us who are mathematically inclined, have a lot of time on our hands, or are just curious, here's a short excursion into walker's mathematics.

The first step of the precision walker is to get a precise measurement of his stride. Here's how:

1. Mark off a distance of twenty-five feet.

2. Count the number of steps required to walk that distance.

3. Mark the position of your last step and measure the distance between that point and the twenty-five-foot line. (See illustration.)

4. Then subtract that distance from three-hundred (the number of inches in twenty-five feet).

5. Divide the remainder by the number of full steps.

6. Multiply by two to convert to strides. The result is the *exact* length of your stride.

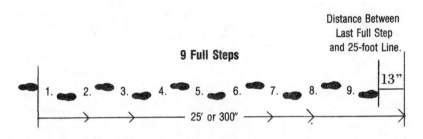

Distance Between Last Full Step and 25-foot Line.

9 Full Steps

13"

1. 2. 3. 4. 5. 6. 7. 8. 9.

25' or 300"

EXAMPLE: The walker in the above illustration took nine full steps with thirteen inches left over. Here's how I calculated the length of his stride.

```
                Inches
        Total   Left
        Inches  Over         31.88              Inches Per Step
No.of 9 ) 300-13   or   9 ) 287        =
Steps

        31.88
        X  2   No. of Steps Per Stride
        63.77  =  Inches Per Stride
```

Here's how to figure your exact speed once you've determined your exact stride length.

1. Count the number of times in one minute that your right foot hits the ground.

2. Multiply the number of strides per minute by the length of your stride.

3. Multiply by sixty to convert to strides per hour.
4. Divide by twelve to convert inches to feet.
5. Divide by 5,280 (the number of feet in a mile) to get miles per hour.

EXAMPLE: My hypothetical walker has a stride of 63.77 inches and a pace of 60 strides per minute. This is how I determined his speed.

Length of Stride 63.77

X 60	Strides Per Minute
3826.20	Inches Per Minute

318.85
12)3826.20   Feet Per Minute

318.85
X 60
19,131   Feet Per Hour

3.62   Miles Per Hour
No. of Feet in Mile   5,280)19,131

The physical rewards of a regular walking program are bountiful. Yet, there's always a gap between intentions and actions and many people (myself included) justify the shortcoming by saying, "I just don't have time." It's a conflict that cannot be dismissed easily. We are all busy. We all have many demands on our time. I was talking with a young business executive about the need for exercise, when he turned to me and said, "People like me are trapped. I have to sit behind this desk all day to make a living. What else can I do?" I suggested that he exercise during his lunch hour, but he had an answer for that one too. "What about the need to fraternize with your associates?" he asked. "Lunch is the only time when you can really get together and exchange ideas." As we grew progressively more depressed about the sedentary life of an office worker, we analyzed the way he spent his time.

```
Work .......................................9 hours
Sleep ......................................8 hours
Driving to and from work.......................1 hour
Meals .....................................3 hours
Household responsibilities,
personal correspondence, etc. ...................2 hours
Total ......................................23 hours
```

What my friend and I learned was that even a busy executive should have one hour a day that he can call his own and that hour could be used for exercise if he planned ahead.

And then there are weekends! I've suggested that you walk for forty-five minutes, four days a week. There's no reason why two of those walks couldn't be taken on a weekend when most people have more free time.

If you still feel you have no time for walking, the only alternative is to make time. Good health is a priceless asset. It shouldn't be exchanged for anything, especially the money you stand to accumulate by working long hours. Ron Laird, a leading American race-walker, once told *Sports Illustrated:* "The most important thing to me is health. People have the choice, health or wealth, and most take wealth. . . . Most people are into making money and accumulating things. I go out for a super workout and I knock out those hostile, poisonous emotions." The significant point here is that you do have a choice. So try to set aside a little time for walking. And remember that some walking is better than none at all. If you can't spare forty-five minutes, four days a week, try to walk a little more than you ordinarily do. Walk all or part of the way to work, take the stairs instead of the elevator at your place of employment—be conscious of the need to walk.

Golf is walking too, if you refrain from riding in a cart. In 1968, Professor Leroy H. Getchell of Ball State University conducted a study of golfers who pulled their clubs in carts. He reported in *The Archives of Physical Medicine and Rehabilitation* that a 150-pound man burns about 223 calories an hour while playing golf. Other studies have shown that the golfer burns as many as three-hundred calories an hour, the rough equivalent of running or walking three miles.

There are several factors that can influence the success of an exercise program. The most important is consistency. Pick a time of day to walk and make it a habit. Many people find that they can get up a little earlier in the morning and walk without disturbing the family routine. Others prefer to walk after work, after dinner, or during their lunch hour. Secondly, keep track of your progress. Draw encouragement from your diminishing waistline, your steadily increasing walking speed, your overall feeling of good health. Follow in the footsteps of the "Great Walkers" and keep a diary to record your progress and observations. Finally, use moderation. Be patient. All good things come to those who wait . . . and walk.

9

The Metropolitan Walker

It's unfortunate that walking in America is so often associated with a rural setting—a country stroll or a wilderness hike. For it's the city-dweller who needs most the physical and mental refreshment of walking. And the city-dweller needs it, not only on the weekends when he can jump into his car and head for the hills, but he needs it every day.

Let's consider our predicament. The American who lives in or around a city usually has a job that calls for very little physical activity. If he is a white-collar worker, he's confined to his desk most of the day; pushing a pencil and picking up the telephone is about all the physical labor the job requires. The same is largely true for blue-collar workers. A little more physical exertion is usually required, but not that much more. Most of the heavy work is done by machines. The family member who remains at home—the housewife or househusband—probably gets more exercise than the one who works outside the home. At least that member of the family is not chained to a desk or lashed to a machine. But even in the home, much of the traditional, physical labor is now done by dishwashers, vacuum cleaners, garbage disposers, washer-dryers, efficient waxes and cleansers, elevators, and automatic garage-door-openers.

But the automation and computerization of the office and the household, haven't eliminated the need for mental exertion. In fact, they've increased it. For now, we have to maintain, repair, and keep up with all the machines and computers that sometimes seem to run our lives. The result is an unnatural imbalance between mental and physical exertion that seems to exacerbate the situation. Some studies have shown that lack of physical fitness inhibits our ability to withstand stress. Dr. Hans Selye, author of *Stress Without Distress* and a noted authority on the subject, once conducted an experiment in which he subjected ten physically inactive rats to a barrage of blinding lights, loud noises, and electrical shocks. Within a month they were all dead. Then Dr. Selye repeated the same experiment with ten rats that were exercised until they were physically fit. At the end of a month, they were still alive and well.

Stress is not something that only people who live in cities have to deal with. It's an unavoidable consequence of living. People in small towns and on farms must deal with it, and even those who flee the cities for the suburbs, cannot escape it. But the city-dweller probably suffers more from it than anyone else. The pace of city life is faster than other places. Cities are crowded. Public transportation is used more often by city-dwellers. Admittedly, it's often advisable to take these experiments on rats with a grain of salt, but the flashing lights and deafening noises these poor rats were exposed to remind me of how it feels to ride a subway. Except the rats probably had a little more room to move around than is available on the average subway car during rush hour.

The effect of all this on the person who lives in a metropolitan area is that he suffers twice for his inactivity. Lack of physical fitness is in itself a perilous situation that leads to an increased risk of heart attacks and several other maladies, but on top of all this, the city-dweller is more susceptible to the stress that is more pronounced in his environment.

And there are other complications. Unless you've been living in a cave for the last several years, you've been told many times in one way or another to get more exercise. But getting exercise can sometimes be quite time-consuming. You must drive somewhere to play tennis (or use a gymnasium) and even after you get there, it may be too crowded to use. At the least, you may have to wait for a short while. You may even have to pay to exercise by joining an athletic club or spa.

Walking provides the city-dweller with a way of solving these problems. First off, it provides a kind of immunity to the stress-producing aspects of an urban environment. You may be somewhat skeptical of this until you've actually tried it, but it's been the experience of many walkers that the simple, natural effort of walking tends to filter out the things that produce stress. As Dr. Selye's experiment would indicate, walking conquers stress. Something happens when you walk that is like the reverse of psychosomatic illness. It's called somato-psychic mental health: The soothing effect of exercise on the central nervous system. So while the walker is improving his physical fitness, he's also reducing his vulnerability to stress. Once you've reached this level of mental relaxation, your way of looking at the city begins to change. What before had seemed a hostile, alien world of concrete, greed, and danger, becomes manageable. It even becomes interesting.

Walking also goes a long way toward solving the problems of where and when to exercise in a city. For most of us, whatever exercise we obtain must be wrapped around or inserted into our work schedule. Many people like to walk in the morning before work. Marshall Eisen, a sixty-year-old salesman who walks every morning, told me: "When I go into the office, I can feel it if I haven't walked. But when I walk, my head clears and I'm ready to go to work." That's the advantage of walking in the morning. It's a great way to start off the day. Other walkers I know get in a half-hour to an hour of walking at noon while everyone is eating lunch. They bring a light lunch that they can eat quickly after they walk. These people get their exercise and keep their weight down at the same time. Others would rather walk after work to unwind. These people usually walk before dinner. And there are some more audacious city-dwellers who walk late in the evening when it's dark. The only way to find out which method works best for you is to try them all for a week. You should always take the path of least resistance. You should pick a walking regimen without going against some essential fiber in your personality. For instance, if you're the kind of person who has a devil-of-a-time getting out of bed in the morning, then you're asking for trouble if you decide that you're going to get up before dawn every morning and walk.

If you decide you can't set aside a specific time period each day for walking, or if you would like to supplement your walking regimen, then you can manipulate your normal daily routine just slightly and come up with a significant amount of walking. For instance, almost everyone who has a job works outside of the home. Consequently, they must drive or ride to work in a car, bus, train, subway, rickshaw, or some other conveyance. They have the option of walking all the way to work, but since that is usually impractical, they can blend walking with their normal method of getting to work.

There are several ways you can do this. You can travel by shank's mare during the first leg of your trip. You can walk to the bus stop, the train station, or the subway station and ride from there. You can control the time and distance of your walk by choosing a subway station or bus stop a certain distance from your home. A second way of using your legs on your way to work is to walk during the last leg of your trip. Again, if you take the train, bus, or subway, then get off a certain distance from your office and walk the rest of the way. If you drive to work, you can park your car some distance away from your office and walk on in. After work, you can reverse this process. You can either board your method of conveyance a certain distance away from your office and ride as close to home as possible, or you can do your walking after you get off the bus or subway. If you drive to work, the choice is simpler. You just walk back to where you parked your car.

There are a lot of possible variations on this theme. On a beautiful spring morning, you may want to walk longer than you would on a bitter winter day. It's always best to try to do as much continuous walking as possible. In other words, if you've allotted a half-hour in the morning and a half-hour in the evening for walking to and from work, then each half-hour should be continuous walking. Try not to walk for fifteen minutes before getting on the bus and then for fifteen minutes after you get off. But whatever system you come up with, even if it's only twenty minutes of continuous walking three or four days a week, it's going to help you if you walk briskly. You'll arrive at your office in the morning and at your home in the evening feeling physically refreshed and mentally relaxed.

The answer to the second logistical problem is simple. You can walk anywhere. When pressed for time, just walk out your door and keep going. But if you have more time to play with, then you have more options.

Many people walk in shopping malls. One winter morning recently, I rose before dawn and drove several miles to a Kansas City shopping mall. It was the kind of morning that makes walking outdoors both painful and hazardous. The streets and sidewalks were icy and a bitter wind cut into my cheeks even during the short trek to my car. When I arrived at the mall, at least a dozen walkers were already there, striding briskly around the perimeters of the climate-controlled, softly-lit promenade. As I started walking myself, the warmth of the mall, the window displays, the conversation, and the smooth, level walking course combined to take the sting out of the morning.

An estimated three-thousand people a year walk regularly in the Ward Parkway Shopping Center in Kansas City and I'm not talking about shoppers. Sure, these people make some purchases at the mall, but that's not why they're there. In fact, many of them come and go long before any stores in the mall open. These people come to the mall as early as 6:00 A.M., Monday through Saturday, because they've found an ideal place to knock out a quick two or three miles. Some of them walk there everyday, all year-round. Others walk there only when the weather forces them.

Photo by Ginzy Schaefer

The shopping mall has become a major factor in American life. There are several hundred really huge malls in this country and perhaps a thousand smaller ones. Sociologists are just now beginning to realize that these are replacing the town square or city center as the main gathering place of Americans. In sprawling, bedroom communities they are often the only possible focal point. And surveys have shown that besides their homes and their offices, Americans spend more time in shopping malls than any other place.

And the malls aren't just in the suburbs. They're springing up everywhere. Observing the drawing power of suburban malls, developers have correctly assumed that the same techniques might work in the inner-cities; and in many of the older cities of the east and midwest, historical landmarks have been rejuvenated by the construction of well-designed shopping areas in, around, and through them.

These two developments—shopping malls and rejuvenation of the inner-cities—benefit no one more than they do the walker. Combined with the many important parks, historical sites, and cultural centers that already exist, these inner-city and suburban facilities have made walking in the city, both for exercise and for pleasure, as satisfying as any country walk and a lot more accessible.

For the person who is devoted to a daily walking regimen, the enclosed shopping mall is ideal. It means that the weather will never interfere with his schedule, that a passing car will never interrupt the rhythm of his stride, and that he will never have to walk alone unless he wants to. There are no hills to negotiate within the confines of the mall, no street curbs waiting to twist an ankle, no dogs ready to nip at your heels, and no suspicious-looking characters lurking in dark corners. In short, the malls are safe, convenient, weatherproof, and friendly.

Although most of the enclosed malls across the country are used by walkers to some degree, few of them cater to the walkers as much as Ward Parkway Shopping Center in Kansas City. There, the mall's management opens the doors to the common area at 6:00 A.M. , an hour earlier than normal, just for the walkers. That gives the exercisers at least three hours of uninterrupted walking before the center begins to fill up with shoppers and store employees. Dick Maloney, an executive of the company that owns the shopping center, told me that it's good business as well as good community relations to accommodate the walkers. There is a marketing theory, he says, called entrainment, which essentially means that if you can attract people to your shopping center for one reason, such as walking, they are likely to come there for other reasons, such as shopping and spending money. "If you're courteous to people, naturally they're going to do more shopping in our center," Maloney says. "If you have good community relations you'll get the shoppers." The theory has apparently worked. Several regular walkers at the center told me they shop there even though they live a long distance away. "You have to give credit to the shopping centers for opening these places," one walker said.

Although special accommodations for walkers are currently the exception rather than the rule, it seems likely that shopping-mall managers, realizing the important role they play in the community, will be doing more for walkers in the future. A spokesman for Shopping Center World, an Atlanta-based publication that keeps an eye on trends in the shopping-mall business, told me that many malls already are sponsoring athletic events and their participation in such events probably will increase in the future.

Malls have to be number one on the list of metropolitan places to walk because they are temperature controlled and free of traffic. But for those people who like to mix a little pleasure with the business of exercise, virtually every city and town is rich in opportunities. There isn't a city in America that doesn't have at least one city park, historic area, or open-air plaza where walkers can find a safe, entertaining place to walk. Not only has the rejuvenation of some parts of America's older cities opened up new avenues for walkers, but better city planning in the nation's newer cities has led to the preservation of greenbelts and other areas where walkers have the right-of-way.

And, of course, there are the suburbs. Many of them are old enough now to be interesting in themselves. Good city planning has resulted in an explosion of parks in suburban areas in recent years. The federal government has provided matching funds in many cases for the purchase of these parks. The suburbs are ideal for people who are interested in a quiet walk close to home. Suburban streets have less traffic than city streets and often are lined with well-kept lawns and greenery. Unfortunately, many suburbs were not designed to facilitate walking. The automobile made suburbs possible and consequently, the automobile is king in the suburbs, even to the point that planners often neglected to include sidewalks in subdivisions. But where there is light traffic, walking in the street is relatively safe. Walkers should know the laws governing pedestrian use of the streets in their locale. They vary from state to state but there is a standard law, the Uniform Vehicle Code, that many states have adopted. Here's what it says about pedestrians. ". . . Where sidewalks are provided it shall be unlawful for any pedestrian to walk along and upon an adjacent roadway. . . . Where sidewalks are not provided any pedestrian walking along and upon a highway shall, when practicable, walk only on the left side of the roadway or its shoulder facing traffic which may approach from the opposite direction." The Uniform Vehicle Code admonishes "drivers to exercise due care. Notwithstanding other provisions of this chapter, every driver of a vehicle shall exercise due care to avoid colliding with any pedestrian upon any roadway and shall give warning by sounding the horn when necessary and shall exercise proper precaution upon observing any child or any obviously confused or incapacitated person upon a roadway." Obviously, the law isn't as threatening as what actually happens on the roads, and you certainly can't argue with a two-thousand-pound automobile when it's bearing down on you. But it's nice to know the law anyway, if only for the sense of moral superiority that the knowledge provides. In reality, the best policy for a walker is one of extreme caution. Walk defensively. Always have a plan for getting off the road quickly in an emergency.

It's also helpful in the enjoyment of city walking to remember that each of us is an explorer; and that the city someone else sees and describes is not the same one we see. Our experience is unique. Christopher Morley wrote in *Travels in Philadelphia:* "I love to be set down haphazard among unknown byways; to saunter with open eyes, watching the moods of men, the shapes of their dwellings, the crisscross of their streets. . . . It is entrancing to walk in such places and catalogue all that may be seen. I jot down on scraps of paper a list of all the shops on a side street; the names of tradesmen that amuse me; the absurd repartees of gutter children. Why? It amuses me and that is sufficient excuse. From now until the end of time no one else will ever see life with my eyes, and I mean to make the most of my chance."

I hesitate to recommend this, but my favorite time to walk in the city is at night. This is partly attributed to the fact that there is more time to walk at night, but it also results from a craving for the curious and for adventure. I usually walk through the parts of the city that are populated at night: The tawdry areas frequented by the night people. I go to these areas because most city streets are deserted after dark. The thousands of people who poured into the city to work have returned to the suburbs, and the city-dwellers themselves are locked into their television sets. But in certain areas, there are people in the streets. They aren't always the kind of people you might invite home for Sunday dinner, but they are nevertheless alive, breathing, and visible. They're interesting to watch.

And then there is the adventure. If you ask a mountain climber, especially the kind who loves nothing more than a sheer precipice, why he risks his life on the side of a mountain, he'll usually say that's the very reason he does—because he risks his life. He craves the exhiliration that comes from the knowledge that one false step, one badly executed maneuver could end it all. I'm not saying that night-walking in the city is equally dangerous, but there is enough danger there to appeal to one's sense of adventure.

The essayist, Edward Hoagland, wrote the following about walking in New York City: "You must have a considerable feel for these things, an extra sense, eyes in the back of your head: or call it a walker's emotional range. You must know when a pistol pointed at you playfully by a ten-year-old is a cap pistol and when it's not; whether someone coming toward you with a broken bottle is really going for you or not. We have grown to be students of police work—watching a bank robber scram as the squad cars converge, watching a burglar tackled, watching four hoodlums unmercifully beating a cop until four patrol cars scream to a halt and eight policemen club down the hoods. Nevertheless, if you ask people who have some choice in the matter why they live in a particular neighborhood, one answer they will give is that they 'like to walk.' "

10

Take a Hike

The practice of walking, like everything else in America, has changed considerably over the years. In Thoreau's day, it was a simple matter to strike out into the country for a day-long jaunt. You simply walked to the edge of town and kept going. Today, it's a day's walk just to the edge of town.

Still, in every part of the country there is a good place to hike within a few hours' drive, at the most, from urban areas and towns. I'm not talking about the High Sierra, mind you, or even the Appalachian Trail, but there's always a good trail for walking. Finding these places usually requires some imagination and asking around. Every state has a department of recreation or conservation that can supply you with leads. Your county and city recreation departments might also be able to help. Then there are the federal agencies: the Bureau of Land Management, the National Park Service, the U.S. Fish and Wildlife Service, and the U.S. Forest Service. Don't forget state and local historical societies, either. They often administer some interesting historical sites or tours.

Many walks in the green world don't require any preparation other than the proper dress and some moderately comfortable shoes. Just throw the kids into the car and you're off. You can have several pleasant hours of walking this way without having to think too much about it.

Or if you're more ambitious and you want to walk longer in rougher country, you can seek out a local hiking club, scout group, or outdoor store and make inquiries about where you should go, what equipment you'll need, and whether you can participate in a group excursion of some sort.

When you start thinking about taking a day-long hike in fairly rough country, then your walking life becomes more complicated. The rewards are great, but you've got to make some preparations both in knowledge and equipment.

The popularity of walking in the country has skyrocketed in the last thirty years. The number of days Americans spent walking with a pack on their back increased from three million to more than forty million between 1945 and 1975. An estimated four-million people hike every year on the beautiful two-thousand-mile Appalachian Trail that runs from Maine to Georgia. Our state and national parks over-flow every summer with campers and hikers. So you're likely to have plenty of company out there during the peak season.

One advantage of joining a local hiking club or getting your walking information from unofficial sources is that you can often avoid this kind of crowded situation. Veteran hikers in every area know out-of-the-way hiking areas that get very little use. Club members also use private property for hiking more often than the average walker. Another way of beating the rush hour in the woods is to plan your hikes for a weekday, when possible, or go during the fall, spring, and winter months when the kids are in school.

When you decide you want to go on a day-long hike, you should prepare the same way that I suggested in my walking program. You need to evaluate your level of fitness. It's no fun to get out on the trail with a fast-moving group of hikers and be the spoil-sport of the bunch. On the other hand, you shouldn't refrain from hiking just because you're out of shape. The trick is to set a reasonable goal and find some people who are at your level. The person who is out of shape can have just as much fun on a hike as a seasoned walker. He has to rest more along the way, but that gives him more time to enjoy the scenery, the companionship, and the escape from civilization. He may not experi-ence that breath-taking view from the mountain top, but beauty is in the eye of the beholder, and the hiker intent upon reaching the top often misses a lot of beauty along the way. For the sake of your health and safety, never push yourself too hard on a hike. It's even more dangerous than overdoing it in a regular exercise program. In the country, help can sometimes be several hours away. So start out slowly when walking in the country. Spend a few days walking in local parks and learning your limitations before planning a full-scale day in the woods.

In terms of equipment, the key is simplicity. We've kept everything fairly simple so far and we might as well be consistent. Besides, most books on outdoor equipment tend to make one's eyes glaze over and roll skyward. Since we need to keep our eyes on the trails, that certainly won't do. Whenever you go for a hike in rough or isolated country, you need to be prepared and follow a few rules. Unfortunately, the rules are becoming more numerous all the time, because increased use of trails means more risk of damage to the environment. Here's a primer on taking a one-day hike. I'm indebted to the Adirondack Mountain Club (AMC) of Glens Falls, New York, for the list of necessities. Their pamphlet, *For the Day Hiker,* is one of the few publications on the subject that doesn't make such a big deal out of hiking that you rapidly become convinced that you'd rather be in Philadelphia.

The AMC equipment list contains twenty-three items.

Good Day Pack.

This is a soft pack that attaches to the shoulders. It has no frame or waist belt like the larger and more expensive backpack. You can get a good one for around thirty dollars at any sporting-goods or outdoor-equipment store. Discount brands are also available, but may not meet the criteria of being a "good day pack."

Map and Guidebook.

Hikers ordinarily use topographic maps which show in great detail the lay of the terrain. If you're walking on well-established trails in heavily used areas, you may never even look at your map. But it's a good idea for at least one person in the group to have one. They are the best guarantee against getting lost and the only accurate way of determining how far you've walked and how high you are (in elevation that is). You can purchase the maps by mail from Branch of Distribution, U.S. Geological Survey, 1200 South Eads Street, Arlington, Va., 22202, if you plan to hike east of the Mississippi River; or from Branch of Distribution, U.S. Geological Survey, Federal Center, Denver, Colo. 80225, for areas west of the Mississippi. You can also find them at your local outdoor-equipment store or obtain them at a park office in the area where you will be walking.

Topographic maps for hiking are available in two scales: Fifteen minutes and seven-and-a-half minutes. The fifteen-minute map, which has a scale of one mile per inch, is better for hikers because it covers more territory, but for many areas they are not available. Maps of either size are marked with brown contour lines which show elevation. These maps won't do you any good unless you know how to read them, so a little practice is advisable. You could, of course, walk deep into the North Woods with a handful of maps and try to find your way out, but I would suggest a somewhat safer method of learning. Buy a topographic map for a park near your home and practice matching natural landmarks, such as small hills and valleys, with the markings on the map. You'll soon find that the map and terrain correspond nicely. Something else you should do with your topographic maps before setting out on a journey is study them. Then you'll know what kind of terrain you'll be covering and what landmarks you should be keeping an eye on as you walk. It's also a good idea to cover your maps with plastic sheets or keep them in a waterproof case. At any rate, make every effort to keep them dry. Wet, they're useless.

In addition to a topographic map, you may want to purchase a guidebook. There are basically two kinds: one you read at your leisure at home and another you carry with you. The first is usually longer, heavier, and more interesting. It includes not only brief descriptions of trails, but lengthy excursions into the history, geology, flower, and fauna of the hiking area. You could take one of these along with you on a hike, but they seem to be an unnecessary burden and some of them are so interesting you might walk off a cliff while reading them. The second kind is usually pamphlet-size and is designed to be taken along. It gives detailed descriptions of the various trails in the area and is helpful in finding your way. Never place absolute trust in a guidebook, however, because trails change, trail-writers make mistakes, and you may have been ripped-off.

Compass.

An astute and expert woodsman can find his way in the woods with nothing more than knowledge of the constellations, the position of the sun, and other natural signs. But even the experts admit that such methods of pathfinding are highly unpredictable und sometimes downright deceiving. For instance, if you've been using the sun to determine your direction, what do you do when suddenly you're wrapped in fog as thick as pea soup? Answer: You sit down and wait for it to go away. Unless you have several weeks to spend sitting in the woods waiting for the fog to rise or help to come, you need to carry a compass.

The main thing you need to know about a compass is that, contrary to everything you've heard, it doesn't point north. It points magnetic north which is not the same as the North Pole or true north—the one that matters. Since your compass doesn't point true north and maps are laid out on the basis of true north, you need to know the declination—the difference between true north and magnetic north—for the area in which you'll be hiking. The declination is often written on topographic maps. Once you know the declination you can orient the compass by turning it so that the needle points to the declination, which will be a certain number of degrees east or west. Then the north symbol on the compass will be pointing toward true north.

To orient your topographical map, you line up the north symbol or mark on the map with the north symbol on the compass. Then rotate the whole shebang until the compass needle is pointing toward the proper declination. Your map should then correspond to the terrain. You can then determine your position by noting carefully the position of several landmarks as you walk or by taking a bearing on those landmarks with your compass. Another advantage of the compass is more casual. Just by looking at it occasionally, you can determine if you are heading generally in the right direction. The compass can tell you when you've missed a bend in the trail and are obviously off course.

The use of a map and compass may sound somewhat complicated and perhaps unnecessary for the casual hiker, but they're really vital for anyone who walks a substantial distance in rough country. If every trail were marked as clearly as a city street you could get along without them. But, unfortunately, trails are often badly marked and difficult to follow. Old trails or other working trails may cross your path from time to time and sometimes it's difficult to know which way to turn. If you decide to walk without a compass and map, choose an area that is heavily used so you can at least ask someone else where you are. And the best protection against getting lost, with or without map and compass, is simply an awareness of what's going on around you. Always watch for landmarks along the trail that you could use in finding your way home.

Canteen.

It's not a good idea to begin a hike without your own water supply. You can survive in the woods for a long time without food, but you won't last long without water. This is especially important in very dry areas.

Water Purification Tablets.

It's still possible in some areas of this country to drink from streams and rivers with impunity, but each water source should be considered carefully.

When I was growing up in Kentucky, I drank from any stream and lake I wanted without any ill effects. But that's a luxury we can no longer afford. Water pollution is here to stay. Even in clear, running water, hikers need to be wary of "backpacker's diarrhea." Writing in *The Physician and Sportsmedicine,* Dr. James W. Brown said: "Most backpackers, in fact, assume that the water is pure and unpolluted and thus drink it without bothering to disinfect it. Unfortunately, this water may be harboring Giardia Lamblia, one of the causes of 'traveler's' diarrhea." To guard against backpacker's diarrhea and other water-carried diseases, you should take a close look at the water you drink. High, swiftly flowing mountain streams generally are considered the safest; stagnant or still pools, the most hazardous. Whenever you drink from a stream, think about what might be upstream. Is there a campground? Does the water flow into the recreation area from private property where livestock wastes may have polluted the stream? When in doubt, use purification tablets.

Trail Lunch and Reserve Food.

You don't have to be very exact about this. Just carry along a hearty lunch and some extra food to keep body and soul together should something go wrong. A loaf of bread or some candy bars serve well as reserve food supply. Don't try to diet when you're hiking. You need a hearty meal to maintain energy. The energy cost of walking increases rapidly with grade, elevation, and the weight of your pack. Dr. Fred W. Kasch reported in *The Physician and Sportsmedicine* that the energy cost of walking more than doubles on a 10 percent grade. At elevations greater than ten-thousand feet, the walker loses 20 to 25 percent of his physical working capacity, he reported. This increase in the energy cost means an equivalent increase in the number of calories you'll burn while walking. So eat abundantly, if not lavishly, on the trail.

Gorp.

Take any high energy snack food that you can munch along the way—fruits, nuts, and granola are good.

Flashlight, Spare Bulb, and Batteries.

These are good for finding your way around in the dark. Sometimes hikers misjudge the distance they've walked and the amount of daylight they have left. That's when a flashlight comes in handy. They're also useful for looking into old, abandoned wells, caves, and other dark, curious places. Unless the on-off switch of the flashlight has a lock of some sort on it, it's a good idea to reverse or remove the batteries from the cylinder so it doesn't switch on in your pack.

Sturdy Hunting or Jack Knife.

Knives are useful for everything from making lunch to cleaning your fingernails on the way home.

Matches.

Even if you don't plan to build a fire (and you shouldn't unless it's absolutely necessary), you need to carry matches in a waterproof container. Most hikers carry several boxes of matches in different places so that if one box gets wet, the other one is still functional. If you carry kitchen matches, remember to bring something along to strike them on. Should you run into trouble, you may need these matches to build a fire for warmth, cooking, and signaling for help.

Candle.

When it's wet or windy, it's hard to start a fire with just a match, but it's easier (sometimes) to light a candle and then start a fire.

First-Aid Kit.

The standard first-aid kit will do for a day's hike. Be sure to bring along an ace bandage in the event of a sprained ankle and some moleskin and a needle for treating blisters. Foot care is perhaps the most important element of comfort on a hike and I'll discuss that in greater detail later. If you're walking in areas where poisonous snakes are fairly common, at least one person in your party should carry a snakebite kit and know how to use it. People walking alone should definitely be prepared for this rare, but sometimes deadly, hazard of walking in the green world.

Insect Repellent.

Bugs, especially mosquitoes, can take the joy out of any hike. Repellents aren't foolproof but they help a little bit.

Salt Tablets.

You should take these only when you have been sweating profusely. Otherwise, the salt in your food should be sufficient to ward off the effects of salt depletion. If you do take salt tablets, you need to drink plenty of water along with them. You lose other body nutrients through perspiration that also need to be replenished. As a result, some hikers take along electrolyte drinks such as Gatorade and ERG. Such drinks are now available in powdered forms.

Windbreaker with Hood.

The effects of a sudden change in temperature on the downside are magnified greatly by the wind. So take along something to shield you from it.

Wool Sweater or Shirt.

Wool is superior to other fabrics for hiking because it continues to provide warmth even when it is wet.

Poncho

This item was invented by our friends south-of-the-border, long before walking became a luxury. The Mexican poncho is nothing more than a small blanket with a hole in the middle for your head. However, hikers use ponchos to protect themselves from rain and snow. You can buy a lightweight nylon poncho that has a hood and snaps on the sides or you can take a piece of rectangular waterproof fabric or plastic and make your own. Ponchos also make good shelters. With some cord, they can be easily suspended between trees to form a tent of sorts.

Hat or Stocking Cap.

You need a broad-brimmed hat to shade your eyes from the sun and protect your face and neck against sunburn. It's also a good idea to pack a stocking cap because an incredible amount of body heat escapes through your head in cold weather. A lot of people don't like wearing hats. If you're one of them, dispense with the sun hat and keep the stocking cap.

Speaking of the sun, most hiking authorities recommend that you wear sunglasses and carry an extra pair. They aren't absolutely essential in ordinary hiking at low elevations, but above the timberline, sunglasses are your only protection against snowblindness. At the least, they can prevent eye strain sometimes caused by walking all day in the sun.

Extra Set of Socks.

Clean, dry socks are the best preventive measure against blisters. An extra pair is also a blessing when you slip and fall into a creek or accidentally step in a puddle. They'll also give you a new lease on walking after a rainstorm.

Space Blanket.

Not really a blanket in the usual sense, a space blanket is an

aluminized sheet about fifty-six by eighty-four inches that, in a pinch, can serve as a signal cloth, an emergency blanket, a heat reflector, a lean-to, and a lot of other things. They are very handy to have around. They are also inexpensive.

Watch.

You wouldn't think you'd need a watch in the woods. After all, the creatures get along perfectly well without one. Yet one easy way for a hiker to get into trouble is by overextending himself. It usually takes longer to return to the trailhead than it does to reach your destination in the woods. So keep tabs on how long you've been walking and leave ample time to return to your camp or car before sundown. Sometimes parties of walkers decide to break up for a while and rendezvous at another point along the trail. The only way you can be sure of returning from the rendezvous on time, and hence avoid worrying your friends, is by using a watch. The hiker also can get a rough idea of direction from a watch. If you point the hour hand in the direction of the sun, north should be about halfway between the hour hand and twelve. When taking readings before noon, you need to count backward on the dial to find direction. After noon, count forward. The watch should be turned back an hour if it's set to daylight-savings time.

A Whistle.

Whistles are a traditional part of the hiker's gear and are supposed to be used for summoning help or scaring off wild animals. Hollering works about as well though.

Toilet Tissue.

The use of this item is rather obvious, but as long as we're on the subject, I might as well discuss some related matters. People-pollution is a big problem in the woods. So when nature calls, be very careful about where you answer. Get as far away from waterways as possible and well away from camping areas. Once you find a suitable spot, dig a small hole six- to eight-inches deep. Afterward, fill the hole with dirt and leaves. If it's possible to do so without risking a fire, burn the toilet tissue.

We've covered the items a day-hiker should put in his pack, but we haven't discussed what he should wear. Your attire depends largely on the weather. The list I just presented applies only to relatively warm weather. Hiking in rough country in the winter is much more complicated and hazardous and it's not for beginners. For warm-weather walking, you need wear only enough clothing to keep comfortable. Jeans or cotton trousers are suitable for both men and women. If you wear jeans, they should be loose fitting. Tight jeans slow you down and chafe. Many walkers prefer to wear shorts in the summer. They're certainly cooler, but you have to be careful about sunburn. Shorts also give you less protection against brush and low-hanging branches that could tear up your legs. If you wear shorts, it's a good idea to pack an extra pair of jeans. Above the waist, anything goes. An undershirt and cotton shirt that buttons down the front allow you some leeway in adjusting to temperature changes. You can unbutton the shirt and cool down without taking your pack off.

More than any other item, shoes or boots determine a walker's comfort. The day-hiker, carrying a light pack, needn't wear a heavy pair of hiking boots unless he wants to. Many people hike in gym shoes, jogging shoes, or street shoes with rubber soles. Others use combat boots or ordinary work boots. If you choose to make a major purchase, special hiking boots are available at outdoor-equipment stores. Some people think they're worth the money. If you buy a pair of boots for walking, be very careful about the fitting. Most people prefer to wear at least two pairs of socks—one of heavy wool and the other of light cotton—when hiking. So you'll need a pair of boots that leaves ample room for socks. Anytime you buy a pair of hiking boots, discuss the purchase at length with either a salesman you can trust or a friend who is an experienced hiker. A heavy pair of boots will put much more strain on your body than an equivalent amount of weight carried on your back. So you need to buy boots that are adequate for the kind of walking you plan to do but not heavier than you need. If you're mainly interested in day hiking, there's no need to buy the kind of heavy boots that backpackers and climbers often wear. Whatever type of footwear you decide to use, break it in well before you do any day-long hiking. You may have to do as much as fifty miles of walking before heavy boots are properly molded to your feet. Some authorities suggest a quick method for breaking in new boots. Soak them in water for about twenty minutes; then walk in them until they're dry. This method is likely to sprout a crop of blisters on your feet, which is what you are trying to avoid in the first place, so I don't advise that you use this method.

Once you've donned a comfortable pair of shoes or boots, then you can begin to do some serious worrying about blisters. A city-walker doesn't have to worry much about blisters. When one of these little fun-destroyer's crops up, the city-walker can just go home and take the load off his feet. But the hiker isn't so fortunate. He may have to walk for hours on feet that feel like they've been through a brushfire. As a result, the hiker has to take care of his feet both before and during a hike. The best method of preventing blisters on a hike is to walk a lot before you go. Gradually, your feet will develop a layer of callus that protects the sensitive underskin from the constant grinding and chafing of walking. The only other way I know of to toughen feet is bathing them in alcohol for a week or two before the hike. That helps some, but not as much as a walking regimen. Once you hit the trail, there's more you can do. First, you can make sure that your socks don't bunch up in your shoes. Occasionally, reach down and pull them up. Secondly, you should act quickly if you begin to feel a blister developing. Don't wait until it's a full-grown, festering monster before you take remedial action. When you've got a hot spot, you need to cover it with something. Moleskin, which is available at any drugstore, is the best material to use. It's a thin pad with a sticky substance on one side that holds it to your foot. You should carry some Moleskin in your first-aid kit. In the absence of such a comforter, a Band-Aid or a piece of adhesive tape will help some. Make sure that the tape fits tightly. Before you put your shoes back on, see if you can discover the cause of the blister and correct it. In most cases, it's a fold in the sock. If so, put on your extra pair. Once a blister emerges, there's nothing you can do but perform some minor surgery. Sterilize a needle with a flame, make a small hole at the edge of the blister, and drain the fluid inside. Then cover it with gauze and an adhesive material.

Yet an even better protection against blisters and other walking maladies, such as sore feet and leg muscles, is to walk with moderation and good sense. You should rest for a few minutes about once every hour. When possible, take your shoes and socks off and let the air dry your feet. Some people even massage their feet to get the blood flowing again. Others bathe their feet at every opportunity. If your socks are damp, change them and attach the old pair to your pack to dry. Many regular rest periods of no more than five or ten minutes an hour are better for you than a long stop—and it's not as hard to get on your feet and walk again. You can avoid sore muscles by walking at a moderate pace. Even if you can walk three miles in forty-five minutes in town, you shouldn't walk that fast on a hike. Set a slow, steady pace that you could keep up all day if need be. Start out walking slowly and you'll have plenty of energy left to end your walk with a sprint. Remember that it requires roughly the same amount of energy to walk at a speed of two miles an hour on a 10 percent grade as it does to walk four miles an hour on level ground. In rough country, most people average only about one-and-one-half miles an hour, counting rest stops.

Unless you're in excellent physical condition, uphill walking will be quite strenuous. There are some tricks, however, that veteran hikers use to move steadily uphill without becoming winded. One trick is the rest step, which as the name implies, is a method of resting between steps. To execute the rest step, you plant the uphill leg, with knee bent, and rest momentarily on the straightened down-hill leg. Then push off with the downhill leg and lean forward on the uphill leg until you've taken another step. Then rest momentarily and so forth. Try to take a deep breath at every resting point in the step. Climbing is not only difficult because of the grade but also because of the altitude. As everyone knows, the higher you go, the thinner the air becomes. Consequently, you need to breathe as deeply as possible and be especially careful of becoming too tired. It takes several days for the body to adjust to high altitudes, so you must always take it easy when you begin walking at a much higher altitude than you are accustomed to. Altitude sickness rarely strikes below an altitude of about nine-thousand feet, but it can become a problem several thousand feet below that. Fortunately for hikers, it doesn't become really severe until you've been high up for at least two days. The hiker usually will feel only a slight headache.

I've already mentioned that this chapter is not meant as a complete guide to hiking in all weather conditions. Yet even in the summer there are certain things that can go wrong while hiking and if you're not at least a little bit knowledgeable about them, you could hurt yourself. Perhaps by discussing them here, I can at least convince you that the list of necessities enumerated in this chapter is more than just idle chatter. They are the minimum daily requirements for a hiker.

The one hazard most summer hikers are familiar with is heat. Normally, our body works as a marvelous cooling system. In order to keep the temperature at our body core around the standard 98.6 degrees, the blood vessels near the skin dilate and heat is radiated from the body to the air around it. Perspiration serves the same purpose. Yet, sometimes this system goes awry and the body cannot dispel a sufficient amount of heat. Two conditions may result. The first and least serious is heat exhaustion. The symptoms of heat exhaustion are pale and clammy skin, excessive perspiration, rapid and shallow breathing, weakness, dizziness and headache. If you, or a member of your group, experience these symptoms, you should immediately get them out of the sun into a cool area. Don't allow the victim to become chilled, however. If he does, cover him with a blanket. Once a victim of heat exhaustion recovers, the group may continue hiking. This procedure is not recommended, however, for victims of a more serious heat-caused affliction, heat stroke. In this malady, the body's cooling system suffers a complete breakdown. The victim's face becomes red and flushed, his skin hot and dry with no perspiration, and he may become unconscious. You must act quickly to save his life. The only way to do so is to cool him down as fast as possible. Lay him in a stream or lake if one is nearby. Otherwise, soak his clothing with water from your canteen. Place a wet cloth on his forehead. Once the victim is cool, you need to watch for symptoms of shock, such as shivering and nausea. If these symptoms occur, you should keep the victim warm (as unlikely as it may sound). Finally, the victim of heat stroke needs medical attention even if he regains the ability to walk. So, end your trek and take him to a doctor despite his contention that he is feeling fine.

Another heat-related, or rather sun-related, problem is sunburn. At high altitudes you burn much more easily than at sea level. Even on a cool day you can get a vicious burn in the mountains. So take steps to protect yourself from the sun by wearing a hat and using either a sun-blocking or tanning lotion. And always carry plenty of water in hot weather or know where water is available along your route. At rest, the average adult needs about two quarts of water a day. When exercising strenuously, as in hiking, the need for water doubles to one gallon a day. Dehydration leads to a loss of stamina, so drink as often as you feel thirsty.

Everyone knows something about the dangers of cold weather and we've all heard stories about people who "died of exposure" or "froze to death." Yet many people are not quite as well informed about what happens when cold, wet, and wind are combined. The effects of all three, or any of the two together, can be devastating.

The outdoor community as a whole was not adequately informed about these perils until a book called *Hypothermia: Killer of the Unprepared* by Dr. Theodore G. Lathrop, was published by the Mazamas, a mountaineering club in Portland, Oregon. Now the twenty-nine-page book is standard fare on the bookshelves of many outdoor-equipment stores. What Dr. Lathrop revealed was that even people hiking at sea level, in above-freezing temperatures, could die from the effects of the cold, the wet, and the wind.

Hypothermia, Dr. Lathrop wrote, "means loss of heat or, more precisely, a lowering of the temperature of the body's inner core. In acute accidental hypothermia, the loss of heat from the body's vital core can result in uncontrollable shivering, followed by increasing clumsiness and loss of judgment, and a fairly rapid descent into unconsciousness and death." In chilling accounts of several tragedies in which both experienced mountaineers and unequipped day-hikers lost their lives, Dr. Lathrop proves that hypothermia is something that casual hikers, as well as mountaineers, need to be aware of. One prime misconception he attempts to dispel is that hypothermia occurs only in extreme cold. "Extreme low temperature is not a necessary precondition for hypothermia," he reported. "It has claimed many victims when the surrounding air temperature was well above 32 degrees Fahrenheit."

The day-hiker should know the astonishing rate at which wet and wind multiply the loss of body heat. One only needs to listen to regular weather reports in the winter to ascertain that wind speed is more important than temperature in determining how cold it will "feel" outdoors. When the temperature is zero and there is no breeze at all, a hiker would be quite comfortable in light clothing, Dr. Lathrop reported, but even a slight bit of wind would rapidly cool him off. ". . . We enter the 'very cold' range of windchill when the temperature is a mild forty degrees and the wind is blowing only twenty-five miles an hour," he reported. Waterchill has similar destructive effects on the body's ability to retain heat. "The thermal conductivity of water (or ice) is thirty-two times as great as that of still air," Dr. Lathrop reported. "This means that wet clothing can extract heat from your body up to thirty-two times as fast as dry clothing." He notes that wool protects the wet hiker much more than other fabrics because it loses only "40 to 60 percent of its protective value when wet." Dr. Lathrop also recommends that people suffering from the cold should eat as much high-energy food as possible to maintain the body's ability to produce heat. They should also keep as active as possible, because activity generates heat. They should also find shelter early, before hypothermia destroys the ability to behave rationally.

What the average hiker should learn from all this is that the list of necessities is really important. They could save your life.

Another bad weather hazard is lightning. Although it results in more deaths per year (about 150) than any other weather phenomenon, lightning can be avoided fairly easy if you know what you're doing. The first thing to remember is that lightning generally will strike the highest point in the area. So when you see a thunderstorm heading your way, try to get down in a valley or into a cave. Avoid peaks, ledges, and trees standing alone in a field or meadow. You can figure roughly how much time you have by counting the seconds between the flash of lightning and the thunder that follows. Light travels at 186,000 miles per second, while sound travels at only 1,100 feet per second, so the storm will be one mile away for every five seconds that passes between lightning and thunder. If you're caught out in the open, crouch as low to the ground as possible, but don't lie down. When possible, stand on an insulated material such as a rope or air mattress. Get rid of metal objects such as keys, canteens, or packs that would tend to conduct electricity. If someone in your party should be struck by lightning, they might be saved by cardiopulmonary resuscitation, if you act quickly.

Another danger of hiking that every walker worries about is getting lost. As long as you carry a map and compass, your chances of getting lost are very slight. You may become disoriented briefly, something that happens to even veteran hikers, but your map and compass should lead you out. If you are really lost, the first thing to do is remain calm. In most wilderness areas in America, you are really not that far from help. Many people get lost in the woods every year and virtually all of them are rescued. When you've grown sufficiently calm to think clearly, you should consider how to find shelter, warmth, and water. Move carefully away from your starting point to a place where you can erect a lean-to with a space blanket (or some other equipment) and build a fire. Try to locate a water source. Once these three essentials are taken care of, you should try to signal for help. Smoke from a fire is one of the best methods of alerting authorities. Three of anything is an emergency signal, so you should blow your whistle or yell in three quick bursts. A pattern of stones on the ground may attract the attention of aerial searchers. In the meantime, continue to study the terrain. You may recognize a landmark that you overlooked before.

Anyone walking in a wilderness area for a day or more should let someone know where he is going. At least a friend or a member of your family should know when you are expected back. For longer trips, you should leave a map of the course you plan to take and a timetable for your trip. They should be instructed to notify the authorities if you don't report in at an appointed time. It's also important to inform a forest ranger or park official of your plans and supply them with a copy of your itinerary.

There's little excuse for a well-equipped hiker or backpacker getting lost and usually they are the ill-equipped and inexperienced walkers who lose their way. Remember that the money you save by not buying a map and compass for your trip would be rapidly spent by the cost of a helicopter rescue.

Yet, more than the weather and getting lost, many novices fear animals in wild country. In almost every case, that fear is totally without foundation.

First, let's consider three carnivorous mammals: the bear, bobcat, and mountain lion. Unless they've been tamed or have lost their fear of man in some other way, these animals are extremely timid. There are exceptions, but in general these animals will not attack humans unless they are caught by surprise in close quarters. The grizzly bear has been cast as the main villain of the wilderness, and undeniably, they have attacked humans. The best precaution you can take against this rare animal is to make plenty of noise when walking through grizzly country. In short, give the bears plenty of warning. Perhaps a more serious threat to hikers are the black bears we find in some heavily used national parks. They have grown accustomed to humans and, although they might appear to be tame, they are not. They should be given a wide berth and reported to park officials when possible.

But the wilderness creatures that really strike fear in the hearts of hikers are the poisonous snakes. Here again, the fear is largely unwarranted. Bites from poisonous snakes are extremely rare, and death from these bites is even more unusual. There are four kinds of poisonous snakes in the United States: the rattlesnake, the copperhead, the water moccasin (sometimes called the cottonmouth), and the coral snake. As an inspirer of fear, nothing that I know of comes close to the buzzing sound produced by the vibration of the horny segments at the end of the rattlesnake's tail. Yet, the characteristic "rattle" is probably only the snake's way of warning you that you're trespassing. Among the most common rattlers in the U.S. are the timber rattler of the eastern and central states, the prairie rattler of the western states, and the diamondback. The reputation of the copperhead was enhanced during the Civil War when it was used as a political epithet to describe those Northerners who opposed war with the Confederacy. Apparently, the inventors of the epithet meant to imply that the political "copperheads" were "sneaky." The copperhead (the snake, that is) is found in the eastern half of the U.S., is usually less than three-feet long, and has a pinkish or reddish color, reddish-brown bands across its back, and a copper-colored head. The water moccasin is limited primarily to the wet areas of the Southeastern states and for that reason is seldom encountered by hikers. They sometimes are as long as five feet and are brown or black, with dark crossbands. They often are called cottonmouths because they threaten humans with their mouths open, revealing the white interior of the mouth. The most dangerous poisonous snake bite in this country is that of the coral snake, because the venom attacks the nerves and affects the body much more rapidly than the venom of the others. The coral snake is found in the southern U.S. and has red, black, and yellow rings running the length of its body. A wonder of nature is the evolutionary process in which creatures sometimes imitate other more powerful creatures. This has occurred in relation to the coral snake. There are several other harmless snakes, including the king snake, which have markings similar to the coral snake. The order of the colored bands on the body, however, is different. A good jingle to remember, in order to distinguish between the real coral snake and the "false" coral snakes (which are harmless), is "red touching yellow, dangerous fellow." (Some snakes, by the way, also will imitate the rattler by beating their tails against dry leaves.) Fortunately, for the hiker, the coral snake is quite timid and docile and is rarely a problem.

Like the warm-blooded creatures of the outdoors, poisonous snakes seldom bother hikers unless they walk within their striking range. Ordinarily, these snakes will lie still or crawl slowly away when they sense danger approaching. (The one exception is the water moccasin, which has a reputation for standing its ground.) Crucial in learning how to avoid poisonous snakes is the fact that they cannot maintain a steady body temperature. If they become too hot, they will die. As the temperature drops, they become sluggish or hibernate. Consequently, on cool days you're likely to find them basking in the sun on a warm rock. On a hot day, they'll be resting in the shade, under a bush or on a rock ledge. These are the places, depending upon the weather, where you should keep your eyes peeled and watch your step. Generally, it's not a good idea to put your foot down anywhere in snake country, without first surveying its destination. Hikers that follow heavily-used trails are much less likely to encounter snakes than people hiking across country. Yet on a cool, sunny day, trails provide snakes with a pleasant, warm surface for basking. I remember one such day when my wife and I were taking a short hike in Rocky Mountain National Park. As usual, I was enthralled by the scenery and nearly stepped on a good-sized snake lying right in the middle of the trail. (I didn't hang around long enough to provide a more detailed description of it here. Snakes have always scared the devil out of me.) If you're really worried about snakes or walking in an area where they're known to be prevalent, you can protect yourself somewhat by wearing high-topped boots and long pants. Otherwise, the best policy is just be aware of them and realize there are some places where they are more likely to be found.

Should the unlikely happen, and you're bitten by a snake, the first thing you need to do is determine if it's poisonous. If you can, kill the snake and inspect it. The rattlesnake, copperhead, and water moccasin are known as pit vipers because they have a small pit, used for sensing heat, between each eye and nostril. They also will have fangs. A rattlesnake, of course, can be identified by the "rattles" at the end of its tail. Poisonous snakes inject their venom into the body through their fangs, so you should always look for one or two puncture marks at the point of the bite. Even if you conclude that you were bitten by a poisonous snake, you need to wait for symptoms to appear. The amount of venom injected into the body varies from a potentially lethal dose to none at all. So watch for spreading, swelling, and redness in the area of the bite. Once you're fairly certain you have a poisonous snakebite on your hands, then consider how to treat it. In recent years, emergency rescue agencies report an increasing number of injuries suffered by persons who have used the standard "cut-and-suck" method of snakebite treatment. Consequently, they recommend whenever possible that the victim remains quiet while a fellow hiker goes for help. When assistance is only a few miles away, this probably is the best way of handling a snakebite unless you're an expert in the use of a snakebite kit. A physician or trained rescuer can easily administer one of the highly effective antivenins.

If you decide to treat the wound yourself, the most commonly used method is to remove as much of the poison from your body as possible, by cutting the wound and sucking out the poison. * It's easier to use this method if you're carrying a snakebite kit, but it's possible to do it with only a knife and some ingenuity. The first step is remain calm and do not waste time, because the first few minutes are crucial. Movement stimulates the spread of the poison. Position yourself so that the wound is lower than the rest of your body. Then you need to place a constricting band just above the swelling caused by the bite. The band should be between the wound and your torso and it should be tight enough to slow the flow of poison, but not so tight that it cuts off circulation totally. Snakebite kits contain a tourniquet, but a belt or a length of cord will work almost as well. If swelling continues past the restricting band, put another band above the swelling and loosen the first one. Once the band is in place, you need to make an incision (either with the blade contained in the kit or with a sterilized knife) through each fang mark. The cuts should be not more than one-eighth-inch deep or more than one-half-inch long. Press the area around the incisions to make them bleed. Be very careful when making these incisions that you do not sever a major blood vessel. The incision should be made lengthwise to your body. The next step is remove the venom. Your snakebite kit includes two suction cups that you can place over the wounds. If you don't have a kit, you can use your mouth and spit out the blood. You shouldn't use your mouth, however, if you have open sores in your mouth or a cut on your lip. Most experts recommend that you continue removing as much venom as possible for about one hour.

Once you've taken these steps and bandaged the wound, then you should send a fellow hiker for help. If you're alone, the decision becomes more difficult. By trying to walk for help yourself, you run the risk of spreading the venom. On the other hand, if you remain, you may face a two-day battle with vomiting, fever, and other symptoms of snakebite. There's no way you can make that decision

---

*This method is not effective in treating the bite of the coral snake.

ahead of time. It depends on how far away you are from civilization and how serious the wound is. In every case, you should get medical attention as soon as possible.

There are two other poisonous "critters" that hikers should know about: The scorpion and the black-widow spider. The scorpion ranges in length from about one-half inch to seven inches, has pincers, and uses its tail to sting its prey. Most varieties are harmless, but two species found in Arizona inject a dangerous nerve poison that may cause death. Although scorpions are rarely seen, and dangerous stings are even more unusual, the hiker should check his boots and equipment every morning when walking in the southwest.

The black-widow spider appears in virtually every area of the country. The most common species in America is black and has a reddish, hour-glass-shaped design or two small spots on its abdomen. The seriousness of their bite varies widely and often causes no more than the redness and swelling similar to that of a bee sting, but the venom sometimes causes severe pain, nausea, and some temporary paralysis of the diaphragm. The bite is very rarely fatal.

In addition to poisonous animals, hikers also should be aware of poisonous plants. It's mildly popular these days to attempt to "survive" in the wilderness by eating the plants found there. There are many excellent books on the subject, vital reading for anyone who's going to be eating a lot of wild plants. Just remember that harmless plants have a way of imitating poisonous ones. So make sure you know damn well what you're eating. Many plants are poisonous when ingested.

Other plants are poisonous when touched. Although "poison" seems a rather strong word to describe what happens when you sit down in a bed of poison ivy, the result can be pretty unpleasant. The most common plants that cause skin irritations of one kind or another are poison oak, poison ivy (actually a variety of poison oak), poison sumac, trumpet creeper, and nettles. I could try to describe them to you, but I don't believe many people could distinguish them from all the imitative varieties without actually seeing them. Have a fellow hiker, who knows the varieties of poisonous plants common to your area, point them out to you. Clothing, of course, is the best protection against irritating plants. Long-sleeved shirts give you more protection that short sleeves; long trousers offer more protection than shorts.

The hazards of hiking shouldn't dampen your enthusiasm. When you consider the number of people who hike and the number of miles they walk, accidents are actually exceedingly rare. And avoiding trouble, once you are aware of the possible dangers, is largely a matter of common sense. I asked Scott Clemons, a hiker who has walked a great deal in the western U.S. and Nepal, what he believed was the key to avoiding disaster in the wilderness. "Know your limits," he replied. "When you're climbing a mountain, you need to know when to turn back. It's a lot easier to climb up something than to climb down."

Most hiking experts and government officials recommend that you never hike alone and that you stay on established trails. The advantages of hiking in groups of two or more are fairly obvious. An injury or a leaky canteen is not nearly as serious when there is another hiker along to go for help or share his water. Similarly, the hiker who remains on the trail runs less chance of getting lost or falling prey to other wilderness hazards. It's certainly a good idea to follow this advice on your first few hiking trips and many people prefer to have someone else along, if only for the company they provide, even after they become expert hikers.

Yet many of America's great walkers—Henry David Thoreau, John Muir, Colin Fletcher—have been solitary walkers. Fletcher walked the length of Grand Canyon mostly alone and he spent an entire summer walking alone in California.

I suspect the question of whether or not to walk alone is resolved after a few trips to the woods. I don't believe many inexperienced hikers feel very comfortable walking alone. But by the time they develop a craving for wilderness solitude, they probably have gained enough experience to take care of themselves. In other words, they've learned their limits.

11

Backpacking: The Ultimate
in Walking

Backpacking is the ultimate walking experience. It's the big payoff for anyone who loves to walk and loves the outdoors. Whether it's a week-long trek planned months in advance or a spur-of-the-moment, weekend outing with rented equipment, backpacking can be a fantastic experience. It's the sun coming up over a snow-capped peak; it's solitude; it's physical challenge; it's falling to sleep with the stars for a blanket. Yet, for the millions of people who backpack all over America every year, it means something different, something unique.

In researching this book, I received letters and local newsletters from hikers and backpackers across the country. Each of them had a story to tell, and each story, be it that of novice or veteran, was a testament to the joys of backpacking.

Here's what one reader of *Frank Ashley's Rag,* a California backpacking newsletter* had to say about her first backpacking experience.

 . . . I had the unique opportunity to take a hike in the "The Narrows" of the East Fork of the San Gabriel River (in Southern California). As a novice backpacker, I thought this trip would give me a chance to "get my feet wet" and find out what the joys of backpacking are all about. Little

---

* *Frank Ashley's Rag,* Box 291, Culver City, California 90230.

did I know that my feet and everything else would get wet on more than one occasion. The stream crossings were refreshing even though it was upstream all the way. Now I have some idea what salmons go through just to get home. The term "day hike" has taken on a whole new meaning for me, especially after taking the whole day to reach our campsite. Four miles in eight hours: Not because I was slow and inexperienced, but because last winter's rains (or tidal waves) washed out the trail. There were rocks to the right of me, rocks to the left of me, rocks above me, rocks below me. I think what I did is called "boulder hopping." . . . After reaching the campsite at long last, the happy hour came with the no-host cocktails served (naturally) on the rocks. Never for one minute did I reach rock bottom. There were a few times I wasn't sure who I was or where I was, but that didn't matter. . . . The outing will be an experience I will long remember and I would like to go again sometime soon. Do I still have rocks in my head?

And this description is of three days of an eleven-day backpack through the Olympic Mountains of Washington. The account is from the annual newsletter of the Olympians, a hiking club in Hoquiam, Washington.

Saturday: The weather looks good—a quick breakfast, we pack up and are on our way. Finding the trail to Scout Lake, it is easy going for about two miles. We have a spectacular view of Scout Lake nestled in a forest-surrounded valley five-hundred feet below us. Now it begins to fog up, so staying above the lake we continue on our way and the fog clears just enough, at the right time, for us to locate St. Peter's Gate, near our destination. Contouring around Boulder Lake, up the snow field, through St. Peter's Gate, then we are on our way down to Lake of the Angels, arriving about 5:30 P.M., a long hard day. The four (other hikers) to meet us here have a nice fire going, a welcome sight. With our tents up, dinner cooked and eaten, dishes washed, we have a pleasant evening around a cheery campfire enjoying the drifting fog.

Sunday: This day starts out being warm and clear. Breakfast of eggs 'n hashbrowns, the climbers take off to conquer Mt. Skokomish. Gordon, Mike and Mary venture on to Hagen Lakes while the rest of us spend the day around Lake of the Angels exploring, taking pictures of many lovely flowers in bloom—beargrass, heather (both white and red), bistort, valerian, butterwort, spring beauty, being a few. As the day progresses the fog blows in and out, so there is not too much to see and we retire early for a good night's rest.

Monday: Leaving Lake of the Angels, a fairly nice morning, we climb on up to the pass and take a short cut down the other side—quite steep so the rope is put to use—cross a large snow field, then a scree slope on up to Hagen Lakes Pass and it's beginning to get *very* foggy. We have a quick lunch and are on our way through the fog with Ned scouting ahead. We more or less follow the narrow rocky bridge, stopping once in a while to check the compass and map. Below the ridge we find sort of a trail and finally find our campsite below Mt. Hopper, and it is still foggy and damp. With a cozy fire, tents up, dinner cooking, the evening is topped off with a birthday celebration. . . .

Six days' later, this group finally reached the end of their journey which had been rather damp and foggy, but fun, nevertheless.

As you can see from these accounts, backpacking is a rugged sport. You can't control bad weather or rough terrain. You can only prepare yourself for it. And that's why backpacking can be a great teacher for people who are used to manipulating their environment. In the wilderness, you can't alleviate boredom by turning on the television set, hunger by popping something in the oven, cold by turning up the thermostat. Backpackers are forced to fall back upon their own resources: advance preparation, ingenuity, and common sense. And what the backpacker can't change, he must suffer through. For this reason, backpacking and hiking have long been used by various groups, such as the Boy Scouts and Girl Scouts, to "build character." It has even been used to rehabilitate juvenile delinquents when all other methods have failed. *Field and Stream* magazine carried an article nearly ten years ago in which a writer described how a group of juvenile delinquents changed from a surly gang of "punks" to a gathering of hopeful young men in only eight days of backpacking. "Perhaps if every American family would spend just one week a year camping together, divorce and juvenile delinquency would become a thing of the past," the writer commented. "Wishful thinking? Maybe . . . but my eyes saw a group of tired exjuvenile delinquents, their faces dirty and their clothing torn from seventy miles of rough hiking. The exterior was dirty, but the boy inside was a heck of a lot cleaner than he was eight days before."

Walking is the backpacker's method of transportation, but there is a great deal more involved in backpacking than simple walking. You should know and use everything I discuss and recommend in the previous chapter on hiking, plus the material in this chapter. What separates hiking from backpacking is that the hiker returns home, to a lodge or to a cabin, where food and shelter are provided for him. The backpacker carries his food and shelter on his back.

As in everything else, there are various levels of backpacking. For instance, you set out on a Saturday morning, camp out for one night, and return home the following day. You can get by with a minimum amount of equipment. If you don't plan to cook, all you need to carry is the pack, the essential equipment I mentioned in the previous chapter, a sleeping bag, and some food. If you decide you need some hot food along the way, any of the small stoves and cooksets now available would probably fit nicely into your ordinary hiking pack. A space blanket or poncho would give you some protection if it should rain. Furthermore, if something should go wrong, you will most likely be only a short way from your car.

In warm weather, backpacking can be pretty simple. Just strap a sleeping bag onto your hiking pack, throw in a few cans of tuna fish and a loaf of bread, plan for adequate water—either by carrying it with you or knowing where you can get it along the way—and you are ready to go backpacking.

When you plan a longer trip, or a trip in less than ideal conditions, your backpacking life becomes more complicated. Then you need to plan more precisely for food, shelter, and walking comfort. A leaky, uncomfortable pair of boots can be tolerated for one or two days, but on a week-long trip, they'd probably drive you mad or, at the least, spoil your hard-earned vacation. The same is true of inadequate food and shelter.

So the backpacker needs to think about equipment and what to do with that equipment when the time comes to use it. Fortunately, the popularity of backpacking has produced an abundance of backpacking equipment. Today, there is a wide selection of excellent equipment on the market. It may be expensive, but it is there, nevertheless. At the same time, as you know, freedom of choice produces its own set of problems. When nothing was available but a packboard, Army surplus tent, and a leaden sleeping bag, outdoorsmen just made the obvious purchases and adjusted to their inadequacies and discomforts. Today, alas, we seek perfection from our equipment and the manufacturers have damned-near reached that elusive state. So why is this a problem? In the first place, it means that we have to choose between all the lines and varieties of equipment. In the second place, it means that we have to decide where to draw the line. How good should our equipment be? In most cases, you get what you pay for and good equipment is more expensive than mediocre or bad equipment. How close should we follow the various innovations and changes in equipment? Is last year's model adequate or should we try that new backpack/tent/sleeping bag/stove that the manufacturers and critics say is lighter/warmer/dryer/more versatile/more durable than "Ole Betsy?" These are tough questions. For nothing is more of a joy to a backpacker than good equipment, equipment that does what it's supposed to do. On the other hand, is it worth taking out a second mortgage on the house, working two jobs, or putting the kids out for hire just to obtain the latest in backpacking equipment?

Such questions were first bandied-about in backpacking circles a few years' ago and the debate still rages. Some backpackers are concerned that preoccupation with equipment tends to overshadow the joys of backpacking, of being outdoors. Others believe that good equipment merely enhances the experience. I asked Jack Scarritt, a backpacking expert and outdoor-equipment inventor in Merriam, Kansas, whether he believes the emphasis on backpacking equipment has become excessive. I knew, being in the business himself, that his reply would be somewhat biased in favor of equipment sales, but I think his answer is interesting, nevertheless. "Equipment freaks," he said, "are always in search of the best. They are very discriminating and they keep on top of the market. The people who buy cheap equipment pay a price in the end in versatility, durability, and comfort. They buy a cheap pack and it fits wrong. We have people come in here all the time with problems like that. People who are interested in the sport are interested in quality equipment." At the other end of the spectrum is my friend, Scott Clemons, the veteran Rocky Mountain and Himalayan backpacker. Clemons told me he has used much of the same equipment for years. He uses a tent he bought at a discount store (although he has a good rain fly to put over it). He seldom buys freeze-dried food, which most backpacking authorities swear by. Instead, Clemons fills his pack with tuna fish and other canned foods. He walks heavy. He doesn't mind carrying a seventy-pound pack and he relies upon the fact that in this day and age, the backpacker is seldom more than a hard day's walk from civilization.

Where does this leave the beginner who's trying to decide what he needs to buy and how much to pay for what he buys? I believe there are several clear choices.

1. You can buy inexpensive equipment. Many brands are available in discount stores and department stores. Some people have good luck with this kind of equipment. Generally, it doesn't last as long as more expensive equipment, but if it works fairly well while it lasts, then you've found a real bargain. Inexpensive equipment may be the best buy for people who plan to use it only occasionally on short walks in fairly good weather. Under those conditions, the discomfort would be brief even if something did go wrong.

2. You can buy topflight equipment. Usually, equipment of this caliber is only available in outdoor-equipment stores or through the mail. Its advantages are many. It usually lasts longer, is more versatile, more reliable, and comfortable. Unfortunately, it can be a great deal more expensive, although there are levels of quality and cost even here. As Scarritt points out, serious backpackers who hike frequently, take long trips, head for rough country and terrain, and take chances with the weather, usually end up buying good equipment, even though they may not always need the very best equipment.

3. You can rent equipment. I believe this is the best route for beginners. You can use good, reliable equipment without a large financial outlay. You can decide how much you like backpacking and how often you think you might be going out; you can test various brands and models of equipment without purchasing them; and, at some stores, you can apply the rental cost to the purchase of new equipment. Many people, who only backpack once or twice a year, never buy equipment; they always rent. Or they may buy a few items and rent others.

Now don't panic; backpacking is not an expensive sport. In fact, it's a real bargain for families who do it year after year because, once you've made the initial outlay for equipment, the cost of subsequent outings is comparatively small. The backpacker, remember, doesn't have to pay for hotel rooms, restaurant meals, transportation, tips, etc. And once safely tucked away in the woods, the backpacker's not constantly tempted by curio shops, entertainments, clothing stores, and other money-gobblers, which often make a vacation much more expensive than you anticipated. So keep that in mind when you recover from the initial shock that usually follows the first trip to the equipment store.

When you begin thinking about backpacking equipment, I believe you should start from the bottom up. As one backpacker told me: "The most important thing is boots. If they're not comfortable and your feet are covered with blisters, you're going to be miserable. If your feet are comfortable, then all the other things that can go wrong don't seem to matter much." Scarritt added: "Boots are the most important purchase. They don't need to be heavyweight but they should be of good quality and a good fit, regardless of the brand." Some authorities might consider my discussion of footwear in the previous chapter somewhat cavalier. As you know, I suggested that some hikers are comfortable in gym, jogging, or street shoes. Most backpacking authorities disagree with that. They believe that boots are essential because a walker carrying a heavy pack on his back needs more support for his feet than light shoes provide, he is more likely to encounter special problems such as snow and rain, and the entire trip might be ruined by inadequate footwear. I concede that good boots do have the aforementioned advantages, but for the short backpack in good weather, something less than expensive hiking boots may still do the job. With footwear, you usually get what you pay for. A well-broken-in hiking boot is the foot's best friend. With less than that, you're taking a chance. It's up to you.

If you do take the boot route, so to speak, most authorities recommend a medium- or lightweight boot, less than seven- or eight-inches tall. It should have a waterproof, durable sole with ruffles, ridges, or some other traction-producing device. Most hiking boots today have rugged soles, constructed of a combination of rubber and synthetic materials. Nearly all leather boots must be treated, both to prevent leakage and preserve the leather. When you buy the boots, find out what treatment the manufacturer recommends for them and follow those directions. The life and effectiveness of the boots are largely dependent upon how well you take care of them. *

*For more information on foot care and footwear, see the previous chapter on hiking.

Yet, even if you buy those boots for walking, there is still a place in backpacking for your dearly beloved sneakers. They're useful for wearing around your campsite at night, for crossing streams, for side trips without a heavy load, and for replacing walking boots should they become lost or damaged. They're also useful for sneaking. So toss a pair into your pack.

Which brings me to the next piece of equipment you'll need to buy, beg, borrow, or rent—the backpack. Most backpacks can be divided into two essential parts: the pack and the frame. The latter is a rectangular device of aluminum or alloy molded to the contours of the human back. Good pack frames are solidly welded at the joints and have strips of material running either vertically or horizontally along the side of the frame closest to your back that prevent the frame itself from digging into your flesh.

The frame is attached to the body at the waist and shoulders. For many years, backpackers, trappers, and mountain men used packs that were attached to their bodies only at the shoulders, but virtually all modern pack frames include an additional strip near the bottom on the frame.

This strap is called the waistbelt or hipbelt and it's the one innovation that has done more than anything else to make it physically bearable to walk with a heavy load on your back. It increases walking comfort by distributing the weight of the pack from the shoulders to the hips. The waistbelt should encircle the body, and most backpackers prefer well-padded belts, especially when carrying heavy loads.

Packframes must be properly fitted. Some firms offer adjustable frames that fit almost all sizes, but always make sure that you are buying a frame suitable for you. Always try on a backpack or frame before you buy it. Even if it is recommended for someone your height, the length of the torso is more important than overall height, and it still may not fit properly. One manufacturer, Camp Trails, recommends this method of insuring the proper fit. "Load the pack with about twenty-five pounds of weight, using sandbags or plastic bottles filled with water. Slip into the backpack while someone holds it for you. Fasten the hipbelt with the horizontal seam at the top of your pelvic bone. Tighten the shoulder straps until the load balances with light shoulder pressure. Try all adjustments until the top of the shoulder straps are level or slightly higher than the top of your shoulder.

Photo by Scott Clemons

This is a correct fit. If the shoulder pads are lower than the top of your shoulder, try a larger size frame. If the shoulder pads are more than two inches higher than the top of your shoulder, try a smaller size frame." Most backpackers buy a packframe and packbag at the same time, but it's possible to buy them separately.

The walker carries his house—kitchen, bedroom, food—and virtually all other necessities either inside, or attached to, his packbag. For this reason, the pack must be purchased carefully, taking into consideration the amount and kind of equipment you might be carrying, weather conditions, and other factors.

Most modern packs are compartmentalized in some fashion. The outside of the packs usually have several zippered pockets or compartments that give you easy access to water, food, compass, map, and other items, without diving into the pack itself. Some packs also contain compartments on the inside that help you organize your load. All these accessories to the basic pack can be helpful on the trail, but it's important to keep in mind that simplicity has its good points, too. A complicated pack with many zippers, belts, and attachments increases the likelihood of something going wrong. It's not a pleasant experience when, far from home, you find your provisions locked away behind an immovable zipper or, conversely, find that a broken zipper allowed breakfast, lunch, and supper to spill onto the trail behind your back, so to speak. So it's a good idea to balance the convenience of gadgetry against the safety of simplicity and arrive at a happy medium that adds to your walking pleasure without jeopardizing vital equipment and food.

Another matter you'll need to consider is the size of the pack. Since you are making a major purchase, it's a good idea to buy a pack that is a little larger than you think you need, but not so large that it adds a lot of unnecessary weight and bulk to your load. A capacity of three-thousand to four-thousand-cubic inches should be adequate for most people, unless they're planning a major expedition. Some packs have extendable tops that accommodate as much as one-thousand-cubic inches of extra equipment.

Most modern bags are made of nylon, but packs made of cotton duck material are still available. The natural fiber is easier to waterproof, but the nylon bags can be equally as water-resistant if sealer is used on the seams. You can also purchase a waterproof cover for your pack. A waterproof pack gives you more flexibility in what you wear on the trail during a rainstorm, because you don't have to cover the pack with a poncho. You can wear a rain jacket, instead, which many walkers find less confining. A waterproof pack may also be left outside the tent at night, a definite advantage when space is a problem.

After proper footwear and a backpack, the next piece of equipment you'll almost certainly need is a sleeping bag. Of the three, the sleeping bag probably will be the most expensive purchase, if you buy a good one.

The initial decision you'll face in selecting a sleeping bag is whether to buy a bag filled with down (either duck or goose feathers) or synthetic fibers. A few years ago, down-filled was widely believed far superior to fiber-filled. But advances in fibers and bag design have narrowed the gap somewhat. Down-filled still provides more warmth, ounce per ounce, than synthetic fibers, because down creates more loft (the displacement between the inside and outside of the bag) and hence, provides more insulation from the cold. Estimates of the difference between the two kinds of fills vary from roughly 15 to 30 percent. In other words, a down bag that is intended to keep you warm at a temperature of 32-degrees Fahrenheit would be roughly 15 to 30 percent lighter than a synthetic sleeping bag with an equal temperature rating. Unfortunately, you get what you pay for and down bags are more expensive than those filled with synthetic fibers. According to one authority, the price of down rose from twelve dollars a pound in 1972 to thirty-five dollars a pound in 1978. Although the price of down is expected to fall, it is doubtful that it will fall far enough to become competitive, on the basis of price, with synthetic fills. The good synthetic sleeping bags, however, have some advantages over down bags besides their lower price. They provide more warmth in wet weather than down bags and are easier to wash. One outdoorsman told me about a canoe trip on which he took a sleeping bag with a synthetic fill and a friend took a down bag. It rained for fourteen straight days, and, although neither sleeping bag became wet from the precipitation, the down bag became uncomfortably damp from the camper's body moisture, while the synthetic bag remained comfortably dry. So in choosing between down or synthetic, you should consider how you intend to use the bag, as well as the difference in price. If you intend to walk in warm or wet weather, the synthetic material may be your best bet. A down bag also may be uncomfortably warm for summer hiking. On the other hand, if you plan to hike in extreme cold for several days, a down bag may be well worth the extra expense. Another factor in determining warmth is the manner in which the fill is sewn into the sleeping bag. Good bags are sewn so that the fill does not slide away from pressure points, such as the hips and shoulders.

Most backpackers these days use a type of sleeping bag called the "mummy," because you look like a mummy when you're sleeping in it. Mummy bags are contoured to fit rather tightly against the body. They're more efficient than ordinary, rectangular bags, because there is less air space between your body and the bag. Mummy bags also have hoods that fit tightly around your head and prevent air from escaping or entering through the top of the bag. Because they're more efficient, mummy bags provide more warmth, ounce per ounce, than rectangular bags. However, some people still prefer the old-fashioned bags because they're roomier.

Sleeping bags, either down or synthetic, are much warmer and more comfortable when they're separated from the ground by an air mattress or a foam pad. The extra thickness of insulation prevents heat from escaping to the cold, cold ground. Also, some sort of pad beneath you and the earth's surface may mean the difference between sleeping and not sleeping if you're accustomed to spending your nights in a comfortable bed. Air mattresses are more versatile—they can be used as rafts or chairs—but foam pads are more durable. Neither item is particularly expensive, so you have some leeway for experimentation even if you buy rather than rent.

Beneath your sleeping bag and pad, you need a ground cloth of some kind to keep your bag clean and dry. Just about anything, from a space blanket to a piece of plastic, will do.

Once you've purchased a backpack—frame and pack—and a sleeping bag, you may want to stop buying and start renting. Assuming that you've acquired all the essentials discussed in the previous chapter, then good boots, a backpack, and a sleeping bag will carry you a long way. It's easy enough to improvise or rent certain additional items when you think you might need them. Often, you won't need anything else besides food and water. If, for instance, you plan a weekend hike in good weather, you'll be cozy enough sleeping under the stars without a tent. You can carry food that does not require cooking, or you can cook over a campfire if the rules and regulations of the area allow it. If it should rain, shelter can be improvised from your ground cloth or poncho and a length of cord. Some careful preparation beforehand, including a visit to an outdoor-equipment store, should yield a variety of ways for staying dry without a tent. In fact, some veteran backpackers never carry tents, preferring to erect some contraption, made up of poncho or plastic or tarp, when the weather warrants it.

Yet, just as many walkers prefer to carry a tent for protection against rain, snow and cold or, sometimes, for privacy and security. Good mountain tents are actually made up of two tents. Although it's possible to get along with only one of them, you need them both to realize full protection. The inner tent is constructed of a material that allows moisture to escape through the walls, thus preventing condensation and dampness on the inside of the tent. The outer tent, usually called a "fly" or "rain fly," is waterproof and prevents moisture from reaching the inner tent. You can choose a tent with or without a floor.

Another piece of equipment that many walkers carry is a stove. This item is both a handy labor-saving device and an implement of wilderness conservation and protection. The walker who carries a stove can camp where he wants without worrying about his fuel supply; he can set up camp while his dinner is cooking; he can cook more easily in wet and windy weather; and he can carry lighter-weight cooking utensils. At the same time, state and federal authorities usually prohibit the use of anything but dead wood in a campfire and that can sometimes be hard to find in heavily-used areas. There is also less danger of forest fires when stoves, rather than campfires, are used for cooking. There are a number of good backpacking stoves on the market that are light, compact, and reliable. So consider buying or renting one when you plan to do some cooking on a hike. Make sure you use the fuel recommended by the manufacturer and find something to use as a windscreen.

If you decide to cook, whether by stove or campfire, you'll need to take along some cooking and eating utensils. This is one area where you can economize. Any lightweight pots or pans will do. Most backpackers cut off the handles and carry a pair of pliers or a pot holder for maneuvering the pots. There are also cook sets that are designed as accessories to certain brands of stoves and fit into a neat, compact container. A spoon, cup, and tin plate are usually all the eating utensils you need.

But all this would be nothing without food. Of course, there are many outdoorsmen who hike for no other purpose than to find food, and in doing so, combine backpacking and hunting or fishing. But I'm assuming that most of us walkers are merely hunting for an exceptional photograph and fishing for a little quiet and peace of mind, so we need to carry everything we're going to eat along the way.

Eating on a hike doesn't really become technical until you begin planning a trip of more than two or three days. You can eat practically anything for a weekend without much damage, as long as you eat enough of it. You can also carry enough canned goods or peanut butter and jelly to last you for a couple of days without adding an unbearable amount of weight to your load.

But when you're planning a week-long walk, you should do a lot of thinking about what you want to eat on the trail. There's one thing you can be sure of: You'll eat at least as much as you do at home. In fact, you will eat a lot more. So you need to plan your meals carefully. Make a list of what you need for every meal and purchase the food well ahead of time so you can check it over and pick up any items you may have overlooked. Try to give your menu as much variety and balance as possible, just like you would at home.

Depending upon your personal feelings about carrying a lot of weight on your back, you also should be concerned about the weight of the food you're going to carry. Some veteran backpackers with strong backs and strong packs disregard this advice with impunity. They're forever carrying cans of sardines or tuna fish, or whatever strikes their fancy, and they say that lightweight foods, specially designed for backpacking, are either not filling or are unappetizing. But us mere mortals, alas, must think about weight, because it's weight, more than anything else, that determines how much we enjoy backpacking.

If you have the money, you can take your proposed menu to an outdoor-equipment store and purchase a combination of freeze-dried and dehydrated foods that will be nutritious and lightweight. But if you don't feel like spending a lot of money on freeze-dried dinners and other backpacking foods, you can easily purchase a tasty, nutritious, walking diet at your neighborhood grocery.

First, in order to keep the weight on your back to a minimum, you need to select foods that contain little or no water—cereals, powdered milk, cocoa, dehydrated fruit, pastas, rice and other grains, instant soups, bouillon cubes, instant fruit drinks, tea bags, coffee, beef jerky and other dried meats. But with a little thought and experimentation you can lengthen the list considerably. Secondly, these foods should be fairly easy to prepare. You should buy instant rice rather than regular rice, for instance. Thirdly, the foods you select should not spoil easily. (Some hikers carry perishable items, even meat, for a treat on the first or second day of a trip, but in hot weather you've got to cook your hamburgers pretty early in the trip or you're in trouble.) Finally, you should try to pick foods that you like to eat. At high altitudes, strange things happen to the appetite and you may have to force yourself to eat. It's easier to do this when you can turn to an old favorite.

Once you've gathered all this food together, you should eliminate weight and bulk as much as possible by transferring it to plastic bags. Some authorities even suggest that you sort out each meal, wrap it in a separate bag, and mark the bag, but this may require more organizational effort than you care to muster.

If you're traveling with a group of people, you can purchase food as a group and then divide it up for packing. Or each person can tend to his own food requirements and tastes. It's certainly easier to obtain more variety at less cost when you buy for the entire group, but it's a good idea to find out beforehand if anyone in the group has a special diet and would rather obtain their own provisions. Sharing food can also result in some pretty unpleasant arguments if you have some big eaters along. So assess the tastes and temperaments of your companions before assuming the role of quartermaster. Remember, they may blame you if something goes wrong with the pea soup.

Since the food you'll be carrying contains no water, you need to be concerned not only about having enough drinking water on the trail, but enough water for cooking as well. I mentioned earlier that a hiker in warm weather should drink as much as a gallon of water a day. So you need to plan for that gallon, plus at least a quart more for cooking.

You needn't carry all this water, however. In fact, you shouldn't carry all the water you're going to need on a backpacking trip unless you think it's unavailable along the way. The trick is to know where you can find water, and if it's scarce, plan carefully. You may even want to hide a water cache along your route ahead of time. Remember, you can boil water for five to ten minutes to purify it.

The backpacker's clothing doesn't differ very much from what you need to take on a day-hike, but you need to take more of it. You need extra pants, shirts, socks, and underwear, so then you can change into dry clothing at the end of a long sweaty or rainy day of hiking. You should try to wear a clean, dry pair of inner socks everyday, but that doesn't mean you have to carry a pair of socks for every day of the trip. If you have one or two extra pairs, you can wash them at night and attach them to your pack for drying. In cool, spring or fall weather, you need to make sure that you have enough warm clothing and rain gear, such as rain chaps or a rain jacket, to keep you relatively warm and dry through a few days of sustained rain. It's also a good idea to wear clothing which is quick-drying. Unless you plan to sleep in the nude, you'll also need some dry clothing, pajamas, or long johns to sleep in. You shouldn't climb into the sleeping bag wearing the damp clothing you've hiked in all day.

There are numerous other items that you may or may not want to take with you. To bring it all together, I'm providing you with a checklist that was provided to me by Camp Trails. I suggest that you evaluate the list closely before making any purchases. I discuss what I believe are the absolute necessities in the previous chapter and all of them are on this list. But beyond the necessities, there is a lot of room for difference of opinion and personal taste. You need only prepare for what you believe will provide adequate food and shelter based on good common sense.

As you gather your equipment together, it's a good idea to keep a running tally of how much everything weighs. Studies have shown that once the weight of your pack exceeds one-third of your body weight there is a significant decrease in walking efficiency. But your goal should be much lower than one-third of your weight. Most experts recommend that you carry no more than one-fifth of your weight. Generally, the best way to approach the matter is to simply keep your pack as light as humanly possible.

FOOD

- ☐ Canteen
- ☐ Water Bag*
- ☐ Pots
- ☐ Fry Pan*
- ☐ Cup Bowl*
- ☐ Tablespoon
- ☐ Foil
- ☐ Matches
- ☐ Pot Tongs*
- ☐ Grill
- ☐ Stove/Fuel
- ☐ Fire Tube*
- ☐ Eating Utensils
- ☐ Salt/Pepper
- ☐ Milk/Sugar
- ☐ Coffee/Tea
- ☐ Cocoa
- ☐ Drink Mix
- ☐ Cooking Oil
- ☐ Trail Snacks

CLOTHING

- ☐ Socks
- ☐ Underwear
- ☐ Sock Cap or Down Hood*
- ☐ Pajamas or Long Johns*
- ☐ Jacket*
- ☐ Wool Shirt*
- ☐ Windbreaker
- ☐ Rainwear*
- ☐ Bandanas*
- ☐ Swim Suit*
- ☐ Gloves*
- ☐ Sneakers*
- ☐ Shirt*
- ☐ Trousers*

SHELTER

- ☐ Tent or Tarp or Tube Tent
- ☐ Sleeping Bag
- ☐ Air Mattress or Foam Pad
- ☐ Ground Cloth
- ☐ Nylon Cord
- ☐ LIGHTWEIGHT TARP
- ☐ _____
- ☐ _____

*Optional Equipment Depending on Weather or Personal Needs
CAPITALIZED ITEMS SHOULD ALSO BE CARRIED ON DAYHIKES.
EMERGENCIES CAN KEEP YOU OVERNIGHT.

TOILETRIES

- ☐ Tooth Brush
- ☐ Tooth Paste
- ☐ Soap
- ☐ Toilet Paper
- ☐ Wash Basin*
- ☐ Towel*
- ☐ Sanitary Supplies*
- ☐ Mirror*
- ☐ _____
- ☐ _____

MEDICAL

- ☐ F.A. Booklet
- ☐ Antiseptic
- ☐ Band Aids
- ☐ Gauze Pads
- ☐ Moleskin
- ☐ Snake Kit
- ☐ 2" Roll Adhesive Tape
- ☐ Tweezers
- ☐ Safety Pins
- ☐ Medication*
- ☐ Sun Burn or Chapstick
- ☐ Extra Glasses
- ☐ Vitamins
- ☐ Bug Repellent
- ☐ Water Purifiers
- ☐ Sun Glasses
- ☐ Protein
- ☐ Allergy Restrictions
- ☐ _____
- ☐ _____

MISCELLANEOUS

- ☐ SURVIVAL KIT
- ☐ Needles
- ☐ Thread
- ☐ MATCHES
- ☐ Candles
- ☐ WHISTLE
- ☐ FLASHLIGHT
- ☐ Extra Batteries and Bulb
- ☐ Plastic Bags
- ☐ Rubber Bands
- ☐ Hiking Staff*
- ☐ Maps
- ☐ NOTEBOOK/PEN
- ☐ Ground/Air Signals
- ☐ Fire Permit
- ☐ Name/Address
- ☐ Camera/Film
- ☐ TWO DIMES (emergency phone calls)
- ☐ _____
- ☐ _____

Courtesy of Camp Trails

HOW TO LOAD A TYPICAL BACKPACK

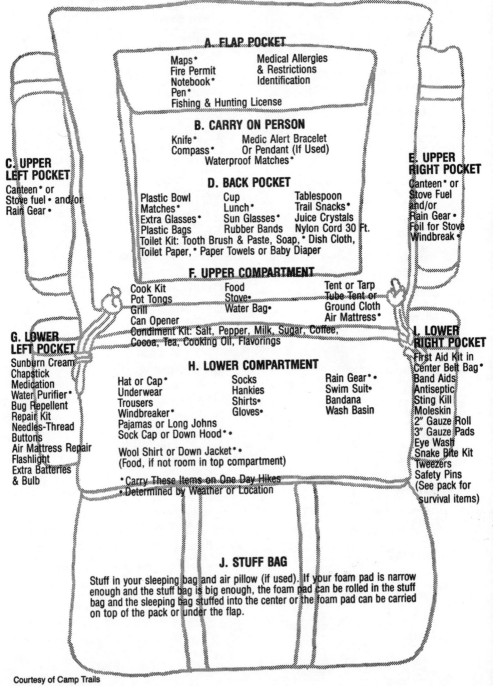

A. FLAP POCKET

Maps*   Medical Allergies
Fire Permit   & Restrictions
Notebook*   Identification
Pen*
Fishing & Hunting License

B. CARRY ON PERSON

Knife*   Medic Alert Bracelet
Compass*   Or Pendant (If Used)
        Waterproof Matches*

C. UPPER LEFT POCKET

Canteen* or
Stove fuel • and/or
Rain Gear •

D. BACK POCKET

Plastic Bowl   Cup   Tablespoon
Matches*   Lunch*   Trail Snacks*
Extra Glasses*   Sun Glasses*   Juice Crystals
Plastic Bags   Rubber Bands   Nylon Cord 30 Ft.
Toilet Kit: Tooth Brush & Paste, Soap,* Dish Cloth,
Toilet Paper,* Paper Towels or Baby Diaper

E. UPPER RIGHT POCKET

Canteen* or
Stove Fuel
and/or
Rain Gear •
Foil for Stove
Windbreak *

F. UPPER COMPARTMENT

Cook Kit   Food   Tent or Tarp
Pot Tongs   Stove•   Tube Tent or
Grill   Water Bag•   Ground Cloth
Can Opener   Air Mattress*
Condiment Kit: Salt, Pepper, Milk, Sugar, Coffee,
Cocoa, Tea, Cooking Oil, Flavorings

G. LOWER LEFT POCKET

Sunburn Cream
Chapstick
Medication
Water Purifier*
Bug Repellent
Repair Kit
Needles-Thread
Buttons
Air Mattress Repair
Flashlight
Extra Batteries
& Bulb

H. LOWER COMPARTMENT

Hat or Cap*   Socks   Rain Gear* •
Underwear   Hankies   Swim Suit*
Trousers   Shirts•   Bandana
Windbreaker*   Gloves•   Wash Basin
Pajamas or Long Johns
Sock Cap or Down Hood* •

Wool Shirt or Down Jacket* •
(Food, if not room in top compartment)

* Carry These Items on One Day Hikes
• Determined by Weather or Location

I. LOWER RIGHT POCKET

First Aid Kit in
Center Belt Bag*
Band Aids
Antiseptic
Sting Kill
Moleskin
2" Gauze Roll
3" Gauze Pads
Eye Wash
Snake Bite Kit
Tweezers
Safety Pins
(See pack for
survival items)

J. STUFF BAG

Stuff in your sleeping bag and air pillow (if used). If your foam pad is narrow
enough and the stuff bag is big enough, the foam pad can be rolled in the stuff
bag and the sleeping bag stuffed into the center or the foam pad can be carried
on top of the pack or under the flap.

After you've loaded the pack, put it on and adjust it properly. If it feels unbearably heavy, weigh it. Then begin reviewing its contents in your mind, item by item. Ask yourself whether you are carrying a particular item because you believe it is a necessity—either for everyday use or for emergencies—or a luxury. Eliminate the luxury items ruthlessly. Remember that the greatest luxury on the trail is a light pack. Once you've pared away the luxuries, begin thinking about how you can cut down on the weight of the necessities. Are you carrying too much food or water? Can you trim some cardboard off the cereal box or transfer the cereal to a plastic bag to eliminate the cardboard altogether? Some backpackers are fanatics about weight, and even resort to cutting handles off of toothbrushes and other, similarly arcane methods of trimming ounces from their load. Some beginners make the mistake of carrying items that could be shared with other members of their party. So make sure you're not carrying more stoves, tents, tarps, and other equipment than the group needs. The problem of weight, and deciding what and what not to carry, is more severe for beginners than experienced backpackers. You can learn a lot about what you really need to carry if you go over your equipment when you return home and eliminate those items you didn't use and wouldn't need in an emergency.

You can make your load somewhat more manageable, whatever its weight, by putting it in your pack so that the center of gravity is as close as possible to your body. You do this by putting the heaviest items on the side of the pack nearest your back, the medium-weight items in the center of the pack, and the lightweight items on the outside of the pack.

Believe it or not, one of your main problems with a loaded pack may be simply putting it on and taking it off. A little care in mounting and dismounting saves wear and tear on your back and your backpack. Basically, there are two ways to mount a pack. I use the sitting method. Here's how it works. Lean the backpack against a tree, rock or a companion. Then sit down against it and put your arms through the shoulder straps. Then slowly, draw your feet up under you and just as slowly stand up. Simply reverse this procedure to remove the pack. I call the second prescription for mounting and dismounting the standing method. Stand over the backpack with the frame facing toward you. Extend one leg forward and drag the pack along your leg until it's resting on the thigh. Then put one arm through a shoulder strap, while supporting the pack with the other arm. Twist the pack around behind you and slip the other arm through. Again, reverse the procedure for dismounting. It's also possible to disregard this advice and put the pack on any damn way you please.

Perhaps, the best way of attaining comfort on a backpacking trip boils down to simple walking. Many a well-planned, well-provisioned excursion has been sidetracked because people try to do too much, too soon, and the body just breaks down. If you walk a good deal on a regular basis, then that experience and physical fitness will carry over into backpacking. If you take some conditioning walks with a loaded pack on your back, the rewards will be even greater once you hit the trail. If you're really out of shape, however, you could be walking into some misery. That doesn't mean that ninety-nine-pound weaklings or two-hundred-pound flablings shouldn't backpack. It just means that you have to realize your limitations and take it easy, especially for the first few days. The best way of making sure you won't overdo it is to set a moderate goal when you're planning your route. The second best way is to set no goal at all. Just walk until you get mildly tired, sit down, cook supper, and go to sleep.

Since I've mentioned big people and little people, I feel compelled to talk briefly about kids. I'm not going to tell you that the family that walks together stays together, or that children should be introduced to wild country at an early age to fully appreciate it later in life, or that children are a lot of fun to have along on a backpacking trip. These things may be true in some cases, not-so-true in other cases, and in a few cases, downright lies. But I will tell you that if you want to take your children hiking or backpacking, there's no reason, in a technical sense, why you shouldn't.

The equipment is available. You can buy a pack that carries a child comfortably and safely on your back. You can buy small backpacks for children to carry themselves. You can buy sleeping bags that can be lengthened as the child grows. You can care for children as young as three months, just about as well in the wilds as you can at home. You need only keep them properly clothed, sheltered, and fed.

The one thing that kids can't do, however, until they're almost teenagers, is carry their own weight. That means that until they can walk well, you have to carry them, and someone else has to carry the equipment you can't carry because you're packing a small child. The burden is alleviated somewhat when the children become competent walkers, but still you must carry their gear at least part of the time.

You have to make other adjustments in the pace and distance of your trek, the terrain, and the climate of your route. On the first two counts, children simply can not walk as far and as fast as adults. Not only are the little people hindered by their very smallness, but they also lack the motivation of adults. They're more easily distracted by the little ant that's carrying a great big piece of bread across the trail or by the tadpoles that are squirting from the sides of a creek. They can not set their minds steadfastly upon yonder mountain in hopes of some day reaching the summit. Consequently, you've got to humor the little darlings by occupying their minds with games and songs and sightseeing. And despite the humoring, there's a fifty-fifty chance they'll just sit down on the trail and do their own thing.

I don't mean to sound discouraging, but what I am trying to say is that you may have to change your style when you take kids along. You should realize from the outset that your goals should be moderate and flexible, that children see the entire excursion in a different way than you do, and that you've got to keep your family happy or you won't be happy. On the third and fourth counts, it's almost always best to take children into an area that is relatively safe from the standpoint of terrain and weather conditions. It's okay to take chances when you're on your own, but don't do it with the kids along.

In summary, kids will be kids and they'll behave about as well on the trail as they do at home. The main thing is to realize ahead of time that you're going to have to make some adjustments in your hardy, full-steam-ahead, backpacking routine and then lean into the load and enjoy it.

I should say something here about the divergence between theory and practice in backpacking. The theorists, that is the people who tell other people how to do it, generally try to prepare beginners for all eventualities. Although their advice is certainly motivated by the knowledge that walking in the wilderness can be dangerous and even fatal, I suspect there is an element of overprotection at work as well. You just don't feel comfortable telling people to go hiking or backpacking unless you send them off well equipped and well warned of the various pitfalls that lay ahead of them. The result is a sometimes excessive preoccupation with equipment and administrative details, while people who don't read books, can't afford equipment, or could care less about traveling first-class seem to get along just fine with nothing more than a laundry bag full of food, a wool blanket, and an old shower curtain for protection against the elements. For that reason, I hope you take the information that I've provided here with a grain of salt, ruminate on it in your own inimitable fashion, and come away with a clear idea of how you want to approach the subject of backpacking. The outdoor-equipment manufacturers and experts did not invent backpacking (although some of them seem to think so). Backpacking was once the natural condition of human beings, in the beginnings of time, when our ancestors were constantly on the move, foraging for food, and carrying everything they had on their backs. Nowadays, of course, we feel out of place at first when we forsake our comfortable homes for a week of walking through some isolated area, but we have it in us to feel just as comfortable in the wilderness as we do at home. And that's the state that every backpacker seeks. If by paving our way with the latest equipment and advice we fail to reach that state of mind, then our equipment has failed us, no matter how advanced and efficient it is. So tread lightly into the equipment maze, keeping in mind all the while that it is only a means to an end.

And there's one more thing. You also owe something to the wilderness from whence cometh your opportunity to go backpacking. Heavy usage of many outdoor areas has made the old hiking maxim—take only pictures; leave only footprints—more important than ever before.

There are many ways you can protect the environment on a backpacking trip. Essentially, it's a matter of leaving things alone. Don't pick, cut, bend, or stomp on any vegetation unnecessarily and don't harass, disturb or harm any wildlife, except in self-defense. If you're going to carry anything out of the wilderness that you didn't carry in, pick up litter on your way out.

A fine book on backpacking, *Walking Softly in the Wilderness* by John Hart, explains in great detail how backpackers can avoid damaging the ecology of wilderness areas. Here are a few of his suggestions, but if you're interested in how to backpack without damaging the environment, and every backpacker should be, read the book.

1. Don't camp in meadows where the balance of nature is fragile.

2. Avoid camping at timberline where vegetation grows very slowly and any wounds to the environment take a long time to heal.

3. Don't modify the landscape to create the perfect campsite. Don't clear the ground, dig trenches or otherwise tear the hell out of the earth.

4. Pack out what you pack in, leaving NOTHING behind, and don't try to fudge by burying what you cannot burn. It soon becomes unburied.

5. Use as little fire as possible and then only where regulations allow it.

6. Follow the rules of the area and obtain a wilderness permit where one is required.

12

Race Walking

Rob Spier is a lean bundle of energy. He talks with the same brisk, even, pacing that he uses to travel incredible distances on foot.

By trade, Rob is an anthropologist. By inspiration, by passion, by whatever prompts men to challenge the impossible, Rob is a race-walker.

Every year when September rolls around, Rob can be found competing in the annual one-hundred-mile championship walk in Columbia, Missouri, one of the most grueling track challenges in the world. At the age of fifty-six, Rob should be long past his peak of athletic excellence, but he has finished the one-hundred-mile walk twice in the last eight years, becoming one of an elite corps of modern American centurions who have walked one-hundred miles in less than twenty-four hours.

Rob and his fellow centurions represent the vanguard of a growing movement toward race walking in America. This once obscure sport is now attracting a substantial following in areas such as New York, California, Colorado, Ohio, and Washington, D.C. Oddly, the sport's obscurity over the years has been a major factor in its revival. Many persons have been attracted to it because it offers an opportunity to compete with the best and be the best.

"In race walking, the bottom is so near the top," said Rob Spier. "I have raced in walks against practically everybody who has been a member of a U.S. team. Can you say that of other sports? Are you going to play against Jack Nicklaus or Jimmy Connors? You're not going to."

Allan Price of Washington, D.C., set a national record in the one-hundred-mile walk in 1978. Before he took up walking four years ago, he continually finished out-of-the-money in his favorite track event, the 880-yard run. He entered his first race-walk because there were so few competitors that he thought he would have a good chance of winning.

"After that, I didn't practice walking," the thirty-one-year-old Price said. "I just participated in meets. I did pretty well without training so I decided I could do a lot better if I trained."

Race walking in the U.S. fell into a state of decline beginning in the late 1920s and it has showed in our performance in the Olympic games. When Larry Young of Columbia, Missouri, won the bronze medal in the fifty-kilometer race-walk in the 1968 Olympic games in Mexico City, he became the first American medalist since 1920. Yet, despite this decline in the international competitiveness of American race-walkers, every major U.S. team has included at least two walkers and sometimes more. Today's race-walkers see this as an advantage of their sport. Less competition for these teams means greater opportunities to compete with the best.

Ron Laird, one of America's top race-walkers, writes in his book, *Competitive Race Walking,* that he was lucky to forsake running for walking early enough in life to become a champion. "I see so many runners who have hopes of becoming great and going on to make the Olympic team," Laird writes. "When I was running in my high school days, I also had those dreams. How fortunate I was to have discovered my sport early enough in life (at seventeen) and then persevered with it through those very trying first couple of years.

"The race walking events are still so wide open today in this country that a person with normal athletic ability, if he has the desire to learn and work, may develop himself into a national champion and/or international team member. I have a closet full of U.S.A. sweatsuits to prove this."

Laird, who has dedicated his life to race walking, recalls that in high school his best time in the half-mile was two minutes, eighteen seconds, and in the mile, five minutes and twelve seconds, hardly the makings of a championship runner. But in race walking, he's one of the best.

Martin Rudow, another race-walking author, laments that his is a neglected sport which has been the target of efforts by the International Olympic Committee to pare the number of events in the Olympic games. But like Laird, Rudow sees that as an opportunity.

"In most national championship race-walks," Rudow writes in his book, *Race Walking*, "the quality thins out after the first few places. There just aren't enough top walkers able to travel to all the big races. This fact opens the way for undertrained and less gifted athletes to pick up medals.

"Even trial races for major teams occasionally have weak fields. If injuries or layoffs take care of only a few of the best walkers, the race is suddenly wide open and berths on the team may go to 'unknowns.' "

I know the Olympic Games, a national championship, or first place in a local walking event seem a long way off if you've just started to take regular walks around the block; but those coveted athletic prizes may be more accessible than you think. At least that's what the experts say.

This is especially true for conditioned hikers and joggers, and for athletes participating in other physically taxing sports. Four years ago, Allan Price was a mediocre runner. Today he's in the record books.

Rob Spier says he often uses runners as his "rabbits" when he is training. No walker is going to beat a well-conditioned runner, of course, but Spier finds it an entertaining and helpful training tool to try to pick up as much ground as possible on the runner.

In Chicago, Augie Hirt, who holds American records for one-hundred- and seventy-five-kilometer walks and for the fifty-mile walk, enters marathons regularly because there are few walking events in the area. In one race, he finished 240 out of 700. But remember, he was walking. The rest were running. "The runners are a little embarrassed," Augie told a reporter afterward. Similarly, in Washington, D.C., Allan Price keeps in shape for race walking during the winter by running ultra-marathons of fifty miles or more.

So walkers and runners are definitely kindred spirits. That does little, however, to appease the walker who sees thousands of runners every year entering the Boston Marathon, but only a handful entering such races as the one-hundred-mile walk in Missouri.

Hirt, sounding slightly bitter, recently told a reporter for the *Chicago Tribune* that "race walking is catching on in other countries, but not here. . . . You can go to another country and walk in a race and they think you are a hero. Here you get no respect at all."

Hirt claimed that running was popularized by the work of Dr. Cooper, who I mentioned earlier, and by television coverage of Frank Shorter's marathon victory in the 1972 Olympics.

"Also, everybody can go out and run, but you have to become very involved and know what you are doing to even start race walking," Hirt said. "The hardest thing is that to most people it looks funny and I can't see something that looks funny being accepted on a large basis."

Well, I've seen some pretty funny-looking joggers lumbering down the street in front of my house and I'm not sure Hirt's assessment of the situation is correct. Our capacity for change and acceptance seems almost unlimited. Clothing that would have seemed outrageous five years ago is in vogue today. Just think back for a moment to what you and the people around you were wearing, doing, and thinking ten years ago, and I think you'll agree we have come a long way.

Besides, I hate the expression "looking funny." I know a lot of people, some of them very close to me, who have hesitated to participate in some sport or activity that could enrich their lives just because of their fear of "looking funny."

Heck, we all "look funny" in our own way. We're short or we're tall or we're skinny or we're fat or we're bow-legged. So forget about "looking funny." If you want to race-walk, do it. If you've got it, flaunt it.

While you're out swiveling your hips, swinging your arms, and walking at a blinding pace, those overweight, grinning, sloths on four wheels are dying at an equally blinding pace and all because they're afraid of "looking funny." I'd rather be a little odd and feel healthy and alive and youthful, than sit back and watch the superb God-given instrument that is the human body dissipate from disease.

Every walker must learn to handle "looking funny" and one of the best ways to do that is to cultivate a sense of humor. Funny things do happen. For instance, Hirt told Dorothy Collin of the *Chicago Tribune* about an incident in which he saw a passing motorist poke his head out of the car window. "I knew I was in trouble," Hirt said. "They threw something at me, and it hit me on the shoulder. I started to chase them, but gave up. Then I noticed my shoulder didn't hurt so I wondered what it was they threw. I walked back and found a marshmallow. I was really laughing when I got home."

The great race-walkers are hardened to this kind of harassment and it's part of the challenge of their sport. If you can learn to fight the crowd and be your own man while race walking, you'll find that you're more independent in the rest of your dealings with mankind, a personality trait that can be extremely valuable—it can even save your life.

A professor of mine in college, a rugged individualist himself, was fond of telling a story about how buffalo hunters would stampede a herd of buffalo over a cliff, thus eliminating the necessity of picking them off with their rifles one by one. Then imploring his students to avoid the herd (something to contemplate during the Boston Marathon), my old professor would say with a grin: "You'll be a lonely little buffalo, but you'll still be alive."

When Larry Young won his first Olympic medal in race walking in Mexico City in 1968, he endured a level of abuse you're not likely to encounter even if you're a resident of Muskogee, Oklahoma, where according to the popular song of a few years' back, they don't tolerate unusual behavior. The course for the fifty-kilometer walk in Mexico City wound through narrow, city streets where masses of Mexicans were lined up within only a few feet of the athletes. As Young passed the Mexican favorite, a man named Pedraza, he fell into an ocean of sound.

"The most hideous screaming and shouting blasted right into my ears," Young later recalled in an interview. "The crowd was yelling 'Mex-i-co, Mex-i-co, Pe-dra-za, Pe-dra-za, Mex-i-co, Pe-dra-za' over and over again at the top of their lungs. The sound pierced me. Imagine yourself walking along a street with people at arms' length away hollering right into your ears. That way lies madness. Pulling away from Pedraza was as crucial to me as catching the leaders."

The abuse didn't end with that incident. When Larry was awarded the bronze medal for placing third in the event, an historic moment for American race walking, the crowd erupted into a chorus of boo's and jerked their thumbs downward to indicate their displeasure. A true walker, Larry stuck out his tongue at the crowd and returned the thumbs-down gesture. A photographer captured the moment and it remains a monument to those walkers who aren't worried about "looking funny."

Many runners have written about their problems with hecklers and how to deal with them. Their exposure is similar to that of race-walkers.

"For reasons best known to themselves, some people can't stand the sight of a runner," James F. Fixx writes in his best-seller, *The Complete Book of Running.* "There aren't many of them, but when one comes along you know it. They shout abuse at you from passing cars, fling objects at you and sometimes drive so erratically that you fear for your life. Others gather in ugly little clots on street corners and mutter about your manhood and the shape of your legs."

Fixx says there are basically three ways to handle hostile humans: Stoicism, fighting back by yelling obscenities, making appropriate gestures or throwing "lethal objects" at the offender.

You'll have to work out your own method of dealing with this phenomenon. I prefer either to ignore the hecklers or use an appropriate hand gesture, mainly because someone passing in a car can't hear you very well, especially if they're going fast, but they can see you in their rear-view mirror. As for hecklers, I keep quiet unless I'm bigger than they are. There is, of course, some danger of violent retaliation by the heckler. It's a good idea to have a plan to escape should something go wrong.

Yet, I suspect that the old adage, "there's strength in numbers," applies here and I doubt that runners are taking as much abuse as they were a few years ago. You'd have to be a fool to hurl insults at a horde of joggers. You might be trampled. Perhaps as the number of race-walkers increases, that sport, too, will achieve greater acceptance by the public, and nonparticipants, sensing that they're outnumbered, will become less openly hostile.

Tremendous changes have taken place in this country in the last fifteen years and the need for regular exercise has become a widely accepted fact. As we progress farther and farther down the road toward socialized medicine and begin paying for everyone else's bad health, this trend is likely to accelerate. It should be accompanied by greater respect for amateur athletes in every sport, including race walking. Ordinary walkers don't face the level of harassment encountered by race-walkers, simply because there's nothing unusual about regular walking. For all the world knows, the avid walker on a ten-mile hike around his city or town is just going about his business.

Only women have serious problems when they're out for a walk at an ordinary pace. Most men don't understand that women aren't necessarily flattered by compliments yelled from a car window.

The odd gait of race walking presents a special problem for women who train on the sidewalk or in any public place frequented by nonathletes. (True sports' persons are seldom intolerant of other athletes). It's sad that women, having hurdled all the cultural obstacles against their participation in strenuous sports, must then be victimized by hostile humans while training. In their case, carrying lethal objects may be warranted if only to preserve their hard-earned self-respect as athletes.

At least one woman race-walker, complaining that people "honk their horns, call you names, throw rocks and bottles, and try to push you off the road," armed herself with a heavy bolt to throw at cars that veered too close to her. But if this approach seems a little risky to you (and I think it is), you can always take comfort in the knowledge that you're bothering them a lot more than they're bothering you. As one race-walker put it, "Maybe they feel threatened or something because they're big fat slobs and we're not." That revenge is as sweet as any.

Women who take up race walking will reap rewards not available in many sports. The record books are wide open for women walkers. Elsie McGarvey of Kalispell, Montana, set a record in 1978 by becoming the first woman walker to complete one-hundred miles in less than twenty-four hours. Researchers have found that based on their weight, women have less muscle and more fat. This puts them at a disadvantage in sports that require great speed and strength. But in matters of endurance, where the body must feed on its reserves of fat, women may even have an advantage. Nowhere is this more true than in walking long distances, and women may someday find themselves breaking walking records set by members of the so-called "stronger sex."

Another aspect of long-distance race walking tends to equalize the traditional dominance of youth in competitive sports. It is the need for mental discipline. "There's some place in that race where you switch over from muscles to head," Rob Spier said of the one-hundred-mile race in Missouri. "There's no place after twenty-five miles where you wouldn't want to just sit down and watch.

"I've talked to marathoners about the wall at eighteen miles. I've walked a marathon and there is no wall. That point in a walk is about 1:00 A.M. or 2:00 A.M. (twelve hours into the race).

"Essentially, you just have to make up your mind to do it. If something hurts, it won't hurt in an hour. Something else will hurt and you will have forgotten about that other pain.

"It's a progression of various aches and pains. It's not a pleasure for anybody. It's an accomplishment."

Paul Hendricks, a thirty-five-year-old high school teacher in San Diego, began race walking at distances over fifty miles in 1976. After only a year of training, he won the one-hundred-mile walk and he placed second in the "big test" in 1978. He agrees that youth is less important than the kind of mental discipline that seems to come with age. "What people don't know about walking is that their prime is in the late thirties or early forties," Hendricks said. "Before that, you don't have the mental discipline. Physically, you've got to get to your best condition, but you have to have the mental discipline to cope with the variations of pain—upset stomach, mental fatigue, sharp leg pains, cramps. . . ."

Spier says any one of a variety of physical aches and pains can drive you out of a long-distance walk if you let them. The people who finish are the people who have the mental discipline and intestinal fortitude to continue to the end. "Some people drop out year after year at the same point. It's not their physical limit. You can predict when they will psyche themselves out. I know one man who gets diarrhea regularly during the race. It's not the travel or the training. It's just psychological."

Art Fleming also emphasized the importance of maintaining your mental balance. "It's so damn easy to step off the track. The psychological boredom is just phenomenal."

Spier says older walkers can't rationalize dropping-out of a race as easily as younger ones. A sixty-year-old race-walker knows he has a limited number of years ahead of him in which to meet the challenge of a long-distance walk. Younger walkers, on the other hand, can tell themselves that they have many years in which to finish the race.

I suspect that it boils down to something as basic as patience. Psychologists have long known that as we grow older, our understanding of time changes. When you celebrated your tenth-birthday anniversary, you looked forward to a year that represented one-tenth of your life. At your fortieth birthday, the ratio has dropped to one-fortieth. This produces a different concept of time, a change that may allow us to deal with long hours of physical and psychological struggle toward a cherished goal, like joining that elite group of centurions.

But whatever the reason behind it, walkers over the age of thirty don't need to be placed in separate categories to achieve victories in long-distance races. They can compete on an equal level and feel confident that the twenty-year-old speedster who laps them in the early going is likely to fade away after thirty-five miles when psychological toughness becomes more important than a young body.

If you still have doubts about the possibility of becoming a first-rate competitor in middle-age, the experience of Larry O'Neil, a lumber executive from Kalispell, Montana, should dispel them once and for all.

When Allan Price set a one-hundred-mile record in 1978 of eighteen hours, fifty-seven minutes, and forty-one seconds, he broke the record for the one-hundred set in 1967 by O'Neil when he was sixty-years old.

Larry is a prime example of the benefits of walking and the potential for remaining competitive in your later years. I can't think of any other sport in which a sixty-year-old set a national record, for all age groups, that stood for eleven years. And Larry still walks in the one-hundred, though he doesn't always finish.

He trains about two hours a day in the mountains around Kalispell, wearing shorts until the temperature drops below freezing. He uses hiking as a conditioner as well.

"It's easier to train in our area where there are so many beautiful mountains and lakes," Larry says. "I like so much to hike up to the high mountains. There's such beautiful fishing in the lakes."

Larry didn't start race walking until 1964, three years before he set a national record in the one-hundred. Like many other walkers, Larry's interest was piqued by the scarcity, rather than the abundance, of walkers. "A friend of mine and I were watching a junior track-and-

Photo by Charles Cancellare

field meet when they announced that they needed two more walkers. My friend asked, 'You'd enter it with me, wouldn't you,' and I thought he was kidding so I said, 'yes.' I couldn't chicken-out, so I had to do it. I entered the race that day and took fifth."

So what began on a dare for Larry O'Neil, developed into a record-setting performance and continues to be a way of participating in competitive sports into his seventies.

It's this universality of race walking and its close relationship to walking for exercise, for pleasure, and for health reasons, that some people believe it's the sport of the future—especially long-distance walks.

As Augie Hirt notes, walking has long been a respected and popular sport in Europe where many trends that eventually sweep this country are sighted first. "It's always been popular in Europe," says Paul Hendricks who has walked in the world's longest race, the three day, three-hundred-mile Strasbourg-to-Paris walk. He says it's "not just race walking but walking in general. It's the natural thing you do all your life."

Martin Rudow reported that "ultra-long distance walking, until recently an obscure branch of the sport, may yet prove to be its mainstay. . . . Already interest is building in these super-endurance affairs."

Rudow notes that distance events of fifty and one-hundred miles, and seventy-five and one-hundred kilometers, are now offered at various sites in this country. And in addition to the Paris-to-Strasbourg, European epic, there is the twenty-eight-hour race in Roubaix, France, and the one-hundred-kilometer race in Lugano, Italy. England offers the popular fifty-three-mile London-to-Brighton contest and a one-hundred-mile walk which guarantees membership in a Centurions Club for those who hoof the distance in less than twenty-four hours. "Genuine ultra-long distance specialists are emerging, especially at the one-hundred-mile distance," writes Rudow. "So far, all these events have been held on tracks. The use of roads has probably been avoided because of officiating and traffic problems. However, such road events have proven to be extremely popular in Europe, and we may see similar races held in the U.S. as interest grows."

I've discussed the problems of road races with many authorities, all of whom verify the dangers. Imagine walkers strung out over a one-hundred-mile course, the stragglers as far as fifty miles behind the leaders. The difficulties are obvious. Somehow, these walkers must be watched by qualified judges to determine if they are following the rules of race walking. Another complication is the need for constant refreshment on long walks. How many people would be needed to man aid stations along a one-hundred-mile course? A hundred or more? Nevertheless, the logistical difficulties of road walks could be solved with proper planning. It's a good idea, most race walkers say, for each walker to bring along his own "handler" to provide him with liquids, food, a change of clothes, and other aid. There's no reason why these "handlers" couldn't follow along in cars during a long road race, providing help when needed and at the same time eliminating the need for numerous aid stations. This would require, of course, that each walker bring a "handler" instead of relying on help from race officials. But walkers who move at about the same speed could team up and use the same "handler."

Judging is a stickier problem. Race walking "purists" contend that poor judging makes a mockery of the sport by robbing it of the important element of technique. But at the risk of offending some of the sport's great supporters, such as Ron Laird, I would suggest that judging is really only important for the top walkers in a long-distance race. Who cares whether those far behind the leaders are meeting technical requirements. If they walk fifty or one-hundred miles, it's still a marvelous accomplishment that should be encouraged.

So as an answer to the problem of judging, I am suggesting that only the leaders be watched carefully by race officials. Let the rest of us amble along at our pace, enjoying our walk and the achievement of our personal goals.

Joe Duncan, president of the Columbia Track Club, has wrestled with this problem since the one-hundred-mile walk was started there in 1967. Initially, entry in the race was wide open, but eventually it had to be limited to those over eighteen-years old, because children on the track interfered with serious walkers.

Now, Columbia track officials seem to practice a policy similar to the one I am suggesting. Race judges keep an eye on the leaders, while other walkers are allowed greater leeway. You see walkers listening to portable radios, chatting with friends, and stopping for a rest on trackside cots. As a result, the race has a delightfully informal flavor which allows each walker to set his own goal in the race and go away with a feeling of accomplishment.

It's this kind of informality that could lead to mass participation in organized walks. Every walker who achieves his or her personal goal could be awarded a small plaque or medallion. Such walks are already popular in Germany.

Getting a walking program started in your area shouldn't be that difficult if you are persistent and methodical about it. You should start by contacting the local track club, track coaches and physical education instructors at the colleges and high schools in your area, and any other organizations or persons that might be interested. Once you've found a few people who want to organize a race-walking program, you can form a committee and assign each member an area of responsibility. The main items you have to take care of are:

A Location for the Race.

This could be a track at a local high school or college. I advise that you hold your first few races on a track, at least until you master the organizational aspects of holding one of these events. Later on, you might want to try a road race. Then you'll have to work out a course which is acceptable to city officials and the police department. Remember that your road course doesn't have to be as long as the race itself. Even if the walkers have to take a few laps around the course, it's going to be more enjoyable than making one-hundred or more laps around a one-quarter-mile track.

Aid Stations.

The rules of the Amateur Athletic Union of the U.S. specify that refreshment stations be provided for the walkers in any race over twenty kilometers (12.4 miles). According to the AAU, the first station should be provided within ten kilometers (6.2 miles) of the starting point, at intervals of five kilometers (3.1 miles) thereafter. In any race of less than twenty kilometers, the organizers of the race may determine if refreshment stations are to be provided. I suggest that you provide at least water and ice to the walkers, especially in hot weather.

Providing refreshments in a race staged on a one-quarter-mile track is a simple matter. Just set up a station at some point along the track with plenty of water and ice. The walkers can drink from paper cups. It's also a good idea to have a tub of water and some sponges handy for the walkers who like to cool themselves externally during the race. You'll find that most walkers have a favorite concoction they want to use, such as ERG, Gator Aide, salted orange juice, flattened soft drinks, etc. Just have them deposit these at the aid station (if they don't bring their own "handlers") and label them so they can ask for them as they pass the station. Race officials also should provide salt pills in hot weather.

In long races of marathon length or more, the walkers will want to eat, as well as drink, while they walk. Here again, each walker has his own preference. I've seen walkers eat grapes, bananas, jello, chicken soup, anything and everything that's nourishing and easily digested. These foods also should be left at the refreshment station by the walkers who don't have their own "handlers." Road races make this a little more complicated because you have to set up more than one aid station along the route. Your best bet is to strongly encourage walkers to make their own arrangements for refreshments so the race organizers can limit themselves to providing only the minimum . number of stations required under AAU rules.

Lap Recording.

In a race as long as one-hundred miles, in which the walkers are going to make four-hundred laps around a one-quarter-mile track, you need to develop a good system for recording their progress. When you've got forty or more walkers going at once, it's easy to miss a lap here and there.

The Columbia Track Club uses a system for monitoring the one-hundred-mile walk that seems to work quite well and is adaptable to races of any length. First, you need at least one recorder for every ten walkers. Set them up at the starting line with a table, some chairs and, if possible, some shade.

Next, get some large pieces of poster paper at least a yard long and a yard wide. At the top of each poster write the names and numbers of the contestants, giving each contestant a separate column marked lengthwise down the paper. Then, mark off horizontal columns for each mile of the race, being sure to leave enough room to write the contestant's time for each quarter-mile lap around the track. Distribute these lap cards to the recorders so that they are responsible for an equal number of walkers. When possible, put the top-seeded walkers on the same card and give that card to the most experienced recorder.

Finally, you need an accurate timing device and someone to announce the time elapsed since the beginning of the race as each walker passes by the recorders. The time for each walker should be noted on the lap cards in the column for the appropriate mile. By recording each lap time, you develop a means of checking possible errors. If a walker has been averaging four minutes per lap all afternoon and suddenly an eight-minute lap shows up on the recorder's card, then a lap has been overlooked. To make this system work, the competitor should always notify his recorder when he is stopping for a break or slowing his pace substantially.

As a race progresses, walker and recorder usually become fast friends. And the recorder eases the walker's fear of doing extra laps by calling his name or nodding each time the walker passes. The recorders should be prepared to advise walkers of their lap times so the walkers can determine if they are maintaining their preferred pace. Especially in long races, where the agony of effort shows clearly on the walkers' faces, the recorders should offer encouragement to the walkers and comment on their style. This shouldn't be discouraged. It makes the race fun for the recorders too.

Judging.

The official AAU rulebook defines race walking as a "progression by steps so taken that unbroken contact with the ground is maintained.

"The advancing foot of the walker must contact the ground before the rear foot leaves the ground. During the period of each step, in which a foot is on the ground, this leg shall be straightened (i.e., not bent at the knee) for at least one moment.

"Competitors may be cautioned once: a second violation of the above shall mean disqualifying and they must leave the track or road."

If you're starting a new walking program in your area, judging is going to be the toughest obstacle to overcome. Ideally, you should find the most experienced race-walkers around and have them obtain certification through the AAU. The experienced walkers are obviously the ones best qualified to judge a race, except for the fact that they're likely to be walking in the race themselves.

So you need to find someone who is interested in the sport but doesn't want to participate in every race. Have them read the chapter on race walking in this book and the two other books that I have mentioned, and they should be able to do a fairly competent job of judging.

But again, at the risk of offending some race-walking authorities, I recommend that you don't get too hung up on this problem. It will work itself out once you get the program well underway and have a few races under your belt. By then you should have a pretty good idea which of your volunteer judges are able to keep the race under control without taking the fun out of it by disqualifying a lot of people who are just out to have a good time. Besides, you won't need a certified judge until your walking group or track club becomes affiliated with a national track association.

Yet the rules are important to the sport of race walking. Without them it wouldn't exist. It's a sport of technique as well as endurance.

Judging the walker's technique has without a doubt been the most controversial aspect of the sport over the years. Race walking at short distances was eliminated from the Olympics many years ago, simply because these events were so difficult to judge and the temptation for walkers to violate the rules were so great.

"I can't imagine how anyone could race-walk a mile," said Rob Spier, a certified walking judge. "There's a tremendous tendency just to get up and run." But for the longer distances, most authorities agree, violation of the rules is not a serious problem because the pace is slow enough to allow compliance without great effort.

The most important rule of race walking, and consequently, the most important aspect of race-walking style, is that one foot must be on the ground at all times. This sounds a little silly until you think about how you run. The rear foot pushes off hard and leaves the ground before the advancing foot touches. Running is a series of small jumps. If you do that in a race-walk, you're disqualified. You're not walking—you're running.

"The heel of the forward stepping foot has to make contact before the toes of the rear foot can leave," writes Ron Laird. "It is at this spread-out 'heel and toe' part of your stride that you will come off the ground if you're going to. Correct terms for this are lifting and floating, not running. The faster the walker moves, the more likely he is to be lifting and floating. It is a physical impossibility to actually detect this because as a judge, you are trying to look for daylight under the advancing foot's heel and trailing foot's toe while the athlete is taking steps at the rate of three or four per second. Because of this fact, the more difficulty there is in judging it."

Laird writes that slow-motion photography, or a lucky shot by a still photographer, can detect illegality but he advises judges to look for several signs of an improper style. "Is his head bouncing? It should proceed along on a smooth and level line," Laird states. "If it doesn't, this would indicate faulty coordination and possibly bad contact. Is there lifting due to too hard an overstride or too high and powerful an arm and shoulder move? How about the high and hard knee thrusting? Is the back kick coming up too high? Does he look like he is sort of jogging because of the lack of a full hip twist, too high a back kick, and the leg locking out too early and high above the ground?"

The walkers, of course, can't be disqualified for these signs of bad style, but these signs can at least indicate to the judges which walkers they should be watching closely. They apply particularly to short races where violations are more common. In a long race, walkers have no trouble making contact unless they're determined to try to jog the distance, something that's pretty easy to detect.

The second part of the rules of race walking—the requirements for straightening legs at some point in each step—is not difficult for a good judge to detect. This offense is called creeping and occurs more commonly in long races where the walkers are more likely to be using a natural walking style. "It's keeping the knee bent all the way back, or rebending at the last instant to push the body forward with the thigh muscles, that makes an illegal stride," Laird writes.

Keeping the knee straight provides race-walkers with additional power and speed, so it's an important technique to learn, both to keep the judges happy and to be an effective walker.

Determining the Distance.

Elliott Denman, a race-walking journalist from New Jersey, recommends in *Race Walking* that you emphasize ten-mile to twenty-kilometer races at first, so you will attract a broader range of persons interested in walking. He also advises that you set a time limit. "Give the competitors some good incentives—as we did in New Jersey by promising medals to all who 'proved their physical fitness by completing a ten-mile walk in two hours or less," writes Denman. "Beating the time limit became an important objective for a big pack of novices."

Publicity.

Once you've decided on the location of your race, made arrangements for refreshment stations and lap recordings, and come to grips with the sticky problem of judging, you're ready to publicize your race.

Prerace publicity is the best way to attract a good turnout of spectators and competitors. Call all the local newspapers, television stations, and radio stations as soon as you set a date. You'll find that the fact that race walking is a little known and little understood sport actually will work to your advantage. It's the kind of story that editors are looking for. It has the stamp of the unusual.

If you can persuade them, get a reporter to meet you at a local track so you can show him what to expect and look for during a race. That way, you'll get better informed coverage before and after the race. Afterward, make sure the media have the names of the top-ten finishers and try to persuade them to print them. One of the great benefits of race walking is that people who have never won recognition for athletic achievement may be able to win it at a walk.

Whether you set out to be a sprinter or a long-distance walker, practicing the techniques of the sport is crucial if you're going to go very far.

Hip Movement.

With each step, the walker moves the hips down and forward, producing the swivel-hipped look that typifies race walking. By moving the hip forward each time you advance your leg, you gain a few inches with each step, thus increasing your speed and reducing effort. You can learn this movement simply by trying to take long steps. As your legs stretch forward, your hips will follow.

It's an important part of the sport, but you'll do better if you don't overemphasize it at first. It will come with practice.

And don't worry about "looking funny." "Hip motion is physically and even emotionally difficult for many athletes to do," writes Laird. "Because of the embarrassment involved, especially when doing it in public, many potential race-walkers never give the sport their sincere efforts or stay with it very long."

I've found that even when I practice race walking in my neighborhood, where I'm sure few of the residents know anything about it, I don't seem to attract much attention. So swivel those hips.

Straightening the Leg.

The rules require that you straighten the advancing leg as it passes under the body, but you can gain power, as well as stay legal, if you lock the knee as soon after the foot touches the ground as possible.

The Feet.

For maximum efficiency of stride, you should always try to touch the ground with the heel of the advancing foot and leave the ground with the toe of the rear foot. Don't walk flat-footed. "Don't push off from the toe," Rudow writes. "Rather, drive with the advancing knee.

In hard sprint walking, the heel is jammed into the ground, and the foot and leg are pulled back powerfully. In distance races, this action is obviously more gentle." Rudow adds that the walker should feel as if he is pulling the ground along underneath him.

Arm Movement.

Your arms and upper body move in the opposite direction of your lower body as you walk. When the right leg advances, the left arm swings to the front and so on. When you walk normally, you allow your arms to hang loosely at your sides, with your elbows slightly bent, and your hands forming an arc centering roughly on the seam of your trousers. Race-walkers hold their arms more like runners. The elbows are bent at roughly ninety-degree angles and the hands go no farther back than the seam of the pants. The arms are as important in race walking as the legs. Walkers with strong arms and upper bodies can drive their legs onward when their legs are virtually unwilling to move. One of these strong-arm-type walkers is Chuck Hunter of Longmont, Colorado. Chuck is built like a professional football player, but he's one of the best distance walkers in the country. He's been called the "Clydesdale" of race walking. So use your arms to control your speed.

The Torso.

Your body should remain relaxed and as erect as possible. If you're leaning forward or backward, you're putting extra strain on your body and cutting down on the power in the legs and arms. "Walk as fast as you can without tightening up," advises Larry O'Neil. "Keep your body relaxed. That's the secret in almost any sport."

Mental Discipline.

Whether you are training for a long race or a sprint, this factor is as important as physical conditioning. Try to keep your mind on your technique, your pace, and your competition. Listen to your body.

No equipment is needed for race walking other than a light pair of shoes and gym clothes. You'll have to experiment with different brands of jogging shoes until you find one that suits you. Many distance walkers wear heel inserts in their shoes to cushion the impact of walking.

Before setting out on a long walk, you should apply lubricating jelly liberally to those areas where the walking motion is likely to cause irritation. You also can cut down on irritation by bringing extra gym suits, shoes, and underwear to a long race. Nothing is more uncomfortable than wearing sweat-soaked clothes for fifty miles.

Long-distance walkers generally try to gain a little weight in the weeks before a big race, but they don't recommend the use of carbohydrate-loading practiced by many marathon runners. After about twenty-five miles of walking, the body relies on its reserves of fat for energy, so carbohydrate-loading has little effect.

Walkers warm-up for a long race by walking a few laps at a leisurely pace. You don't want to burn up any more energy or put any more miles on your feet than necessary. Warmups for sprints should include walking slowly, stretching exercises, and even a few short sprints at less than full speed. Obviously, the walker has to be much more careful about warming-up when he is getting ready for a sprint race, where his body is going to be moving much faster on much shorter notice.

Photo by Charles Cancellare

13

The Long Haul

In 1970, David Kunst, a hard-working family man from Waseca, Minnesota, decided he wanted to walk around the world. "Something snapped," Kunst said later. He was tired of his job as a surveyor for the county and he was tired of Waseca. So accompanied by his younger brother, John, and a mule donated by the local Chamber of Commerce, Kunst simply walked out of town.

He walked and he walked and he walked. He walked across America, Europe, and Asia. He was entertained by Princess Grace of Monaco, mistaken for a smuggler in Spain, and attacked by anti-American mobs in Turkey and Iran. He kept body and soul together by mooching meals and lodging from dignitaries and ordinary citizens in the thirteen countries he crossed. Everywhere he went, Kunst collected pledges for UNICEF and newspapers reported his fund-raising efforts. But the reports soon revealed tragedy. Bandits in Afghanistan, who believed the brothers were carrying large sums of money, killed John and wounded David.

Yet even his brother's death didn't stop the older Kunst. After recuperating in Waseca, he flew back to Afghanistan to continue his journey. On October 5, 1974, the journey ended. He was greeted by a throng of townspeople as he trudged into Waseca and drank a champagne toast to the four-year, 14,500-mile trek that earned him a place in the *Guinness Book of World Records* as the first man to walk around the world.

185

As he ended his journey, Kunst walked in the footsteps of a long line of people who for one reason or another, both in war and peace, have accomplished incredible feats of endurance and tenacity on foot.

Although men at war have performed many great feats of walking endurance, few have matched The Long March of the Red Army across China in the 1930s. Led by MaoTse-tung, 100,000 troops marched eight-thousand miles from the Kiangsi republic to Peking, in about a year's time. That's an average of about twenty-two miles a day, no mean feat in itself, but remarkable when you consider that full-scale battles were fought along the way and much of the walking was done at night. The American journalist, Edgar Snow, wrote that "the whole journey was covered on foot, across some of the world's most impassable trails, most of them unfit for wheeled traffic, across some of the highest mountains and the greatest rivers of Asia." Only twenty-thousand men survived The Long March.

Another notable military feat-of-foot was the march out of Burma in 1942 led by General Joseph Stilwell. After the fall of Burma to the Japanese, Stilwell astonished the world by leading his men through the jungle to the safety of India. The sixty-year-old Stilwell maintained a pace of 106 steps per minute.

In peacetime, people who walk long distances are usually trying to prove a point. Sometimes the point is health-related. More often, it's simply to prove they have what it takes to finish a long-distance walk.

The popularity of walking great distances, like everything else, seems to rise and fall in cycles. The middle years of the Nineteenth Century produced the pedestrian movement in Europe and America and there has been a similar revival in the last twenty years. One indication that we're going through another feat-of-foot cycle is the number of people each year who walk the entire 2,050 miles of the Appalachian Trail from Maine to Georgia. According to the Appalachian Trail Conference, the number of end-to-enders, as they're called, was negligible from 1936, when someone began keeping track, until 1971. Then the pace picked up rapidly. In the thirty-four years between 1936 and 1970, only thirty people reported walking the trail from end to end in one trip. In 1971 alone, twenty-three people walked the length of the trail; in 1972, thirty-three people made the trip; in 1973, seventy-four people; in 1974, forty-five people; in 1975, fifty-six people; and in 1976 about ninety people. The total of end-to-enders is now well over three-hundred and rising rapidly. The Appalachian Trails's western counterpart, the 2,300-mile Pacific Crest Trail, from Canada to Mexico, has become an equally busy wilderness expressway.

Road-walkers haven't been neglecting their duties in the last twenty years, either. A notable road-walker of our era was Dr. Barbara Moore, who at the age of fifty-six, walked the one-thousand-mile length of Great Britain—from Northern Scotland to Land's End—in twenty-three days. "I have proved, I hope, that we women can do all that men can," she said after completing the trek on February 5, 1960. Dr. Moore wasn't satisfied, however, with the conquest of Britain and less than a month afterward, announced that she was going to the colonies to set a new transcontinental walking record. But two British sergeants beat her to it when they walked from San Francisco to New York in sixty-six days, four hours, and seven minutes. Dr. Moore, who left San Francisco one day behind the sergeants, arrived in New York on July 7, 1960, after eighty-five days on the road. In route, she was hit by a car, suffered a twisted ankle and severe sunburn, and was forced to don snowshoes for twenty miles in a Colorado snowstorm. As she was mobbed by New York crowds, she claimed that the walk was proof of the effectiveness of her vegetarian diet.

Other record-setting walks in the last twenty years, according to *Guinness*, follow.

———David Kwan, then twenty-two-years old, walked from Singapore to London in 1957. He made the 18,500-mile trip in eighty-one weeks, averaging thirty-two miles a day.

———Astronaut Edward H. White II took the first walk in space on June 3, 1965.

———A new transcontinental record was set by John Lees of Brighton, England, who walked from Los Angeles to New York in fifty-three days, twelve hours, and fifteen minutes. He averaged 53.7 miles a day during the 2,876-mile walk.

———David Ryder, of Essex, England, walked from Los Angeles to New York, leaving the West Coast on March 30, and arriving in the East on August 14, 1970. He broke no speed records, but he had a handicap. As a polio victim, he walked with crutches.

———And last, but hardly least, was Plennie Wingo's 452-mile

walk from Santa Monica to San Francisco in 1976. Wingo, eighty-one-years old, covered the distance in eighty-five days, a pretty slow pace unless you take into consideration the fact that he was walking backward. The trek was a celebration of the forty-fifth anniversary of Wingo's eight-thousand-mile backward walk from Santa Monica to Istanbul.

The modern-day walkers I've mentioned are fine specimens of the pedestrian breed, but you have to go back to the Nineteenth Century to discover the man, whom I believe was the greatest walker of all time. The Nineteenth Century produced many great walkers— Wordsworth, Thoreau, Muir—who were more interested in what they saw or thought along the way than the actual process of walking. They were thinkers, poets, and naturalists, rather than athletes. In fact, they looked down their noses at people who measured the success of their walks in terms of time and distance, instead of beauty and clarity of thought. But despite the disdain of the intellectuals, there sprung up in the Nineteenth Century an awareness of walking as a sport, as a feat of discipline and endurance. In 1809, a British man, Captain Robert Barclay Allardice, walked one-thousand miles in one-thousand consecutive hours. That's more than forty-one straight days and nights of walking. Of course, the walker only had to cover one mile in each hour, leaving him at least forty minutes of free time for eating, sleeping, or whatever. Perhaps, the greater feat was accomplished by the poor soul who had the task of waking the pedestrian up once every hour for more than a month. Fifty years later, a Chicago man matched the British performance, and two women from Brooklyn topped both gentlemen by doing four-thousand quarter-mile-stints in as many quarter-hours. The female feat seems to be the more difficult because it didn't allow for even a half-hour of uninterrupted rest.

It's odd that Pedestrianism, as the walking movement was called, seems to have caught on in America around the time of the Civil War. You would think that folks during that most difficult period in American history would have had more serious ways to spend their time than walking around in circles for four-thousand consecutive quarter-hours. Although one never knows for sure about such things, I attribute the spread of Pedestrianism to the influence of one man, Edward Payson Weston, my choice for the world's number-one walker.

Weston and the pedestrians were professionals. They walked for

purses, packing in huge crowds at major arenas in the U.S. and Britain. In fact, walking was so lucrative that some of the pedestrians became extremely wealthy, so wealthy that a newspaper ran a cartoon which showed the walkers earning as much as twenty-five-thousand-dollars a week. The *New York Times* wrote of the pedestrians in 1867: "A kind of pedestrian mania seems to afflict this country just now. We hear of erratic pedestrians rushing across the continent in every direction, just as the recent meteors traversed the heavens. Side by side with telegrams announcing the progress of events in Italy we find, day after day, telegrams announcing that of a pedestrian walking so many miles a day for so many thousand dollars. Mayors greet him, roughs assail him, police protect him, children are kissed by him, and every detail is telegraphed with pre-Raphaelite minuteness." The editors of the *Times* were not pleased with the new "pedestrian mania" and they applauded Cornelius Vanderbilt, the railroad magnate, when he cancelled a walking event, featuring Weston and several other walkers, at Madison Square Garden.

Weston was the first man to walk five-hundred miles in six days, and he had incredible stamina and consistency throughout his long walking career. He was a spy for the Union forces during the Civil War and a reporter for the *New York Herald* before becoming a professional walker. He apparently made the decision to turn professional after walking from Boston to New York for the inauguration of Abraham Lincoln.

Weston reached the height of his prowess and popularity in the twenty-years after the Civil War. In 1879, he walked two-thousand miles in one-thousand hours and the same year he won the Astley belt, then the most coveted prize in walking, by going 550 miles in 141 hours and 56 minutes. Only two weeks prior to the match, he had walked 562 miles in the same time period. He went on a walking tour of England in 1884 in which he covered five-thousand miles in one-hundred days and lectured on the virtues of temperance every night before large crowds. Weston was capable of both speed and endurance. He once walked the five-hundreth mile of a race in seven minutes and fifty-one seconds (7.5 miles an hour) and he walked 127 miles in one day.

After a period of retirement, Weston made a comeback in the 1900s and again fueled the American fascination with walkers. In 1906, he walked from Philadelphia to New York in twenty-three hours and thirty-one minutes, beating the record for the trek that he, himself, had set forty years before. He was sixty-seven-years old at the time. At the age of sixty-nine, Weston took another anniversary walk from Portland, Maine, to Chicago. Again, he broke a record he had set forty years' earlier. Encouraged by the massive crowds that turned out to see him walk and the apparent preservation of his walking prowess, despite his age, Weston decided to make his longest walk and announced that he would walk to San Francisco along a circuitous route that totaled more than 4,400 miles. A revival of the old six-day walking contests was scheduled in Madison Square Garden for the week before Weston's transcontinental walk was to begin.

Today, we're somewhat more accustomed to seeing septuagenarians perform remarkable athletic feats but, in the early 1900s, it was unheard of. As a result, Weston's announcement that he would make the longest walk of his career became a national event. He was perhaps the first American athlete to gain the kind of public recognition that we take for granted today. His personal habits were examined in minute detail. Some physicians believed that he would never survive the transcontinental walk while others, looking at his record, were believers. Weston attributed his good health to temperance, moderate eating habits, and walks of twelve to fifteen miles a day. He never walked on Sunday, however.

Weston left New York for San Francisco on March 15, 1909. It was his seventy-first birthday. He filed exclusive reports on his journey to the *New York Times.* A dashing figure with his long, white mustache and his wide-brimmed hat, cocked slightly to the side, he was cheered and given milk and eggnog by the crowds that gathered along his route. Many of the people who cheered him had witnessed his other city-to-city walks forty years earlier. But as he progressed further west, the going got tougher. He walked for miles without seeing anyone but the tramps that rode the rails in those days. The lack of suitable roads forced him to walk along the railroad tracks for more than two-thousand miles, slowing him down. He walked through slush and snow a foot deep and bucked fifty-mile-an-hour winds, which on one occasion blew him over a thirty-foot embankment. He arrived in San Francisco on July 15, 105 walking days out of New York. He was disappointed because he had intended to walk all the way to Seattle in only one-hundred days. Weston's final big walk was from New York to Minneapolis for the dedication of the new Minneapolis Athletic Club. He planned to make the 1,500 mile trek in sixty days, but he arrived four days ahead of schedule. He was seventy-five-years old.

Weston died in 1929 at the age of ninety. He apparently had set that as his longevity goal, and even though he had been hit by a cab in New York City several years earlier, he hung on until he made ninety. It was typical of the man, who although endowed with marvelous athletic gifts and an extremely rapid, bent-kneed gait, was also, above all, a man with a will of steel.

14

The Walking Writers

What do Aristotle, Sigmund Freud, Albert Einstein, William Wordsworth, Samuel Taylor Coleridge, William Shakespeare, Charles Dickens, Vachel Lindsay, Robert Louis Stevenson, Saul Bellow, William O. Douglas, Oliver Wendell Holmes, Ray Bradbury, Aldous Huxley, Ralph Waldo Emerson, Henry David Thoreau, Edna St. Vincent Millay, Thomas Mann, James Michener, Vladimir Nabokov, John Keats, Edward Hoagland, John Muir, Alfred Kazin, C.S. Lewis, John Burroughs, and Edwin Way Teale have in common?

That's simple. They are walkers. They all loved to walk. And they are only a few of the many writers and thinkers across the ages, who for one reason or another, or perhaps no reason at all, have been drawn to walking.

Aristotle lectured to his students while walking around a sacred grove in Athens in the Third Century Before Christ. The students in his school of philosophy were called Peripatetics, from the Greek words *peri*, meaning "around," and *patein*, meaning "to walk."

Sigmund Freud sometimes sauntered through the streets of Vienna with his patients or students, searching for a path through some mental labyrinth.

Einstein was said to become so immersed in thought in his walks around Princeton, New Jersey, that he sometimes lost his way.

Many of the world's literati were and are, avid walkers. What better way to observe and assimilate the life, both human and nonhuman, of the city and the country? Leslie Stephen, wrote that walking "is the natural recreation for a man who desires not absolutely to suppress his intellect but to turn it out to play for a season. All great men of letters have, therefore, been enthusiastic walkers (exceptions, of course, excepted)." Stephen, a walker himself, was particularly impressed by the effect walking may have had on the literary movement in England in the latter part of the Eighteenth Century. He wrote that it "was obviously due in great part, if not mainly, to the renewed practice of walking."

By all accounts, the most prodigious walker of the writers of that period was William Wordsworth. The poet's biographer, Thomas De Quincey wrote: "I calculate, upon good data, that with these identical legs Wordsworth must have traversed a distance of 175,000 or 180,000 English miles, a mode of exertion which to him stood in the stead of alcohol and all stimulants whatsoever to the animal spirits; to which indeed he was indebted for a life of unclouded happiness, and we for much of what was most excellent in his writings."

Early in his career, while still a student at Cambridge University and shortly thereafter, Wordsworth went on two, long walking tours, one through France and the Alps and the other through Wales, with his friend, Robert Jones. Wordsworth described the continental walking tour in one of his first poems, "Descriptive Sketches," published in 1793. Both walks were used later in Wordsworth's other great works, either directly or indirectly. Many were actually composed in his head during the walks. In a note to one of his poems, Wordsworth wrote: "I began it [the poem] upon leaving Tintern, after crossing the Wye, and concluded it just as I was entering Bristol in the evening, after a ramble of four or five days, with my sister. Not a line of it was altered, and not any part written down till I reached Bristol."

Wordsworth was occasionally accompanied on his walks by Samuel Taylor Coleridge, the great poet who is perhaps best known for "The Rime of the Ancient Mariner." The first stanza of that poem was said to have been composed while the two poets were walking. And the work, itself, was intended to earn money for a walking tour planned by Coleridge, Wordsworth, and his sister, Dorothy Wordsworth.

Other walking literati of the period were Sir Walter Scott, whose novels and poetry drew heavily upon the lore he gathered on walks of twenty to thirty miles a day; John Keats, whose beautifully crafted poems were often inspired by his country walks; and Jonathan Swift, who was said to have walked ten miles a day, stopping at roadhouses along the way to talk with the tramps that frequented the highways in those days.

Although most of the Eighteenth and Nineteenth Century Englishmen of letters were country walkers, the island's greatest novelist, Charles Dickens, did his sauntering through the streets of London, where teeming humanity served as fodder for his prolific pen. Dickens's essay, "Night Walks," is an account of several nights he spent wandering the streets of London. He used these walks, prompted by his inability to sleep, as an opportunity to build "sympathetic relations with people who have no other object every night in the year" other than "to get through the night." The nights were filled with a mixture of coarse entertainment and boredom. When the bars closed for the night, he yearned for the sounds of a policeman breaking up a fight or other entertainments provided by the people of the night. But often he walked through silent streets. To communicate the sense and feeling of these all-night walks, Dickens created the personna, "Houselessness." This character saw men peaking furtively from doorways "intent upon no particular service to society"; stopped by the door of a debtor's prison to ponder the fate of those poor souls who had sweated out their years within its walls; and at the entrance to an insane asylum raised the age-old question of whether the lunatics inside were any less sane than their fellow men on the outside.

In general, "Houselessness" spent the night wandering in search of company, but found that the people of the night were much too strange and threatening to provide much companionship.

While the English walkers were sauntering through the Lake Country and London, the Nineteenth Century was producing America's greatest walker, Henry David Thoreau. A passionate naturalist, Thoreau's ample contribution to the literature of the world is filled with references to his walks in New England. His essay, "Walking," published in 1862, is probably the most widely quoted work on walking and the most eloquent summary of its pleasures and purposes. Walkers in those days often used the word "sauntering" to describe their walks and Thoreau believed that "sauntering" was derived from the French "a la Saint Terre" or "to the Holy Land." True walkers, he

Photo by Ginzy Schaefer

believed, were people who sought something holy in their walks.

Thoreau's book, *Cape Cod*, is an account of three walking tours on the Cape. It is filled with descriptions of his moods, the passing scenery, the people, and the history of the area. In one chapter he describes his method of walking a beach (near the water, where the sand is hard) and his encounter with a driftwood gatherer. Many naturalists have written about the Cape, but none has captured the feeling of it being a fragile bit of sand jutting into the stormy North Atlantic better than Thoreau. (Legend has it that the Cape was formed when some mythical giant sat on Massachusetts to empty the sand from his moccasins.) The Cape, of course, has changed a great deal since Thoreau's day. The great walker found houses "few and far between" and even they were only simple shacks punctuated by an occasional clapboard mansion. Now, there are many, many substantial dwellings, along with the golden arches of McDonalds, cut-rate gasoline stations, discount stores, portable toilets, and souvenir stands. There are massive traffic jams, too, as the tourists and weekend residents pour out to the Cape from the cities of the Northeast. But it's still possible to find places on the Cape where it's an easy mental journey back to the days of Thoreau. There is a beautiful nature trail near Eastham that winds through Red Maple Swamp; and Nauset Beach, one of Thoreau's favorite spots, is now Cape Cod National Seashore.

Yet, Thoreau was merely the first of a long line of American naturalists who have traversed large areas of the country on foot, exploring, enlightening, and cataloging as they went. If Thoreau was the seminal walker-writer-naturalist of the Northeast, John Muir was his counterpart for the mountains and deserts of the American West. Neither man was the first to explore the American wilderness. They were preceded by the early settlers, trappers, and adventurers, but they were part of the first wave of Americans to see "nature" as something other than a vehicle for the prosperity of mankind. To these writing walkers, "nature" in itself was a source of great good, great wisdom, and great mystery. It was something to be preserved and cherished and studied rather than exploited.

Muir immigrated to the U.S. from Scotland when he was eleven years old. In 1849, his family settled in the backwoods of Wisconsin. He attended the University of Wisconsin, where he studied botany, and began preparing himself for his lifelong study of the American wilderness. He took long walking tours hrough Wisconsin, Iowa, and Illinois, and later walked one-thousand miles from Indiana to the Gulf of Mexico. He then headed west where he spent many years wandering through the mountains, recording everything he saw and experienced in his journals.

Muir spent his first years in the west living like a hermit in Yosemite Valley. From there he explored the surrounding mountains, partly in an effort to prove they were formed by receding glaciers. While living in Yosemite, he was visited by the elderly poet, Ralph Waldo Emerson, who also walked from time to time with Thoreau.

Muir wrote later that Emerson "seemed as serene as a sequoia," but the poet was prevented from hiking into the backcountry with Muir by other members of Emerson's party who were concerned about his health and safety. Years later, Muir showed another famous American, Teddy Roosevelt, the splendors of Yosemite. Roosevelt was said to have commented on the tour: "This is bully." Eventually, Muir's tours through the mountains evolved into an organization, the Sierra Club, whose members were the leading spokesmen for wilderness preservation.

In his later years, Muir began editing and publishing his journals and working for the preservation of the areas he wandered through in his years of walking. Today, we have a rich collection of his writings available to the reading walker. But far more important, we have Yosemite National Park, John Muir Trail, the John Muir Wilderness Area in the Inyo and Sierra National Forests, and many other expanses of wilderness that were saved from exploitation by Muir's eloquent evocation of their unspoiled beauty.

Virtually all naturalists are walkers and there are so many American naturalists that it is impossible to mention them all and it seems discriminatory to mention only a few. There is one contemporary naturalist, however, who has been such a prolific writer that his output rivals even Thoreau and Muir. As I write this, a stack of books by Edwin Way Teale casts a shadow across my typewriter: *The American Seasons, Days Without Time, The Lost Woods, Green Treasury, Autumn Across America, A Naturalist Buys an Old Farm.* . . . In the latter work, Teale describes a walk he took one afternoon around the boundaries of a farm he eventually purchased near Hampton, Connecticut. His description of the walk shows that even in the Twentieth Century, with the American wilderness reduced to a mere reminder of its virgin splendor, it is possible to find places where age-old, natural processes are relatively undisturbed. "In a time when 'pedestrian' is most often used to describe someone hit by an automobile, it was pleasant that afternoon to walk on mossy trails through the spring woods—sometimes beside a brook, sometimes along an old stone wall, sometimes skirting the edge of a swamp, Teale wrote. "Everywhere we went what we saw exceeded our expectations."

The naturalists such as Thoreau, Muir, and Teale have looked first and foremost at the plants, animals, and geological nature of

America, but there are two great American walkers, both of them poets, who attempted to describe the beliefs and people of America as well.

The first is Walt Whitman. Many authorities regard Whitman as the first great American poet, and he is widely thought to have been the first bard to establish a distinctly American voice in the poetry of the world. To classify Whitman as a walker is somewhat of an understatement, a diminution of his great talent. For surely, his years of country and city walking were only the means to an end: The end of seeing America in all its rough grandeur and variety and compressing and refining it into lines of poetry.

But Walt Whitman was undeniably an avid walker. Born in West Hills, Long Island, in 1819, the poet spent much of the first thirty-six years of his life sauntering around Long Island, New York, observing and loafing as he went. In his poetry, Whitman preached the need for comradeship, openness, and honesty, even about sexual matters. His poetry is athletic; and the voice in such works as "Leaves of Grass" is that of a person who is isolated, yet feels a common bond with the life around him. Whitman's famous lines in "Leaves of Grass" are perhaps the best expression in the English language of the exhilaration and anticipation of setting out on a walking tour.

"Afoot and light-hearted I take to the open road,

Healthy, free, the world before me,

The long brown path before me leading wherever I choose."

Like Whitman, Vachel Lindsay was a poet who loved the common man and common things. He tried to be the voice of a genuine, raucous, teeming, democratic America. And he learned about America on foot.

Born in Springfield, Illinois, in 1879, Lindsay's first ambition was to become an artist. He studied art in Chicago and New York for several years but he found no market for his drawings. It was only then that he saw his poetry as a way of making a living. Being a simple man in the tradition of all the walkers who had forsaken the comforts of the sedentary life for the perils and pleasures of pedestrianism, Lindsay came up with a rather novel idea for surviving as a poet. In 1905, he became what was called in those days a "tramp." He toured the country exchanging recitations of his poetry for the necessities of life and everywhere he went, he passed out a little booklet of his poems called *Rhymes to Be Traded for Bread*. Even today the booklet serves as an excellent manual for anyone yearning to revive the dying art of "tramping."

The tour in 1905 was only the first of many such tours Lindsay was to make in his lifetime and he spent virtually his entire life reciting his poetry and lecturing. In 1916, Lindsay published a book of prose, *A Handy Guide for Beggars*, based on his walking tours in 1906 and 1908 through Georgia, North Carolina, Tennessee, Kentucky, New Jersey, Pennsylvania, and Ohio. Lindsay dedicated his *Handy Guide* to the "one-hundred new poets in the villages of the land." He saw "tramping" as a way of cleansing his soul of city life. While on the road, he was fed and housed by simple folk, and in return, he heaped praise upon the lowly and turned his satirical style upon the more sophisticated elements of American society: professors, businessmen, preachers, and politicians. "I took to the road once, long ago, because people said if I staid [sic] rhymer and artist I would be a beggar and die in the poor-house. My most intimate friends prophesied it incessantly for years, after nourishing themselves on businessmen's clubs and office-supply advertisements," Lindsay wrote. "Therefore, in no sentimental mood, but actually to try out this beggary, and deliberately calling myself 'a beggar to the end of my days,' I took to the road and tried, as it were, the 'poor-house,' at its worst, that I might get used to it."

Lindsay also published another book of prose, *Adventures While Preaching the Gospel of Beauty*, about his tours through Missouri and Kansas. The book reflects his disgust with urban life and Lindsay calls upon all of America's artists to return to the villages for inspiration. Much of the book is devoted to a description of the Kansas wheat harvest and it is perhaps the best writing ever done about that aspect of America.

In the same way that Thoreau elevated the practice of "sauntering" into the search for something "holy," Lindsay linked "tramping" with the tradition of Saint Francis of Assisi. Lindsay considered the founder of the Franciscan Order, with its rules of poverty and charity, his patron saint and Lindsay in turn showed great compassion for the poor and down-trodden.

"But seldom are keepers of engine-stables as unfortunate as these," Lindsay wrote in *Adventures*. "The best they can get from the world is cruel laughter. Yet this woman, crippled in brain, her soul only half alive, this dull man, crippled in body, had God's gift of the liberal heart. If they are supremely absurd, so are all of us. We must include ourselves in the farce. These two, tottering through the dimness and vexation of our queer world, were willing the stranger should lean upon them. I say they had the good gift of the liberal heart. One thing was theirs to divide. That was a roof. They gave me my third and they helped me to hide from the rain. In the name of St. Francis I laid me down. May that saint of all saints be with them, with all the gentle and innocent and weary and broken."

Twentieth Century novelists, short-story writers, and journalists have often used walkers as characters in their fiction or have used the process of walking as a way of telling a story or describing places and people. Two writers, both avid walkers themselves, who have used walkers as fictional characters, are the late C. S. Lewis and Ray Bradbury.

Lewis, an Englishman, wrote more than fifty books of poetry, literary criticism, and fiction before his death in 1963. He never owned a car and in addition to his daily walks, often along a path called Addison's Walk in Oxford, he went on a walking tour every year from the 1920s until 1939. As he walked, he soaked up the beauty of the English and Irish landscapes and seacoasts. Later, the scenes appeared in some form in his poetry, fiction, and nonfiction. In his science-fiction novel, *Out of the Silent Planet*, Lewis begins the first chapter by describing a character, known at first only as the "Pedestrian," who has set out on a walking tour of England. The Pedestrian has waited out a thunderstorm and when it's over refers to his map, adjusting his pack, and strides briskly down the road in search of a place to spend the night. The Pedestrian, later identified as a professor at Cambridge, runs into trouble when he is abducted by two scientists and finds himself enroute to the planet, "Malacandra." He seals his own fate by informing his captors that he is not the kind of walker who lets anyone know where he is going. Lewis obviously drew upon his experience as a walker in creating the character, Ransom, and it must have occurred to him that a man on a long walking tour would be an ideal target for an abduction because he wouldn't be missed for some time.

Ray Bradbury's "Pedestrian" is also abducted, but he is abducted by the police rather than two mad scientists. In his short story, "The Pedestrian," Bradbury tells of a man in the year 2052 A.D., who loves to take long walks in the city. The streets are empty as he strolls along in the moonlight. The residents of the city are camped in front of their television sets, protected by dogs that sometimes snarl at the pedestrian as he walks by. "In ten years of walking by night or day, for thousands of miles, he had never met another person walking, not one in all that time." In the end, the pedestrian is arrested by the city's lone patrol car (operated by remote control) simply because he cannot give a "rational" explanation for why he is walking.

Bradbury wrote in the introduction to the 1967 edition of his novel, *Fahrenheit 451*, that "The Pedestrian" was written in anger after a policeman stopped him for walking at night. His story carried "the entire ridiculous episode one step further, into a future where all pedestrians are suspect and criminal."

And Bradbury has stumbled across other stories on his walks. In the same introduction, he wrote of an idea that came to him while walking on the beach with some friends. ". . . I drew with a Popsicle stick in the sand and said, idly, 'Wouldn't it be terrible if we, Picasso lovers one and all, always desiring a Picasso, suddenly stumbled on him there, drawing on the beach, late one day?' " That same night Bradbury wrote the story, "In a Season of Calm Weather," about a man who does meet Picasso drawing on a beach in Spain.

The literary critic, journalist, and autobiographical writer, Alfred Kazin, used walking to recall his childhood in the Brownsville section of New York City. Kazin used his walks through the east Brooklyn neighborhood as a framework for recounting his childhood memories in *A Walker in the City*. Kazin told his publisher that the walks in the book "serve two purposes: to recapture the aliveness of the moment described and to describe walking itself as an exercise in human delight." He used walking to recall an entire network of experiences: His own and those of the Jewish immigrants from which he sprang.

The novelist, Saul Bellow, explored the city of Jerusalem on foot in writing *To Jerusalem and Back*, published in 1976. Although Bellow relied on personal interviews and other research in compiling his account of that ancient city, it is clear that he absorbed much of its atmosphere and history while walking through the streets with friends. " . . . we ask our way through endless lanes, where kids ride donkeys, kick rubber balls, scream, fall from wagons, and build small fires to warm their fingers, for the weather is cold," Bellow wrote of one of his walks in Jerusalem.

I've given you only a smattering of information about the great writers and thinkers of the world who have found something of value in walking. I could go on and on, listing and explaining, but that might rob you of much of the satisfaction of making your own discoveries. I hope you will use this book as a kind of appetizer to stimulate your hunger for more reading about, and by, the great walkers. Once you've devoured those works listed here, I'm sure the card catalog of your local library will yield an even greater harvest of books by walkers. So good hunting!

15

On Foot

I remember one snowy, cold day when I was feeling as stale as a month-old slice of bread; I decided the only way to throw off the staleness, the tedium, and the stiffness in my bones was to go for a walk. I put on my long underwear, my jeans, my boots, about four shirts, a stocking cap, and a wool sweater, and stepped out the door.

The sidewalk was slick with snow and it took a while for the stiffness to wear off. The wind burned my face and I realized that a heavy beard was no luxury or self-indulgence, that facial hair is our natural guard against the cold in places that are otherwise most difficult to protect.

As I crossed streets and negotiated slippery sidewalks, I yearned for a long, straight stretch where I could pick up speed and experience that natural, rhythmic pace that's known as "hitting your stride." Finally, I climbed down into a creek bed where back in the days when Kansas City was known as "Tom's Town," the city administration had laid down a wide strip of concrete that was tailor-made for the kind of level, fast walking that I most enjoy. The creek bed was a little slippery in places, but I was soon able to hit my stride, to enjoy that natural, God-given pace that separates man from his primate ancestors. The pace is so natural that once in good shape, you become a well-oiled machine, the kind of machine that improves with time, with use, with wear, and with little or no servicing or repairs. It can change your life. It can bring out that feeling of sheer joy, of freedom, of effortlessness that is a reminder of childhood, when motion was everything. That's how it was for me on that snowy day. I forgot that I was walking, that my arms and legs were churning like pistons. I watched the snowflakes drift lazily to the pavement. I waved at the people on the bridges above me as I steamed through. I danced a little jig. I slid in the snow, spun around, and generally behaved like a three-year-old.

My body was generating its own warmth. I was a warm spot in what was rapidly becoming a full-scale blizzard. My accelerated metabolism was chewing away at sausage and eggs and toast and coffee and at the same time the muscles of my legs and arms were massaging the vessels that carry the blood, filled with oxygen and nutrients, to the cells stacked one upon another side by side that were me. The overall result was that I felt good: vital and alive.

I hadn't a care in the world. I had shaken them all loose, one by one, and they had been replaced by a feeling that all things were possible if I could walk when I needed to, when my worries and frustrations began to weigh me down again. I realized how simple life really is, how we attempt to hide behind the complexities of modern life out of fear of our natural selves. I realized how senseless and hopeless and wrong-headed is that attempt to hide. I saw how the plants along the creek bed neither spun nor toiled, how they seemed to accept a cycle that dictates that they should germinate, grow, reproduce, and die. I saw our kinship with them.

After leaving my walker's expressway, I walked along a busy street and wondered what people in their cars were thinking. I was convinced they thought me a fool. I wished I could tell them what fun I was having sauntering through the snow; how my heart and lungs were becoming stronger right before their very eyes; how I was losing weight effortlessly without the tension and frustration of dieting; how my mind was free of worries; how I was training myself for a long walk through a still forest. I thought of how much I could tell them about their city, how you see the city in a new way when you walk it. Then I thought about the people who someday might be reading this book and I hoped that I would be able to convince them that, in the words of Ralph Waldo Emerson, "tis the best of humanity that goes out to walk."

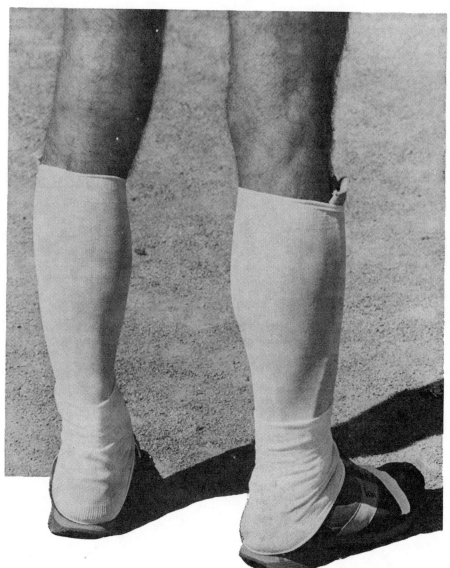

Photo by Charles Cancellare

A GUIDE TO WALKING IN ALL FIFTY STATES

There are over 185,000 miles of trails in the United States and although some authorities believe the American trail system is inadequate, there are far too many trails to list each one in this book. What I have attempted to do in this Walker's Guide is to give you enough information to get you started. The rest is up to you.

For most of the states and the District of Columbia I have listed and described to some extent the National Recreation Trails. This list of trails, which is lengthening rapidly, has its origins in the National Trails Systems Act of 1968. When Congress adopted this landmark piece of outdoor legislation, it wanted to be certain that the National Trails System would include some trails either within, or close to, urban areas. These trails are now called National Recreation Trails.

I have also listed certain national parks for each state. I have by no means included every national park in America, only those which the National Park Service considers appropriate for hiking. There are many others, of course, which would be suitable for short walks and strolls.

In the listings for each state, I have also included the address of the state agency which administers and maintains state parks and forests. Although it varies from state to state, these agencies are generally excellent sources of information about places to walk. This is especially true in states where federal facilities are scarce.

Lastly, I have listed at least one private organization for each state. The role of each of these organizations is somewhat different, but generally they are in some way involved in outdoor activities. They may be a small club of walkers or nature lovers, a trail maintenance organization, a trail-guide publishing house, an umbrella corporation with many chapters or member clubs, or all these things wrapped into one. Whether or not you're interested in joining an organization, these groups are often the best sources of information about places to walk in their bailiwicks.

There is some danger of distortion and omission when one attempts to make a state-by-state list of trails and walking organizations. The trails simply don't conform to arbitrary state boundaries. The most obvious instances of omission are the two great north-south trails: The Appalachian Trail and the Pacific Crest Trail.

The Appalachian Trail runs for more than 2,000 miles through the most scenic areas of the Appalachian Mountain region of the eastern United States. It passes through Georgia, Tennessee, North Carolina, Virginia, West Virginia, Maryland, Pennsylvania, New York, Massachusetts, Vermont, New Hampshire, and Maine. Along many parts of the trail, campsites and shelters have been constructed for overnight campers, but the trail passes within striking distance of many urban areas and is most widely used by people who want to spend a few hours or a day hiking in a scenic area. The trail is maintained by hiking clubs situated along the route from Maine to Georgia, but there are several large organizations which publish guides to the trail, serve as umbrella organizations for the smaller clubs, and raise funds for maintenance and expansion of the trail. They are:

THE APPALACHIAN TRAIL CONFERENCE, P.O. Box 236, Harpers Ferry, WV 25425.
THE APPALACHIAN MOUNTAIN CLUB, 5 Joy Street, Boston, MA 02108.
THE POTOMAC APPALACHIAN TRAIL CLUB, INC., 1718 N Street, N.W., Washington, DC 20036.

The Pacific Crest Trail, when completed, will run roughly 2,400 miles from Mexico to Canada along the mountain ranges of California, Oregon, and Washington. The trail is still being pieced together, however, and it is incomplete in some places. For further information on the Pacific Crest Trail contact:

REGIONAL FORESTER, Pacific Northwest Region, Forest Service, 319 S.W. Pine St., Portland, OR 97208.
REGIONAL FORESTER, California Region, Forest Service, 630 Sansome St., San Francisco, CA 94111.
PACIFIC CREST FOUNDATION, Box 115, Mill City, OR 97360.

There are also several national and regional organizations whose influence and activities cross state lines. Some of them are mentioned in the state-by-state listings, but I do them an injustice unless I list them again here because their impact is regional and national. *

THE ADIRONDACK MOUNTAIN CLUB, INC., 172 Ridge St., Glens Falls, NY 12801.

THE APPALACHIAN MOUNTAIN CLUB, 5 Joy Street, Boston MA 02108.

THE APPALACHIAN TRAIL CONFERENCE, P.O. Box 236, Harpers Ferry, WV 25425.

BOY SCOUTS OF AMERICA, National Council, North Brunswick, NJ 08902.

FEDERATION OF WESTERN OUTDOOR CLUBS, 4534½ University Way N.E., Seattle WA 98105.

THE GREEN MOUNTAIN CLUB, INC., P.O. Box 889, 43 State St., Montpelier, VT 05602.

INTERNATIONAL BACKPACKERS ASSOCIATION, P.O. Box 85, Lincoln Center, ME 04458.

KEYSTONE TRAILS ASSOCIATION, R.D. 3, Box 261, Cogan Station, PA 17728.

NATIONAL HIKING AND SKI TOURING ASSOCIATION, P.O. Box 7421, Colorado Springs, CO 80933.

NATIONAL TRAILS COUNCIL, P.O. Box 1042, St. Charles, IL 60174.

NEW YORK-NEW JERSEY TRAIL CONFERENCE, 15 East 40th St., New York, NY 10016.

THE POTOMAC APPALACHIAN TRAIL CLUB, INC., 1718 N Street, N.W., Washington, DC 20036.

SIERRA CLUB, 530 Bush Street, San Francisco, CA 94108 (National Headquarters).

WALKING NEWS, INC., Box 352, New York, NY 10013.

THE WILDERNESS SOCIETY, 1901 Pennsylvania Avenue, N.W., Washington, DC 20006.

Other excellent sources of information about places to walk are the two federal agencies which administer most of the wilderness areas in America: The National Park Service and the Forest Service.

The addresses of the national and regional offices of the National Park Service:

NATIONAL PARK SERVICE, Room 1013, U.S. Department of the Interior, 18th and C Streets, N.W., Washington, DC 20240.

NORTH ATLANTIC REGION, 15 State St., Boston, MA 02109.

MID-ATLANTIC REGION, 143 South Third St., Philadelphia, PA 19106.

MIDWEST REGION, 1709 Jackson St., Omaha, NE 68102.

---

*Most of these organizations have member clubs or chapters. Because the addresses of the smaller groups in the state-by-state listings may change, you should write one of the regional groups if you are unable to contact a particular club or chapter listed in this guide.

NATIONAL CAPITOL REGION, 1100 Ohio Drive, S.W., Washington, DC 20242.
PACIFIC NORTHWEST REGION, 601 Fourth and Pike Building, Seattle, WA 98101.
ROCKY MOUNTAIN REGION, 655 Parfet St., P.O. Box 25287, Lakewood, CO 80225.
SOUTHEAST REGION, 1895 Phoenix Blvd., Atlanta, GA 30349.
SOUTHWEST REGION, Old Santa Fe Trail, P.O. Box 728, Santa Fe, NM 87501.
WESTERN REGION, 450 Golden Gate Ave., P.O. Box 36063, San Francisco, CA 94102.

The addresses of the national and regional offices of the Forest Service:
U.S. DEPARTMENT OF AGRICULTURE, Washington, DC 20250.
ALASKA REGION, Federal Office Building, Box 1628, Juneau, AK 99802.
CALIFORNIA REGION, 630 Sansome St., San Francisco, CA 94111.
EASTERN REGION, 633 West Wisconsin Ave., Milwaukee, WI 53203.
INTERMOUNTAIN REGION, 324 25th Street, Ogden, UT 84401.
NORTHERN REGION, Federal Building, Missoula, MT 59801.
PACIFIC NORTHWEST REGION, 319 S.W. Pine St., P.O. Box 3623, Portland, OR 97208.
SOUTHERN REGION, 1720 Peachtree Rd., N.W., Atlanta, GA 30309.
SOUTHWESTERN REGION, Federal Building, 517 Gold Ave., S.W., Albuquerque, NM 87102.

ALABAMA

National Recreation Trails:
BARTRAM TRAIL—A 1-mile foot trail in Tuskegee National Forest.
GEORGE WARD PARK EXERCISE TRAIL—A 1.5-mile trail in Birmingham.
PINHOTI TRAILS SYSTEM—28 miles in two segments in the Talladega National Forest and the Cheaha State Park, about 80 miles east of Birmingham.

National Parks:
HORSESHOE BEND NATIONAL MILITARY PARK, Route 1, Box 103, Daviston 36256.
NATCHEZ TRACE PARKWAY (See Mississippi).
RUSSELL CAVE NATIONAL MONUMENT, Route 1, Box 175, Bridgeport 35740.

State Trails:
DIVISION OF PARKS, Department of Conservation and Natural Resources, Administration Building, Montgomery 36130.

Organizations:
BARTRAM TRAIL CONFERENCE, 3815 Interstate Ct., Suite 202-A, Montgomery 36109.
SIERRA CLUB, Chattahoochee Chapter, P.O. Box 19574, Station N, Atlanta, Ga. 30325.

ALASKA

National Recreation Trail:
PINNELL MOUNTAIN TRAIL—A 24-mile trail, about 90 miles north of Fairbanks off the Steese Highway.

National Parks:
GLACIER BAY NATIONAL MONUMENT, P.O. Box 1089, Juneau 99802.
KATMAI NATIONAL MONUMENT, P.O. Box 7, King Salmon 99613.
KLONDIKE GOLD RUSH NATIONAL HISTORICAL PARK, P.O. Box 517, Skagway 99840.
MOUNT McKINLEY NATIONAL PARK, P.O. Box 9, McKinley Park 99755.

State Trails:
DEPARTMENT OF NATURAL RESOURCES, Division of Parks, 619 Warehouse Ave., Suite 210, Anchorage 99501.

Organizations:
THE MOUNTAINEERING CLUB OF ALASKA, 613 West Sixth Ave., Anchorage 99510.
SIERRA CLUB, Alaska Chapter, P.O. Box 2025, Anchorage 99501.

ARIZONA

National Recreation Trails:
HUNTER TRAIL—A 2.3-mile trail that ascends to the summit of Picacho Peak in Picacho State Park about 45 miles west of Tucson.
NORTH MOUNTAIN TRAIL—A .9-mile trail in North Mountain Park about 10 miles north of downtown Phoenix.
SOUTH MOUNTAIN PARK TRAIL—A 14-mile trail in the center of South Mountain Park in the Phoenix area. There is an extensive network of connecting trails in the park.
SQUAW PEAK TRAIL—A 1.2-mile trail that ascends Squaw Peak through fissured ledges to the bare rock summit. The trail is in Squaw Peak Park in Phoenix.
SUN CIRCLE TRAIL—This 68-mile trail links the South Mountain Park Trail and the Squaw Peak Trail and passes through the cities of Phoenix, Tempe, Gilbert, Mesa, Scottsdale and other communities.

National Parks:
CANYON DE CHELLY NATIONAL MONUMENT, P.O. Box 588, Chinle 86503.
CHIRICAHUA NATIONAL MONUMENT, Dos Cabezas Star Route, Willcox 85643.

GLEN CANYON NATIONAL RECREATION AREA (See Utah).
GRAND CANYON NATIONAL PARK, P.O. Box 129, Grand Canyon 86023.
LAKE MEAD NATIONAL RECREATION AREA (See Nevada).
NAVAHO NATIONAL MONUMENT, Tonalea 86044.
ORGAN PIPE CACTUS NATIONAL MONUMENT, P.O. Box 38, Ajo 85321.
PETRIFIED FOREST NATIONAL PARK, Petrified Forest National Park 86028.
SAGUARO NATIONAL MONUMENT, P.O. Box 17210, Tucson 85731.
WALNUT CANYON NATIONAL MONUMENT, Route 1, Box 25, Flagstaff 86001.
WUPATKI NATIONAL MONUMENT, Tuba Star Route, Flagstaff 86001.

State Trails:
ARIZONA PARKS BOARD, Room 122, 1688 West Adams, Phoenix 85007.

Organizations:
SIERRA CLUB, Grand Canyon Chapter, 6413 S. 26th St., Phoenix 85040.
SOUTHERN ARIZONA HIKING CLUB, P.O. Box 12122, Tucson 85732.

ARKANSAS

National Recreation Trails:
BRIDGE ROCK TRAIL—A 1-mile foot trail on Lake Dardanelle about 15 miles west of Dardanelle.
CEDAR CREEK SELF-GUIDING TRAIL—A 1.5-mile foot trail in Petit Jean State Park.
CEDAR FALLS TRAIL—A 2.2-mile trail in Petit Jean State Park.
DAM MOUNTAIN TRAIL—A 4.5-mile trail in Lake Catherine State Park, about 15 miles southeast of Hot Springs.
DEVIL'S DEN SELF-GUIDED TRAIL—A 1.5-mile trail in Devil's Den State Park, off U.S. 71 between Fayetteville and Fort Smith.
FALLS BRANCH TRAIL—A 2-mile trail in Lake Catherine State Park.
FOREST HILLS TRAIL—A 1.5-mile trail at Nimrod Lake about 9 miles east of Plainview.
HORSESHOE MOUNTAIN TRAIL—A 3.5-mile trail in Lake Catherine State Park.
ROBINSON POINT NATURE TRAIL—A 3-mile trail at Norfolk Lake, about 9 miles east of Mountain Home.
SEVEN HOLLOWS TRAIL—A 3.5-mile trail in Petit Jean State Park.
SUGAR LOAF MOUNTAIN NATURE TRAIL—A 1-mile trail at Greers Ferry Lake.
SUMMIT PARK SELF-GUIDED TRAIL—A 1.75-mile trail in Mount Nebo State Park, about 7 miles west of Dardanelle.
TOLLANTUSKY TRAIL—A 1.4-mile foot and wheelchair trail in Cadron Settlement Park, about 6 miles west of Conway.
YELLOW ROCK TRAIL—A 2-mile trail in Devil's Den State Park.

National Parks:
ARKANSAS POST NATIONAL MEMORIAL, Route 1, Box 16, Gillett 72055.

BUFFALO NATIONAL RIVER, P.O. Box 1173, Harrison 72601.
HOT SPRINGS NATIONAL PARK, P.O. Box 1860, Hot Springs National Park 71901.

State Trails:
DEPARTMENT OF PARKS AND TOURISM, Director, 149 State Capitol, Little Rock 72201.

Organizations:
ARKANSAS TRAILS COUNCIL, 1510 Broadway, Little Rock 72202.
SIERRA CLUB, Ozark Chapter, P.O. Box 12424, Olivette 63132.

CALIFORNIA

National Recreation Trails:
CALIFORNIA AQUEDUCT BIKEWAY—A 67-mile foot and bicycle trail from Bethany Reservoir to O'Neil Forebay in the San Luis Creek State Recreation Area.
EAST BAY SKYLINE TRAIL—A 14-mile trail between Redwood Regional Park and Anthony Chabot Park along the eastern skyline of the San Francisco Bay.
GABRIELINO TRAIL—A 28-mile trail in Angeles National Forest, near Pasadena.
JEDEDIAH SMITH TRAIL—A 26-mile trail in Sacramento.
KING RANGE TRAIL—Two segments of a 10-mile trail in the King Range National Conservation Area near Eureka.
LAKE TAHOE BICYCLE AND PEDESTRIAN WAY—A 5-mile trail along the northwestern shore of Lake Tahoe.
LOST LAKE NATURE TRAIL—A 2-mile trail in the Lost Lake Recreation Area in Fresno County.
PENITENCIA CREEK TRAIL—A 5.5-mile trail in San Jose.
PIEDRA BLANCA TRAIL—An 18.2-mile trail in the southern part of the Los Padres National Forest.
SANTA ANA RIVER TRAIL—A 10-mile trail along the banks of the Santa Ana River in Riverside County.
SOUTH YUBA TRAIL—A 6-mile trail along the north side of the South Yuba River Canyon near Nevada City.
TORO RIDING AND HIKING TRAILS—A 6-mile trail in Monterey County.
TWENTY MULE TEAM TRAIL—A 12-mile trail through Galileo Park at California City.
WESTERN STATES PIONEER EXPRESS TRAIL—A 50-mile trail from the Folsom Lake State Recreation Area to Tahoe National Forest.
YORK TRAIL—A 3.5-mile trail from Leona Park to Skyline Boulevard in Oakland.

National Parks:
CHANNEL ISLANDS NATIONAL MONUMENT, 1699 Anchors Way Dr., Ventura 93003.

DEATH VALLEY NATIONAL MONUMENT, Death Valley 92328.
GOLDEN GATE NATIONAL RECREATION AREA, Fort Mason, San Francisco 94123.
JOHN MUIR NATIONAL HISTORIC SITE, 4202 Alhambra Ave., Martinez 94553.
JOSHUA TREE NATIONAL MONUMENT, 74485 Palm Vista Dr., Twentynine Palms 92277.
KINGS CANYON NATIONAL PARK, Three Rivers 93271.
LASSEN VOLCANIC NATIONAL PARK, Mineral 96063.
LAVA BEDS NATIONAL MONUMENT, P.O. Box 867, Tulelake 96134.
MUIR WOODS NATIONAL MONUMENT, Mill Valley 94941.
PINNACLES NATIONAL MONUMENT, Paicines 95043.
POINT REYES NATIONAL SEASHORE, Point Reyes 94956.
REDWOOD NATIONAL PARK, Drawer N, Crescent City 95531.
SEQUOIA NATIONAL PARK, Three Rivers 93271.
WHISKEYTOWN-SHASTA-TRINITY NATIONAL RECREATION AREA, P.O. Box 188, Whiskeytown 96095.
YOSEMITE NATIONAL PARK, P.O. Box 577, Yosemite National Park 95389.

State Trails:
DEPARTMENT OF PARKS AND RECREATION, P.O. Box 2390, Sacramento 95811.

Organizations:
BERKELEY HIKING CLUB, P.O. Box 147, Berkeley 94701.
CALIFORNIA ALPINE CLUB, 562 Flood Building, 870 Market Street, San Francisco 94102.
DESOMOUNT CLUB, c/o W. J. Walker, 19511 Sunken Trail, Topange 90290.
SANTA BARBARA TRAILS COUNCIL, 4140 Marina Drive, Santa Barbara 93105.
SOUTHERN CALIFORNIA TRAIL RAMBLERS, Box 15582, Long Beach 90815.
TAMALPAIS CONSERVATION CLUB, 850 Pacific Building, San Francisco 94103.
VAGMARKEN CLUB, Box 643, Saugus 91350.
THE SIERRA CLUB CHAPTERS: REDWOOD, P.O. Box 466, Santa Rosa 95402.
ANGELES, 2410 W. Beverly Blvd, Suite 2, Los Angeles 90057.
KERN-KAWEAH, c/o Love, 5805 Dagget Ave., Bakersfield 93309.
LOMA PRIETA, 1176 Emerson St., Palo Alto 94301.
LOS PADRES, P.O. Box 30222, Santa Barbara 93105.
MOTHER LODE, Box 1335, Sacramento 95806.
SAN DIEGO, 1549 El Prado, San Diego 92101.
SAN FRANCISCO BAY, 6014 College Ave., Oakland 94618.
SAN GORGONIO, P.O. Box 1023, Riverside 92502.
SANTA LUCIA, Eco Slo, 985 Palm St., San Luis Obispo 93401.
TEHIPITE, P.O. Box 5396, Fresno 93755.
VENTANA, P.O. Box 5667, Carmel 93921.

COLORADO

National Recreation Trails:
CRAG CREST TRAIL—An 11-mile trail in Grand Mesa National Forest.
HIGHLINE CANAL TRAIL—A 35-mile trail along the Highline Canal in metropolitan Denver.
HIGHLINE CANAL TRAIL—A 13-mile trail along another segment of the canal in Aurora.
PLATTE RIVER GREENWAY TRAIL—A 7-mile trail from the northern city limits of Denver to Mississippi Avenue.

National Parks:
BLACK CANYON OF THE GUNNISON NATIONAL MONUMENT, P.O. Box 1648, Montrose 81401.
COLORADO NATIONAL MONUMENT, Fruita 81521.
CURECANTI NATIONAL RECREATION AREA, P.O. Box 1040, Gunnison 81230.
DINOSAUR NATIONAL MONUMENT, P.O. Box 210, Dinosaur 81610.
FLORISSANT FOSSIL BEDS NATIONAL MONUMENT, P.O. Box 185, Florissant 80816.
GREAT SAND DUNES NATIONAL MONUMENT, P.O. Box 60, Alamosa 81101.
HOVENWEEP NATIONAL MONUMENT, c/o Mesa Verde National Park.
MESA VERDE NATIONAL PARK, Mesa Verde National Park 81330.
ROCKY MOUNTAIN NATIONAL PARK, Estes Park 80517.
SHADOW MOUNTAIN NATIONAL RECREATION AREA, P.O. Box 100, Grand Lake 80447.

State Trails:
DIVISION OF PARKS AND OUTDOOR RECREATION, Department of Natural Resources, 1313 Sherman St., Room 618, Denver 80203.

Organizations:
SIERRA CLUB ROCKY MOUNTAIN CHAPTER, 1325 Delaware, Denver 80204.

CONNECTICUT

National Recreation Trails:
SLEEPING GIANT TRAILS—25 miles of trails in Sleeping Giant State Park near Hamden.

State Trails:
PARKS AND RECREATION UNIT, Department of Environmental Protection, 165 Capitol Avenue, Hartford 06115.

Organizations:
APPALACHIAN MOUNTAIN CLUB, Connecticut Chapter, c/o Richard A. Whitehouse, 1543 Manchester Road, Glastonbury 06033.
CONNECTICUT FOREST AND PARK ASSOCIATION, P.O. Box 389, 1010 Main Street, East Hartford 06108.

SIERRA CLUB, Connecticut Chapter, 60 Washington Street, Suite 611, Hartford 06106.

DELAWARE

State Parks and Forests:
DEPARTMENT OF NATURAL RESOURCES AND ENVIRONMENTAL CONTROL, Edward Tatnall Building, P.O. Box 1401, Dover 19901.

Organizations:
BRANDYWINE VALLEY OUTING CLUB, Box 7033, Wilmington 19803.
SIERRA CLUB, Potomac Chapter, c/o Clark, 402 Burgundy Road, Rockville, Md. 20850.
WILMINGTON TRAIL CLUB, 36 Augusta Drive, Newark 19711.

DISTRICT OF COLUMBIA

National Recreation Trails:
FORT CIRCLE PARKS TRAIL—Segments of trails totaling 19.5 miles through Rock Creek Park, Fort Dupont Park and Anacostia Park.

National Parks:
NATIONAL MALL, c/o National Park Service, 1100 Ohio Dr., S.W., Washington 20242.
ROCK CREEK PARK, 1800 Beach Dr. N.W., Washington 20015.
THEODORE ROOSEVELT ISLAND, c/o George Washington Memorial Parkway, Turkey Run Park, McLean, Va. 22101.

Organizations:
CAPITOL HIKING CLUB, c/o Jerry Williamson, 2002 Columbia Pike, Arlington, Va. 22204.
POTOMAC APPALACHIAN TRAIL CLUB, 1718 N Street, N.W., Washington 20036.
SIERRA CLUB, Potomac Chapter, c/o Clarke, 402 Burgundy Rd, Rockville, Md. 20850.
WANDERBIRDS HIKING CLUB, c/o Dan Risley, 2939 Van Ness St., Washington 20008.

FLORIDA

National Recreation Trails:
JACKSON TRAIL—A 21-mile trail in the Blackwater River State Forest, 20 miles northeast of Milton.
OCALA TRAIL—A 68-mile trail through the Ocala National Forest from State Highway 42 near the Clearwater Recreation Area to the Oklawaha River at Rodman Dam.
RICE CREEK TRAIL—A 3-mile trail in the Rice Creek Wildlife Sanctuary, 6 miles west of Palatka.

UNIVERSITY OF NORTH FLORIDA NATURE TRAILS—12 miles of trails on the University campus in Jacksonville.

National Parks:
BIG CYPRESS NATIONAL PRESERVE, P.O. Box 1247, Naples 33940.
CANAVERAL NATIONAL SEASHORE, P.O. Box 2583, Titusville 32780.
GULF ISLANDS NATIONAL SEASHORE, P.O. Box 100, Gulf Breeze 32561 (See also Mississippi).

State Trails:
DIVISION OF RECREATION AND PARKS, Department of Natural Resources, 601 Larson Building, Tallahasee 32304.

Organizations:
FLORIDA TRAIL ASSOCIATION, INC.,Box 13708, Gainesville 32605.
SIERRA CLUB, Florida Chapter, c/o Coleman, 203 Lake Pansy Dr., Winter Haven 33880.

GEORGIA

National Recreation Trails:
BARTRAM TRAIL—A 22-mile trail in two segments through the Chattahoochee-Oconee National Forest, near Clayton.
BUSH MOUNTAIN TRAIL—A .75-mile trail in a 20 acre natural area in southwest Atlanta.
STONE MOUNTAIN TRAIL—A 6.5-mile trail in Stone Mountain Memorial Park, near Atlanta.

National Parks:
CHICKAMAUGA AND CHATTANOOGA NATIONAL MILITARY PARK, P.O. Box 2126, Fort Oglethorpe 30742.
CUMBERLAND ISLAND NATIONAL SEASHORE, P.O. Box 806, St. Marys 31558.
KENNESAW MOUNTAIN NATIONAL BATTLEFIELD PARK, P.O. Box 1167, Marietta 30061.
OCMULGEE NATIONAL MONUMENT, 1207 Emery Highway, Macon 31201.

State Trails:
TRAILS PLANNER, Department of Natural Resources, 270 Washington St., S.W., Atlanta 30334.

Organizations:
GEORGIA APPALACHIAN TRAIL CLUB, c/o Ms. Margaret Drummond, 1351 Springdale Rd., Atlanta 30306.
SIERRA CLUB, Chattahoochee Chapter, Box 19574, Station N, Atlanta 30325.

HAWAII

National Parks:
CITY OF REFUGE NATIONAL HISTORICAL PARK, P.O. Box 128, Honaunau, Kona 96726.
WALEAKALA NATIONAL PARK, P.O. Box 537, Makawao 96768.
HAWAII VOLCANOES NATIONAL PARK, Hawaii National Park 96718.

State Trails:
HAWAII DEPARTMENT OF LAND AND NATURAL RESOURCES, 1151 Punchbowl St., Honolulu 96813.

Organizations:
HAWAII GEOGRAPHIC SOCIETY, P.O. Box 1698, Honolulu 96806.
HAWAII TRAIL AND MOUNTAIN CLUB, P.O. Box 2238, Honolulu 96804.
SIERRA CLUB, Hawaii Chapter, P.O. Box 22897, Honolulu 96822.

IDAHO

National Recreation Trails:
COEUR D'ALENE RIVER TRAIL—A 14-mile trail from Forest Road No. 208 to Marten Creek in the Coeur D'Alene National Forest in Shoshone County.
LAKESHORE TRAIL—A 7-mile trail that follows the west shore of Priest Lake from Granite Creek to Tule Bay in Bonner County in the Kaniksu National Forest.
MAJOR FENN NATURE TRAIL—A .6-mile trail with interpretative signs in Clearwater National Forest in Idaho County about 33 miles east of Kooskia.
I.P. SMITH EXPERIENCE LANE—A .33-mile braille trail on the banks of the Snake River in Idaho Falls.

National Parks:
CRATERS OF THE MOON NATIONAL MONUMENT, P.O. Box 29, Arco 83213.

State Trails:
STATE TRAILS COORDINATOR, Idaho Department of Parks and Recreation, 2263 Warm Springs Avenue, Boise 83720.

Organizations:
SIERRA CLUB, Northern Rockies Chapter, c/o Bond, P.O. Box 424, Spokane, WA 99210.

ILLINOIS

National Recreation Trails:
THE ILLINOIS PRAIRIE PATH—A 27.76-mile trail in the Chicago area that runs from Dunham Road, near Elgin, to Wheaton, from Wheaton to Elmhurst and from Wheaton to the west line of DuPage County, near

Aurora. Trail is located on part of an abandoned railroad right-of-way.

State Parks and other Trail Information:
A list of Illinois Trails, "Trails in Illinois Guide" is available from the
ILLINOIS DEPARTMENT OF CONSERVATION, 605 State Office Building, 400 South Spring Street, Springfield 62706.

Organizations:
AMERICAN YOUTH HOSTELS, 2948 N. Pine Grove, Chicago 60657.
SIERRA CLUB, Heart of Illinois Chapter, 2610 W. Greenbrier Lane, Peoria 61614.
ILLINOIS PRAIRIE PATH, INC., P.O. Box 1086, 616 Delles, Wheaton 60187.

INDIANA

National Recreation Trails:
CALUMET TRAIL — A 9.2-mile trail from Dune Acres to Michigan City.

National Parks:
INDIANA DUNES NATIONAL LAKESHORE, R. R. 2, Box 139-A, Chesterton 46304.

State Trails:
STREAMS AND TRAILS COORDINATOR, Division of Outdoor Recreation, Department of Natural Resources, 612 State Office Building, Indianapolis 46204.

Organizations:
INDIANAPOLIS HIKING CLUB, c/o Harrison Feldman, 4622 Evanston Avenue, Indianapolis.
SIERRA CLUB, Hossier Chapter, P. O. Box 40275, Indianapolis 46240.
WHITE RIVER HERITAGE AND CONSERVATION TRAILS, P. O. Box 1823, Anderson 46014.

IOWA

National Recreation Trails:
SAC AND FOX TRAIL — A 5-mile trail along Cedar River and Indian Creek in Cedar Rapids.

National Parks:
EFFIGY MOUNDS NATIONAL MONUMENT, P. O. Box K, McGregor 52157.

State Trails:
IOWA CONSERVATION COMMISSION, 300 4th St., Des Moines 50319.

Organizations:
IOWA MOUNTAINEERS, Box 163, 30 Prospect Place, Iowa City 52240.
SIERRA CLUB, Iowa Chapter, P. O. Box 171, Des Moines 50301.

KANSAS

National Recreation Trails:
INTERNATIONAL FOREST OF FRIENDSHIP TRAIL—A .56-mile trail in Atchison.
PERRY LAKE TRAIL—A 10-mile trail along Perry Lake, near Topeka.

State Trails:
KANSAS PARK AND RESOURCES AUTHORITY, 503 Kansas Avenue, P. O. Box 977, Topeka 66603.

Organizations:
JOHNSON COUNTY OUTDOOR SOCIETY, 6501 Antioch Rd., Shawnee Mission 66202.
KANSAS TRAILS COUNCIL, 1906 Jamaica, El Dorado 67042.
SIERRA CLUB, Kansas Chapter, 807 Sandusky Avenue, Kansas City 66101.

KENTUCKY

National Recreation Trails:
HILLMAN HERITAGE TRAIL—A 10-mile trail in the land between the Lakes in western Kentucky.

National Parks:
BIG SOUTH FORK NATIONAL RIVER AND RECREATION AREA (See Tennessee).
CUMBERLAND GAP NATIONAL HISTORICAL PARK, P. O. Box 840, Middlesboro 40965. (Also in Virginia and Tennessee.)
MAMMOTH CAVE NATIONAL PARK, Mammoth Cave 42259.

State Trails:
DIVISION OF PLANNING AND GRANTS, Department of Parks, Capital Plaza Tower, Frankfort 40601.

Organizations:
SIERRA CLUB, Cumberland Chapter, c/o Crouch, 1362 Bordeaux Dr., Lexington 40504.

LOUISIANA

National Recreation Trails:
RED RIVER TRAIL—A 5.25-mile trail along the Red River in the Shreveport area.
WILD AZALEA TRAIL—A 30-mile trail in the Kisatchie National Forest that begins at a roadside rest about 6 miles south of Alexandria.

State Trails:
LOUISIANA STATE PARKS AND RECREATION COMMISSION, P. O. Drawer 1111, Baton Rouge 70821.

Organizations:
SIERRA CLUB, Delta Chapter, 111 S. Hennessey St., New Orleans 70119.

MAINE

National Parks:
ACADIA NATIONAL PARK, Route 1, Box 1, Bar Harbor 04609.
APPALACHIAN NATIONAL SCENIC TRAIL.
SAINT CROIX ISLAND NATIONAL MONUMENT, c/o Acadia National Park. (See above).

State Trails:
DIRECTOR, BUREAU OF PARKS AND RECREATION, Maine Department of Conservation, State Office Building, Augusta 04333.

Organizations:
APPALACHIAN MOUNTAIN CLUB, Maine Chapter, c/o Peter Madeira, Box 326, Lee 04455.
BATES COLLEGE OUTING CLUB, Bates College, Box 389, Lewiston 04240.
BOWDOIN OUTING CLUB, Moulton Union Box, Brunswick 04011.
COLBY OUTING CLUB, Colby College, Box 913, Roberts Union, Waterville 04901.
FAIRFIELD TROOP #470, c/o Harold Hanson, RFD #1, Box 284-A, Fairfield 04937.
GOULD ACADEMY OUTING CLUB, Gould Academy, Bethel 04217.
MAINE APPALACHIAN TRAIL CLUB, Box 183-A, RFD #2, Bangor 04401.
MAINE OUTING CLUB, Memorial Union Building, University of Maine at Orono, Orono 04473.
MAINE TRAIL TROTTERS, RFD #3, Winthrop 04364.
SIERRA CLUB GROUP, c/o Gerald R. Ireland, River Road, RFD #2, Orrington 04474.

MARYLAND

National Recreation Trails:
TOUCH OF NATURE TRAIL—A .32-mile braille trail in Patapsco State Park.

National Parks:
ANTIETAM NATIONAL BATTLEFIELD SITE, Box 158, Sharpsburg 21782.
APPALACHIAN NATIONAL SCENIC TRAIL.
ASSATEAGUE ISLAND NATIONAL SEASHORE, Route 2, Box 294, Berlin 21811. (Also in Virginia).
CATOCTIN MOUNTAIN PARK, Thurmont 21788.
CHESAPEAKE AND OHIO CANAL NATIONAL HISTORICAL PARK, Box 158, Sharpsburg 21782. (Also in the District of Columbia and West Virginia.)
FORT WASHINGTON PARK, National Capital Parks-East, 5210 Indian Head Highway, Oxon Hill 20021.
GEORGE WASHINGTON MEMORIAL PARKWAY (See Virginia).

GREENBELT PARK, 6501 Greenbelt Rd., Greenbelt 20770.

State Trails:
MARYLAND PARK SERVICE, Department of Natural Resources, Tawes State Office Building, Annapolis 21401.

Organizations:
MARYLAND APPALACHIAN TRAIL CLUB, 202T Waverley Drive, Frederick 21701.
MOUNTAIN CLUB OF MARYLAND, 802 Kingston Rd., Baltimore 21212.
SIERRA CLUB, Potomac Chapter, 402 Burgundy Road, Rockville 20850.

MASSACHUSETTS

National Recreation Trails:
DR. PAUL DUDLEY WHITE BICYCLE PATH — A 6.5-mile bicycle and foot trail along the Charles River from the dam on the river to Watertown Square in the heart of metropolitan Boston.
FREEDOM TRAIL — This 2.5-mile trail links 19 historic sites in downtown Boston.
NORTHFIELD MOUNTAIN TRAIL SYSTEM — A 30-mile trail near the Northfield Mountain Pumped Storage Station on property owned by the Northeast Utilities Service.

National Parks:
APPALACHIAN NATIONAL SCENIC TRAIL.
CAPE COD NATIONAL SEASHORE, South Wellfleet 02663.
MINUTE MAN NATIONAL HISTORICAL PARK, P. O. Box 160, Concord 01742.

State Trails:
FOREST AND PARKS DIVISION, Department of Environmental Management, Executive Office of Environmental Affairs, 100 Cambridge St., Boston 02202.

Organizations:
APPALACHIAN MOUNTAIN CLUB (A.M.C.), 5 Joy St., Boston 02108.
A.M.C., BERKSHIRE CHAPTER, 17 State Street, Northampton 01060.
A.M.C., BOSTON CHAPTER, 71 Simpson Avenue, Somerville 02144.
A.M.C., SOUTHEAST MASSACHUSETTS CHAPTER, 159 Franklin St., Halifax 02338.
A.M.C., WORCESTER CHAPTER, 11 Candlewood St., Worcester 01602.

MICHIGAN

National Parks:
ISLE ROYALE NATIONAL PARK, 87 North Ripley St., Houghton 49931.
PICTURED ROCKS NATIONAL LAKESHORE, P. O. Box 40, Munising 49862.

SLEEPING BEAR DUNES NATIONAL LAKESHORE, 400½ Main Street, Frankfort 49635.

State Parks and Forests:
DEPARTMENT OF NATURAL RESOURCES, Information Services Center, Box 30028, Lansing 48909.

Organizations:
SIERRA CLUB, Mackinac Chapter, 590 Hollister Building, 106 West Allegan, Lansing 48933.
SIERRA CLUB, Mackinac Chapter, Detroit Group, 37241 Eisenhower #543, Farmington Hills 48024.

MINNESOTA

National Recreation Trails:
CONGDON CREEK PARK TRAIL—A .75-mile self-guided nature trail in Duluth.
LESTER PARK NATURE TRAIL—A .8-mile trail along the Lester River in Duluth.

National Parks:
GRAND PORTAGE NATIONAL MONUMENT, P. O. Box 666, Grand Marais 55604.
LOWER ST. CROIX NATIONAL SCENIC RIVER (See Wisconsin).
ST. CROIX NATIONAL SCENIC RIVER (See Wisconsin).
VOYAGEURS NATIONAL PARK, P. O. Drawer 50, International Falls 56649.

State Trails:
DIRECTOR, DIVISION OF PARKS AND RECREATION, Department of Natural Resources, Centennial Office Building, St. Paul 55155.

Organizations:
SIERRA CLUB, North Star Chapter, 812 Midland Bank Building, Minneapolis 55401.

MISSISSIPPI

National Recreation Trails:
BURNSIDE PARK NATURE TRAIL—A 2-mile trail in Burnside Lake Water Park, 5 miles north of Philadelphia.
RIVERSIDE PARK NATURE TRAIL—A 2-mile trail in the Pearl River Floodplain in Jackson.
SHOCKALOE TRAIL—A 23-mile loop trail in the Bienville National Forest, within 50 miles of Jackson and Meridian.

National Parks:
BRICES CROSS ROADS NATIONAL BATTLEFIELD SITE, c/o Natchez Trace Parkway, R.R. 1, NT-143, Tupelo 38801.

GULF ISLANDS NATIONAL SEASHORE, P. O. Box T, Ocean Springs 39564. (See also Florida.)
NATCHEZ TRACE PARKWAY, R.R. 1, NT-143 Tupelo 38801. (Also in Alabama and Tennessee.)
TUPELO NATIONAL BATTLEFIELD, c/o Natchez Trace Parkway. (See above.)

State Trails:
MISSISSIPPI PARK COMMISSION, 717 Robert E. Lee Building, Jackson 39201.

Organizations:
SIERRA CLUB, Mississippi Chapter, Box 4335, Jackson 39216.

MISSOURI

National Recreation Trails:
ELEPHANT ROCKS BRAILLE TRAIL—A 1-mile trail in Elephant Rocks State Park.

National Parks:
GEORGE WASHINGTON CARVER NATIONAL MONUMENT, P. O. Box 38, Diamond 64840.
OZARK NATIONAL SCENIC RIVERWAYS, Box 490, Van Buren 63965.
WILSON'S CREEK NATIONAL BATTLEFIELD, Route 2, P. O. Box 75, Republic 65738.

State Trails:
MISSOURI DEPARTMENT OF NATURAL RESOURCES, P. O. Box 176, Jefferson City 65101.

Organizations:
SIERRA CLUB, Ozark Chapter, Box 12424, Olivette 63132.

MONTANA

National Recreation Trails:
BLUE MOUNTAIN EQUESTRIAN AND HIKING TRAIL—A 6-mile trail in the Lolo National Forest, near Missoula.
BLUE MOUNTAIN NATURE TRAIL—A .25-mile nature trail in Lolo National Forest, near Missoula.
PALISADE FALLS TRAIL—A .33-mile braille trail in Gallatin National Forest.

National Parks:
BIGHORN CANYON NATIONAL RECREATION AREA, P. O. Box 458, Fort Smith 59035.
CUSTER BATTLEFIELD NATIONAL MONUMENT, P. O. Box 39, Crow Agency 59022.

GLACIER NATIONAL PARK, West Glacier 59936.
GRANT-KOHRS RANCH NATIONAL HISTORIC SITE, P. O. Box 799, Deer Lodge 59722.
YELLOWSTONE NATIONAL PARK (See Wyoming).

State Trails:
RECREATION AND PARKS DIVISION, Montana Department of Fish and Game, Mitchell Building, 1420 E. Sixth Ave., Helena 59601.

Organizations:
SIERRA CLUB, Northern Rockies Chapter, c/o Bond, Box 424, Spokane, Wa. 99210.

NEBRASKA

National Recreation Trails:
FONTENELLE FOREST TRAIL—A 3.9-mile trail along the Missouri River in the Omaha-Council Bluffs area. Connects with a network of trails in the 1,200 acre Fontenelle Forest.
WILDERNESS PARK HIKING TRAIL—A 13-mile trail from the southwest edge of Lincoln at S.W, 1st Street and W. Van Dorn to Saltillo Road and S. 27th Street.

National Parks:
AGATE FOSSIL BEDS NATIONAL MONUMENT, P. O. Box 427, Gering 69341.
HOMESTEAD NATIONAL MONUMENT OF AMERICA, Route 3, Beatrice 68310.
SCOTTS BLUFF NATIONAL MONUMENT, P. O. Box 427, Gering 69341.

State Trails:
NEBRASKA GAME AND PARKS COMMISSION, P. O. Box 30370, Lincoln 68503.

Organizations:
SIERRA CLUB, Nebraska Chapter, c/o Warrick, Meadow Grove 68752.

NEVADA

National Recreation Trails:
GRIMES POINT PETROGLYPH TRAIL—A .37-mile trail in Churchhill County about 10 miles southeast of Fallon.

National Parks:
DEATH VALLEY NATIONAL MONUMENT (See California).
LAKE MEAD NATIONAL RECREATION AREA, 601 Nevada Hwy., Boulder City 89005.
LEHMAN CAVES NATIONAL MONUMENT, Baker 89311.

State Trails:
NEVADA DIVISION OF STATE PARKS, Room 221, Nye Building, 201 S. Fall Street, Capitol Complex, Carson City 89710.

Organizations:
SIERRA CLUB, Toiyabe Chapter, P. O. Box 8096, University Station, Reno 89507.

NEW HAMPSHIRE

National Parks:
APPALACHIAN NATIONAL SCENIC TRAIL.

State Trails:
NEW HAMPSHIRE DEPARTMENT OF RESOURCES AND ECONOMIC DEVELOP-MENT, Division of Parks and Recreation, P. O. Box 856, Concord 03301.

Organizations:
APPALACHIAN MOUNTAIN CLUB, New Hampshire Chapter, c/o Marjorie Kneeland, RFD #1, Concord 03301.
DARTMOUTH OUTING CLUB, P. O. Box 9, Hanover 03755.
SIERRA CLUB, New England Chapter, 3 Joy Street, Boston 02108.

NEW JERSEY

National Recreation Trails:
PALISADES LOG PATH—This 11-mile trail offers a spectacular view of New York City and the Hudson River Valley. It begins at the New Jersey Side of the George Washington Bridge and climbs to the top of the Palisade cliffs.
PALISADES SHORE TRAIL—An 11.25-mile trail that runs along the shore of the Hudson River at the foot of the Palisades and passes under the George Washington Bridge.

National Parks:
MORRISTOWN NATIONAL HISTORICAL PARK, P. O. Box 1136R, Morristown 07960.

State Trails:
BUREAU OF PARKS, Division of Parks and Forestry, Department of Environmental Protection, P. O. Box 1420, Trenton 08625.

Organizations:
ADIRONDACK MOUNTAIN CLUB, North Jersey Chapter, P. O. Box 185, Ridgewood 07451.
BATONA HIKING CLUB, 301 Broadway, Westville 08093.
NEW YORK-NEW JERSEY TRAIL CONFERENCE, INC., 15 East 40th Street, New York, NY 10016.
SHORT HILLS OUTING CLUB, Box 1127, Union 07083.
SIERRA CLUB, New Jersey Chapter, 360 Nassau Street, Princeton 08540.
WEST JERSEY HIKING CLUB, 34 Laurie Road, Landing 07850.
WOODLAND TRAIL WALKERS, 34 Hillcrest Drive, Wayne 07471.

NEW MEXICO

National Recreation Trails:
ORGAN MOUNTAIN TRAILS—Two trail segments totaling 8.7 miles that lead from the Acquirre Spring Recreation Area into the area of Organ Mountain in southern New Mexico. The trail is about an hour's drive north of El Paso, Texas.
PASEO DEL BOSQUE BICYCLE TRAIL—A 5-mile bicycle and foot trail along the east bank of the Rio Grande River in the center of Albuquerque.

National Parks:
BANDELIER NATIONAL MONUMENT, Los Alamos 87544.
CAPULIN MOUNTAIN NATIONAL MONUMENT, Capulin 88414.
CARLSBAD CAVERNS NATIONAL PARK, 3225 National Parks Highway, Carlsbad 88220.
CHACO CANYON NATIONAL MONUMENT, Star Route 4, Box 6500, Bloomfield 87413.
EL MORRO NATIONAL MONUMENT, Ramah 87321.
WHITE SANDS NATIONAL MONUMENT, P. O. Box 458, Alamogordo 88310.

State Trails:
STATE OF NEW MEXICO, Planning and Management Bureau, Natural Resources Department, Administrative Services Division, Villagra Building, Santa Fe 87503.

Organizations:
NEW MEXICO MOUNTAIN CLUB, 10212 Chapala Place, N.E., Albuquerque 87111.
SIERRA CLUB, Rio Grande Chapter, 338 E. De Vargas, Santa Fe 87501.

NEW YORK

CRANDALL PARK INTERNATIONAL SKI TRAILS—A 2.2-mile loop system of trails for ski, foot and bicycle travel that include a .5-mile interpretative nature trail. The walks are located in a 49-acre forest in the Glens Falls area.
HARRIMAN LONG PATH—A 16-mile trail in Harriman State Park about 20 miles northwest of New York City. The trail winds along ridge tops and crosses the Appalachian National Scenic Trail.

National Parks:
FIRE ISLAND NATIONAL SEASHORE, 120 Laurel St., Patchogue 11772.
SARATOGA NATIONAL HISTORIC PARK, R.D. 1, Box 113-C, Stillwater 12170.

State Trails:
NEW YORK STATE PARKS AND RECREATION, Agency Building 1, Empire

State Plaza, Albany 12238; or New York State Department of Environmental Conservation, Room 602, Albany 12233.

Organizations: *

ADIRONDACK FORTY-SIXERS, Morrisonville 12962.

ADIRONDACK MOUNTAIN CLUB, INC. (Headquarters), 172 Ridge Street, Glens Falls 12801.

ADIRONDACK MOUNTAIN CLUB, Long Island Chapter, c/o Herb Coles, 101-17 97th St., Jamaica 11416.

ADIRONDACK MOUNTAIN CLUB, Knickerbocker Chapter, 957 Park Avenue, New York 10028.

ADIRONDACK MOUNTAIN CLUB, Mid-Hudson Chapter, c/o Mary Forman, 72 Hudson View Drive, Beacon 12508.

ADIRONDACK MOUNTAIN CLUB, New York Chapter, c/o Edward Cymes, 54 Orange Street, Brooklyn 11201.

ADIRONDACK TRAIL IMPROVEMENT SOCIETY, INC., Box 64, Keene Valley 12943.

AMERICAN YOUTH HOSTELS, Metropolitan New York Council, 132 Spring Street, New York 10012.

APPALACHIAN MOUNTAIN CLUB, New York Chapter, c/o Julianna Irelan, 26 Crest Drive, Cresskill, NJ 07626.

ARDSLEY OUTING CLUB, c/o Bob Sillman, 18 Larchmont St., Ardsley 10502.

CATSKILL 3500 CLUB, 20 Cedar Lane, Cornwall 12518.

CHALET CLUB, 135 East 55th Street, New York.

COLLEGE ALUMNI HIKING CLUB, 290 9th Ave., New York 10001.

FRIENDS OF CENTRAL PARK, 799 Broadway, New York.

GREEN MOUNTAIN CLUB, New York Section, 1522 W. 5th Street, Brooklyn 11204.

NASSAU HIKING AND OUTDOOR CLUB, 3 Rosedale Road, Valley Stream 11581.

NEW YORK HIKING CLUB, 404 E. 18th St., Brooklyn 11226.

NEW YORK-NEW JERSEY TRAIL CONFERENCE, 15 East 40th Street, New York 10016.

NEW YORK RAMBLERS, 508 East 78th Street, New York 10021.

NEW YORK UNIVERSITY OUTDOOR CLUB, Box 1, 566 LaGuardia Pl., New York 10012.

SIERRA CLUB, Atlantic Chapter, 800 Second Ave., New York 10017.

OPEN ROAD CLUB, Brooklyn College, Brooklyn 11210.

TORREY BOTANICAL CLUB, The New York Botanical Garden, Bronx 10458.

TRAMP AND TRAIL CLUB OF NEW YORK, 229 E. 12th St., New York 10003.

WESTCHESTER TRAILS ASSOCIATION, 632 Warburton Ave., Apt. 6K, Yonkers 10701.

---

*Information on many clubs in the New York area was provided by Walking News, Inc., P. O. Box 352, New York, NY 10013.

WOODLAND TRAIL WALKERS, 350 E. 65th St., New York 10021.

NORTH CAROLINA

National Recreation Trails:
BILTMORE CAMPUS TRAIL—A 1-mile trail that begins at the Cradle of Forestry Visitor Center on U.S. 276 about 30 miles from Asheville in the Pisgah National Forest.
BOB'S CREEK TRAIL—An 8-mile loop trail containing a smaller 3.5-mile loop that runs through a 500-acre pocket wilderness area in McDowell County.
HISTORIC EDENTON TRAIL.—A 1.9-mile trail through historic sections of Edenton.

National Parks:
BLUE RIDGE PARKWAY, 700 Northwestern Bank Building, Asheville 28801. (Also in Virginia.)
CAPE LOOKOUT NATIONAL SEASHORE, P.O. Box 690, Beaufort 28516.
CARL SANDBURG HOME NATIONAL HISTORIC SITE, P.O. Box 395, Flat Rock 28731.
GREAT SMOKY MOUNTAINS NATIONAL PARK (See Tennessee).

State Trails:
NORTH CAROLINA DIVISION OF TRAVEL AND TOURISM, Department of Commerce, 430 North Salisbury Street, Raleigh 27611.

Organizations:
CAROLINA MOUNTAIN CLUB, P.O. Box 68, Asheville 28802.
NANTAHALA HIKING CLUB, Route 1, Box 162, Franklin 28734.
PIEDMONT A.T. HIKERS, 307 S. Chapman, Greensboro 27403.
SIERRA CLUB, Joseph LeConte Chapter, c/o Lieberman, 7111 Carosan Lane, Charlotte 28211.

NORTH DAKOTA

National Recreation Trails:
OLD OAK TRAIL—A 3-mile nature trail named for a 200-year-old oak tree along the route. The trail is 13 miles north of Bottineau in the Lake Metigoshe State Park.

National Parks:
THEODORE ROOSEVELT NATIONAL MEMORIAL PARK, Medora 58645.

State Trails:
NORTH DAKOTA PARKS AND RECREATION DEPARTMENT, Fort Lincoln State Park, Box 139, R.R. 2, Mandan 58554.

Organizations:
SIERRA CLUB, Dacotah Chapter, P.O. Box 1624, Rapid City 57701.

OHIO

National Recreation Trails:
CUYAHOGA VALLEY TOWPATH—A 2.8-mile trail between the Brecksville Reservation and the Bedford Reservation in the Cleveland area.
HARRIET L. KEELER WOODLAND TRAIL—A .5-mile braille trail in the Brecksville Reservation in the Cleveland area.
ROCKY RIVER BICYCLE TRAIL—A 5-mile trail through the Rocky River Reservation in the Cleveland metropolitan area.

National Parks:
CUYAHOGA VALLEY NATIONAL RECREATION AREA, P.O. Box 158, Peninsula 44264.

State Trails:
OHIO DEPARTMENT OF NATURAL RESOURCES, Division of Parks and Recreation, Fountain Square, Columbus 43224.

Organizations:
AMERICAN YOUTH HOSTELS, Columbus Council, P.O. Box 23111, Columbus 43223.
BUCKEYE TRAIL ASSOCIATION, INC., P.O. Box 254, Worthington 43085.
CENTRAL OHIO HIKING CLUB, Central YMCA, 40 Long St., Columbus 43215.
SIERRA CLUB, Ohio Chapter, c/o Rice, 1325 Westminster Dr., Cincinnati 45229.

OKLAHOMA

National Recreation Trails:
INDIAN NATIONS TRAIL—A 20-mile trail through dense forests that begins in the southern part of Beavers Bend State Park in southeastern Oklahoma and extends along the banks of Broken Bow Reservoir.
PATHFINDER PARKWAY—A 4.7-mile trail along the Caney River from Johnstone Park to Hillcrest Heights in the Bartlesville area.
RED STICK TRAIL—A 1.5-mile trail in the Dr. J.T. Martin Park Nature Center in the Oklahoma City area.

National Parks:
CHICKASAW NATIONAL RECREATION AREA, P.O. Box 201, Sulphur 73086.

State Trails:
OKLAHOMA TOURISM AND RECREATION DEPARTMENT, Division of State Parks, 500 Will Rogers Building, Oklahoma City 73105.

Organizations:
OZARK SOCIETY, 2811 East 22nd, Tulsa 74114.
SIERRA CLUB, Oklahoma Chapter, c/o Wesner, 616 Tulsa, Norman 73071.

OREGON

National Recreation Trails:
BEAR CREEK BIKEWAY AND NATURE TRAIL—A 3.4-mile paved trail along Bear Creek in Medford.
McKENZIE RIVER TRAIL—A 13-mile trail that follows the scenic McKenzie River in the Willamette National Forest.
TILLAMOOK HEAD TRAIL—A 6-mile trail between Seaside and Cannon Beach along the northern Oregon coast in Ecola State Park.
WILDWOOD TRAIL—A 14-mile trail through 5,000-acre Forest Park in the Portland area.
WILLAMETTE RIVER TRAIL—A 1.84-mile trail on the southwest bank of the Willamette River from Briarcliff Street to the Ferry Street Bridge in Eugene.

National Parks:
CRATER LAKE NATIONAL PARK, P.O. Box 7, Crater Lake 97604.
JOHN DAY FOSSIL BEDS NATIONAL MONUMENT, 420 W. Main St., John Day 97845.
OREGON CAVES NATIONAL MONUMENT, P.O. Box 649, Cave Junction 97523.

State Trails:
COORDINATOR, RECREATION TRAILS SYSTEM, State Parks and Recreation Branch, Oregon Department of Transportation, 525 Trade St., S.E., Salem 97310.

Organizations:
THE ANGORAS, P.O. Box 12, Astoria 97103.
CHEMEKETANS, 360½ State Street, Salem 97301.
DESERT TRAIL ASSOCIATION, P.O. Box 589, Burns 97720.
HOOD RIVER CRAG RATS, Route 1, Box 84, Hood River 97031.
MAZAMAS, 909 N.W. Nineteenth Ave., Portland 97209.
OBSIDIANS, INC., P.O. Box 322, Eugene 97401.
SANTIAM ALPINE CLUB, P.O. Box 1041, Salem 97308.
SIERRA CLUB, Oregon Chapter, c/o Mintkeski, 6815 S.E. 31st St., Portland 97202.
TRAILS CLUB OF OREGON, P.O. 1243, Portland 97207.

PENNSYLVANIA

National Recreation Trails:
FAIRMOUNT PARK BIKE PATH—An 8.5-mile foot and bicycle path in Fairmount Park in Philadelphia. There are also 5.5 miles of connecting trails in the park, one of the oldest and largest urban parks in the country, which in addition to the natural setting offers walkers a chance to tour several country estates and an internationally famous art museum.
FLOUR SAK BATTLE BICENTENNIAL TRAIL—A 1-mile braille trail through

the Bushy Run Battlefield State Park in the Jeannette area.

HARRISBURG RIVERFRONT BIKEWAY—A 4-mile trail from Division Street to the South Bridge along the Susuquehanna River in Harrisburg. The trail is part of the 18-mile-long Harrisburg Bikeway.

KELLYS RUN-PINNACLE TRAIL SYSTEM—A 4.75-mile system of four interconnecting loop trails in the Susquehanna River Valley near Holtwood.

UNION CANAL WALKING AND BICYCLE TRAIL—This trail is a 2.3-mile portion of the Union Canal Towpath in Reading.

WISSAHICKON TRAIL—A 5.4-mile nature trail in the Wissahickon Valley in the Philadelphia area.

National Parks:

ALLEGHENY PORTAGE RAILROAD NATIONAL HISTORIC SITE, P.O. Box 247, Cresson 16630.

APPALACHIAN NATIONAL SCENIC TRAIL.

DELAWARE WATER GAP NATIONAL RECREATION AREA, Bushkill 18324 (Also in New Jersey).

FORT NECESSITY NATIONAL BATTLEFIELD, The National Pike, Farmington 15437.

GETTYSBURG NATIONAL MILITARY PARK, Gettysburg 17235.

HOPEWELL VILLAGE NATIONAL HISTORIC SITE, R.D. 1, Box 345, Elverson 19520.

VALLEY FORGE NATIONAL HISTORICAL PARK, VALLEY FORGE 19481.

State Trails:

PENNSYLVANIA DEPARTMENT OF ENVIRONMENTAL RESOURCES, Office of Public Information, P.O. Box 1467, Harrisburg 17120.

Organizations:

ALLENTOWN HIKING CLUB, 124 W. 16th St., Allentown 18102.

ALPINE CLUB OF WILLIAMSPORT, PA., P.O. Box 501, Williamsport 17701.

APPALACHIAN MOUNTAIN CLUB, Delaware Chapter, c/o George F. Heckler, 115 Sourwood Drive, Hatboro 19040.

BLUE MOUNTAIN EAGLE CLIMBING CLUB AND WILDERNESS PARK ASSOCIATION, INC., P.O. Box 3523, Reading 19605.

HORSE-SHOE TRAIL CLUB, INC., c/o Mrs. Robert L. Chalfant, 1325 Jericho Road, Abington 19001.

KEYSTONE TRAILS ASSOCIATION, R.D. 3, Box 261, Cogan Station 17728.

LEBANON VALLEY HIKING CLUB, c/o Emmett V. Mariano, R.D. 1, Bethel 19507.

PHILADELPHIA TRAIL CLUB, 1522 Huntington Road, Abington 19001.

PENN STATE OUTING CLUB, Student Intramural Building, Pennsylvania State University, University Park 16802.

SIERRA CLUB, Pennsylvania Chapter, P.O. Box 135, Cogan Station 17728.

SPRINGFIELD TRAIL CLUB, c/o Ms. Wilma Flaig, P.O. Box 441, Media 19063.

SUSUQUEHANNA APPALACHIAN TRAIL CLUB, 87 Greenwood Circle, Wormlesbury 17043.

WARRIOR TRAIL ASSOCIATION OF GREENE COUNTY, PENNSYLVANIA, INC., R.D. 2, Waynesburg 15370.
YORK HIKING CLUB, 347 S. George St., York 17403.

RHODE ISLAND

National Recreation Trails:
CLIFF WALK—A 3.5-mile trail along the shoreline of the Atlantic Ocean in the historic city of Newport.

State Trails:
STATE OF RHODE ISLAND AND PROVIDENCE PLANTATIONS, Department of Natural. Resources, Division of Planning and Development, 83 Park Street, Providence 02903.

Organizations:
APPALACHIAN MOUNTAIN CLUB, Narragansett Chapter, c/o Bettey Cooley, 78 Indian Road, East Providence 02915.
HIKERS CLUB OF RHODE ISLAND, c/o Dr. John Mulleedy, 709 Hope St., Providence 02906.
SIERRA CLUB, New England Chapter, 3 Joy St., Boston, MA 02108.

SOUTH CAROLINA

National Recreation Trails:
EDISTO NATURE TRAIL—A 1.5-mile self-guided nature trail just off U.S. 17 in the Jacksonboro area.
TABLE ROCK TRAIL—A rugged 9-mile loop trail that runs along mountain ridges in Table Rock State Park in Pickens County.

National Parks:
KINGS MOUNTAIN NATIONAL MILITARY PARK, P.O. Box 31, Kings Mountain 28086.
NINETY SIX NATIONAL HISTORIC SITE, P.O. 357, Ninety Six 29666.

State Trails:
CHIEF NATURALIST, SOUTH CAROLINA DEPARTMENT OF PARKS, Recreation and Tourism, Division of State Parks, Edgar Brown Building, Columbia 29201.

Organizations:
PINE ISLAND CAMP, P.O. Box 10128, Greenville 29603.
SIERRA CLUB, South Carolina Chapter, P.O. Box 12112, Columbia 29211.

SOUTH DAKOTA

National Recreation Trails:
BEAR BUTTE TRAIL—A 3.5-mile trail in Bear Butte State Park near Sturgis that runs from Indian ceremonial grounds to the top of Bear Butte, a registered National Natural Landmark.

SUNDAY GULCH TRAIL—A 4-mile loop trail along the shore of Sylvan Lake in Custer State Park near Rapid City.

TRAIL OF SPIRITS—A .5-mile self-guided trail in the Seiche Hollow State Park near Aberdeen that runs past several colored springs, rich in Indian lore.

WOODLAND TRAIL—A 1.33-mile trail across glacier-altered terrain in Newton Hills State Park about 20 miles south of Sioux Falls.

National Parks:
BADLANDS NATIONAL MONUMENT, P.O. Box 6, Interior 57750.

State Trails:
SOUTH DAKOTA DEPARTMENT OF GAME, FISH AND PARKS, Division of Parks and Recreation, Anderson Building, Pierre 57501.

Organizations:
THE SIERRA CLUB, Dacotah Chapter, P.O. Box 1624, Rapid City 57701.

TENNESSEE

National Recreation Trails:
BEARWALLER GAP HIKING TRAIL—A 6-mile trail along the Cordell Hull Lake on the Cumberland River about 8 miles north of Carthage.

BLUE BEAVER TRAIL—A 10.5-mile trail that begins at the base of Lookout Mountain in the Chattanooga area and climbs to Park Point.

FORT HENRY HIKING TRAILS—A 26-mile system of trails in the Land Between the Lakes about 80 miles northwest of Nashville. The trails generally follow the route taken by General Grant's troops from Fort Henry to Fort Donelson during the Civil War.

GREAT SMOKY MOUNTAINS NATIONAL PARK, Gatlinburg 37738 (Also in North Carolina).

HONEY CREEK TRAIL—A 5-mile loop trail along the scenic gorges of two streams in a 109-acre pocket wilderness in Scott County.

HONEYSUCKLE TRAIL—A .5-mile braille trail in T.O. Fuller State Park near Memphis.

LADY FINGER BLUFF TRAIL—A 2.7-mile trail on land abutting Kentucky Lake near Linden in Perry County about 100 miles southwest of Nashville.

LAUREL-SNOW TRAIL—An 8-mile trail in the 710-acre Laurel-Snow Pocket Wilderness in the Dayton area.

NORTH RIDGE TRAIL—A 7.5-mile trail along Black Oak Ridge on the northern boundary of Oak Ridge.

OLD HICKORY TRAIL—A 1.66-mile trail below the Old Hickory Dam in the Nashville metropolitan area.

PINEY RIVER TRAIL—A 10-mile trail along the Piney River between the Piney River Picnic Area and the Newby Branch Forest Camp near Spring City.

RED LEAVES OVERNIGHT TRAIL—A 30-mile trail in the 44,000-acre Natchez Trace State Resort Park and Forest midway between Memphis and Nashville.

RIVER BLUFF TRAIL—A 3.1-mile trail on the Norris Dam reservation that overlooks the Clinch River.

THIRD CREEK BICYCLE TRAIL—A foot and bicycle trail that runs 2.3 miles from the rear of the University of Tennessee housing complex to the intersection of Painter Ave. and Concord St. in Knoxville.

VIRGIN FALLS TRAIL—An 8-mile trail that begins about eight miles south of DeRossett in White County.

SHILOH NATIONAL MILITARY PARK, Shiloh 38376.

STONES RIVER NATIONAL BATTLEFIELD, Route 2, Old Nashville Highway, Murfreesboro 37130.

National Parks:
FORT DONELSON NATIONAL MILITARY PARK, P.O. Box F, Dover 37058.

State Trails:
TRAILS PROJECT ADMINISTRATOR, Tennessee Department of Conservation, 2611 West End Ave., Nashville 37203.

Organizations:
BOWATER SOUTHERN PAPER CORPORATION, Public Relations Department, Calhoun 37309.

THE CUMBERLANDS CLUB, c/o Mrs. Eleonore Williams, 1701 Crestwood Dr., Chattanooga 37405.

SIERRA CLUB, Tennessee Chapter, c/o Kelly, 107 Vista Dr., Chattanooga 37411.

SMOKY MOUNTAINS HIKING CLUB, P.O. Box 1454, Knoxville 37901.

TENNESSEE EASTMAN RECREATION CLUB, Eastman Employee Center, Kingsport 37662.

TENNESSEE TRAILS ASSOCIATION, INC., P.O. Box 4913, Chattanooga 37405.

TRI-STATES HIKING CLUB, c/o Bill Stutz, 1705 McCallie Ave., Chattanooga 37404.

TEXAS

National Recreation Trails:
CARGILL LONG PARK TRAIL—A 2.5-mile trail along an abandoned railroad right-of-way in Longview. The trail is lighted for use at night.

GREER ISLAND NATURE TRAIL—A 3-mile trail on a 32-acre island in Lake Worth within the city of Fort Worth.

SAN ANTONIO RIVER TRAIL—This 8-mile trail begins about three miles south of downtown San Antonio and runs along the San Antonio River corridor to the Espada Mission.

TOWN LAKE WALK AND BIKEWAY—A 9.75-mile trail that follows the bed of the Colorado River through the center of Austin.

National Parks:
AMISTAD NATIONAL RECREATION AREA, P.O. Box 1463, Del Rio 78840.
BIG BEND NATIONAL PARK, Big Bend National Park 79834.
BIG THICKET NATIONAL PRESERVE, P.O. Box 7408, Beaumont 77706.
FORT DAVIS NATIONAL HISTORIC SITE, P.O. Box 1456, Fort Davis 79734.
GUADALUPE MOUNTAINS NATIONAL PARK, 3225 National Parks Highway, Carlsbad, NM 82220.
PADRE ISLAND NATIONAL SEASHORE, 9405 S. Padre Island Dr., Corpus Christi 78418.

State Trails:
TEXAS PARKS AND WILDLIFE DEPARTMENT, 4200 Smith School Road, Austin 78744.

Organizations:
SIERRA CLUB, Lone Star Chapter, P.O. Box 1931, Austin 78767.

UTAH

National Parks:
ARCHES NATIONAL PARK, 446 S. Main St., Moab 84532.
BRYCE CANYON NATIONAL PARK, Bryce Canyon 84717.
CANYONLANDS NATIONAL PARK, 446 S. Main St., Moab 84532.
CAPITOL REEF NATIONAL PARK, Torrey 84775.
CEDAR BREAKS NATIONAL MONUMENT, P.O. Box 749, Cedar City 84720.
GLEN CANYON NATIONAL RECREATION AREA, P.O. Box 1507, Page AZ 86040.
NATURAL BRIDGES NATIONAL MONUMENT, c/o Canyonlands National Park.
RAINBOW BRIDGE NATIONAL MONUMENT, c/o Glen Canyon National Recreation Area.
TIMPANOGOS CAVE NATIONAL MONUMENT, R.R. 2, Box 200, American Fork 84003.
ZION NATIONAL PARK, Springdale 84767.

State Trails:
STATE OF UTAH, Department of Development Services, Utah Travel Council, Council Hall, Capitol Hill, Salt Lake City 84114.

Organizations:
BYU ALPINE CLUB, Brigham Young University, Provo.
SIERRA CLUB, Utah Chapter, Utah Environmental Center, P.O. Box 8393, Salt Lake City 84108.
UTE ALPINE CLUB, University of Utah, Salt Lake City 84115.
WASATCH MOUNTAIN CLUB, 425 South 900 West, Salt Lake City 84104.

VERMONT

National Parks:
APPALACHIAN NATIONAL SCENIC TRAIL.

State Trails:
THE LONG TRAIL system runs some 435 miles along ridges of the Green
Mountains from the Massachusetts line to the Canadian border. For other
information on state trails: Vermont Department of Forests, Parks and
Recreation, Agency of Environmental Conservation, 5 Court St.,
Montpelier 05602.

Organizations:
GREEN MOUNTAIN CLUB, INC., P.O. Box 889, Montpelier 05602 (Founder
and protector of the Long Trail).
SIERRA CLUB, New England Chapter, 3 Joy St., Boston 02108.

VIRGINIA

National Recreation Trails:
CASCADES TRAIL. A 4-mile trail that follows the banks of Little Stoney
Creek and an old logging road through the Jefferson National Forest near
Pearisburg.
SEASHORE STATE PARK NATURAL AREA TRAILS SYSTEM—A 23-mile system
of trails within the Seashore State Park at Virginia Beach.

National Parks:
APPALACHIAN NATIONAL SCENIC TRAIL.
ASSATEAGUE ISLAND NATIONAL SEASHORE (See Maryland).
BLUE RIDGE PARKWAY (See North Carolina).
BOOKER T. WASHINGTON NATIONAL MONUMENT, Route 1, Box 195, Hardy
24101.
COLONIAL NATIONAL HISTORICAL PARK, P.O. Box 210, Yorktown 23690.
FREDERICKSBURG NATIONAL MILITARY PARK, P.O. Box 679, Fred-
ericksburg 22401.
GEORGE WASHINGTON BIRTHPLACE NATIONAL MONUMENT, Washington's
Birthplace 22575.
GEORGE WASHINGTON MEMORIAL PARKWAY, Turkey Run Park, McLean
22101.
MANASSAS NATIONAL BATTLEFIELD PARK, P.O. Box 350, Manassas 22110.
PETERSBURG NATIONAL BATTLEFIELD, P.O. Box 549, Petersburg 23803.
PRINCE WILLIAM FOREST PARK, P.O. Box 208, Triangle 22172.
SHENANDOAH NATIONAL PARK, Route 4, Box 292, Luray 22835.

State Trails:
COMMONWEALTH OF VIRGINIA, Department of Conservation and Economic
Development, Division of Parks, 1201 State Office Building, Capitol
Square, Richmond 23219.

Organizations:
MT. ROGERS APPALACHIAN TRAIL CLUB, 29 Shadow Grove Circle, Bristol
24201.
NATURAL BRIDGE APPALACHIAN TRAIL CLUB, P.O. Box 32, Madison
Heights 24572.

OLD DOMINION APPALACHIAN TRAIL CLUB, P.O. Box 25283, Richmond 23260.

ROANOKE APPALACHIAN TRAIL CLUB, 2416 Stanley Avenue, S.E., Roanoke 24014.

SHENANDOAH-ROCKFISH APPALACHIAN TRAIL CLUB, 1520 Mulberry St., Waynesboro 22980.

SIERRA CLUB, Old Dominion Chapter, c/o Fulghum, 13412 Woodbriar Ridge, Midlothian 23113.

TIDEWATER APPALACHIAN TRAIL CLUB, Box 62044, Virginia Beach 23462.

VIRGINIA TECH OUTING CLUB, P.O. Box 459, Blacksburg 24060.

WASHINGTON

National Recreation Trails:

BAYSIDE GREENBELT TRAIL—A 2.5-mile trail that begins near the central business district of Tacoma and runs along a bluff overlooking Commencement Bay and Puget Sound.

DISCOVERY PARK LOOP TRAIL—A 2.8-mile trail in 400-acre Discovery Park in Seattle.

FRED CLEATOR INTERPRETATIVE TRAIL—A 1.3-mile trail in Federation Forest State Park 35 miles from Tacoma and 45 miles from Seattle on old Naches Trail.

ICE CAVES TRAIL—A .9-mile trail that begins at the Big Four Picnic Ground, adjacent to Forest Highway 7, and ends at the Ice Caves at the foot of Big Four Mountain. The trail is in Mount Baker National Forest about 74 miles northeast of Seattle.

LAKE WASHINGTON BICYCLE PATH—A 3.2-mile segment of a longer trail along the west shore of Lake Washington in Seattle.

RAINY LAKE TRAIL—An .8-mile trail that begins at the Rainy Pass Rest Area on State Highway 20 and ends at Rainy Lake in Chelan County. The trail is in the Okanogan National Forest.

National Parks:

LAKE CHELAN NATIONAL RECREATION AREA, 800 State St., Sedro Woolley 98284.

MOUNT RANIER NATIONAL PARK, Tahoma Woods, Star Route, Ashford 98304.

NORTH CASCADES NATIONAL PARK, 800 State St., Sedro Woolley 98284.

OLYMPIC NATIONAL PARK, 600 East Park Ave., Port Angeles 98362.

ROSS LAKE NATIONAL RECREATION AREA, 800 State St., Sedro Woolley 98284.

State Parks:

WASHINGTON STATE PARKS AND RECREATION COMMISSION, Public Information Office, 7150 Clean Water Lane KY-11, Olympia 98504.

Organizations:

KLAHANE CLUB, P.O. Box 494, Port Angeles.

THE MOUNTAINEERS, 719 Pike St., Seattle 98101.
OLYMPIANS, INC., P.O. Box 401, Hoquiam 98550.
SIERRA CLUB, Northwest Office, 4534½ University Way, N.E., Seattle 98105.

WEST VIRGINIA

National Recreation Trails:
THE GENTLE TRAIL—A .4-mile braille trail maintained by the Huntington Galleries in Huntington.

National Parks:
HARPERS FERRY NATIONAL HISTORICAL PARK, P.O. Box 65, Harpers Ferry 25425.

State Trails:
STATE OF WEST VIRGINIA, Department of Natural Resources, Charleston 25305.

Organizations:
BUCKSKIN BOY SCOUT COUNCIL, 1319 Quarrier Street, Charleston 25301.
SIERRA CLUB, Potomac Chapter, c/o Clarke, 402 Burgundy Road, Rockville 20850.
TRI-STATE BOY SCOUT COUNCIL, 733 7th Ave., Huntington 25701.
WEST VIRGINIA HIGHLAND CONSERVANCY, 1605-D Quarrier St., Charleston 25311.
WEST VIRGINIA SCENIC TRAILS ASSOCIATION, P.O. Box 4042, Charleston 25304.
WEST VIRGINIA UNIVERSITY OUTINGS CLUB, West Virginia University, Lair Student Union, Morgantown 26506.

WISCONSIN

National Recreation Trails:
AHNAPEE STATE PARK TRAIL—A 15-mile trail on an abandoned railroad right-of-way in the scenic Door Peninsula in Door County.
ELROY-SPARTA TRAIL—A 30-mile section of the Wisconsin Bikeway that runs along an abandoned railway between Elroy and Sparta.
ICE AGE TRAIL—182.5 miles of this trail have been designated as National Recreation Trails. A 25-mile segment of the trail passes several glacial geological features in the Kettle Moraine State Forest about 40 miles north of Milwaukee. Four other segments of the trail, totaling 39 miles, are located in Langlade County. The 14-mile Chippewa Moraine Segment is in northern Chippewa County and the 9.5-mile Blue Hills Segment is in northwestern Rusk County. Two other segments, totaling 15 miles are in the Marathon County Forest. A 40-mile segment crosses the Medford Ranger District in Chequamegon National Forest.
LAKE PARK BICYCLE TRAIL—A 3.1-mile trail in the Milwaukee area that

swings around Lake Park in a residential area bordering Lake Michigan.
SUGAR RIVER STATE TRAIL—A 23-mile trail on an abandoned railroad
right-of-way in the scenic Sugar River Valley in Greene County about a
half-hour's drive from Madison.

National Parks:
APOSTLE ISLANDS NATIONAL LAKESHORE, Route 1, Box 152, Bayfield
54814.
LOWER ST. CROIX NATIONAL SCENIC RIVER, c/o St. Croix National Scenic
River (Also in Minnesota).
ST. CROIX NATIONAL SCENIC RIVER, P.O. Box 708, St. Croix Falls 54024
(Also in Minnesota).

State Trails:
WISCONSIN DEPARTMENT OF NATURAL RESOURCES, Box 7921, Madison
53707.

Organizations:
THE HOOFERS HIKING CLUB, University of Wisconsin-Madison, Madison
53706.
SIERRA CLUB, John Muir Chapter, 444 W. Main St., Madison 53703.

WYOMING

National Recreation Trails:
GRASSROOTS TRAIL—A .94-mile trail that runs through the center of
Torrington along a greenbelt of mini-parks.
LEE McCUNE BRAILLE TRAIL—A .3-mile braille trail in the Casper Moun-
tain Park near Casper.

National Parks:
DEVILS TOWER NATIONAL MONUMENT, Devils Tower 82714.
FOSSIL BUTTE NATIONAL MONUMENT, P.O. Box 527, Kemmerer 83101.
GRAND TETON NATIONAL PARK, P.O. Box 67, Moose 83012.
JOHN D. ROCKEFELLER, JR., MEMORIAL PARKWAY, c/o Grand Teton Na-
tional Park.
YELLOWSTONE NATIONAL PARK, P.O. Box 168, Yellowstone National
Park, 82190 (Also in Idaho and Montana).

State Trails:
WYOMING RECREATION COMMISSION, Cheyenne 82002.

Organizations:
SIERRA CLUB, Wyoming Chapter, P.O. Box 1595, Cody 82414.
WYOMING OUTDOOR COUNCIL, 202½ S. Second, Laramie 82070.

SOURCE LIST AND OTHER READINGS

Abrams, M.H., ed. *The Norton Anthology of English Literature* (revised). New York: W.W. Norton & Company, Inc., 1968.

Advancedata, ed. "Exercise and Participation in Sports Among Persons 20 Years of Age and Over: United States, 1975." *Advancedata*, March 15, 1978.

American Heart Association. "Heart Facts, 1978." Dallas: American Heart Association.

American Medical Association. *Basic Bodywork . . . For Fitness and Health*. Chicago: American Medical Association.

——. *The ABC's of Perfect Posture*. Chicago: American Medical Association.

Angier, Bradford. *Survival with Style*. New York: Vintage Books, 1974.

Angle, Paul M., ed. *The Lincoln Reader*. New Brunswick, N.J.: Rutgers University Press, 1947.

Baekeland, Frederick. "Exercise Deprivation." *Archives of General Psychiatry*, Vol. 22, April 1970.

Bellow, Saul. *To Jerusalem and Back: A Personal Account*. New York: The Viking Press, 1976.

Berg, Kris. "Exercise Prescription: A Practitioner's View." *The Physician and Sportsmedicine*, February 1978.

Better Homes and Gardens, ed. "What to Do for Your Aching Feet." *Better Homes and Gardens*, September 1977.

Blackburn, Henry. "Role of Exercise in Patients with Coronary Disease." *Geriatrics*, April 1971.

Borland, Hal. "To Own the Streets and Fields." *New York Times*, October 6, 1946.

Boyer, John L. and Kasch, Fred W. "Exercise Therapy in Hypertensive Men." *Journal of the American Medical Association*, March 9, 1970.

Bradbury, Ray. *Fahrenheit 451*. New York: Simon and Schuster, 1967.

————. *Golden Apples of the Sun*. Westport, Conn.: Greenwood 1971.

Brown, James W. " 'Pure' Streams May Cause 'Backpacker's Diarrhea.' " *The Physician and Sportsmedicine*, May 1976.

Burroughs, John. *Winter Sunshine*. Boston and New York: Houghton, Mifflin and Company, 1901.

Caldwell, George S., ed. *Good Old Harry*. New York: Hawthorne Books, Inc., 1966.

Clark, Ronald W. *Instructions to Young Ramblers*. London: Museum Press Limited, 1958.

Colby, C.B. "Join the Backpack Boom?" *Outdoor Life*, Vol. 148:12, October 1971.

Committee on Exercise of the American Heart Association. *Exercise Testing and Training of Apparently Healthy Individuals: A Handbook for Physicians*. Dallas: American Heart Association, 1972.

Cooper, Kenneth H., et. al. "Physical Fitness Levels vs. Selected Coronary Risk Factors." *Journal of the American Medical Association*, Vol. 236, No. 2, July 12, 1976.

————. *The Aerobics Way*. New York: M. Evans and Company, Inc., 1977.

————. "Guidelines in the Management of the Exercising Patient." *Journal of the American Medical Association*, March 9, 1970.

Cooper, Mildred and Cooper, Kenneth H. *Aerobics for Women*. New York: M. Evans and Company, Inc., 1972.

Culliton, Barbara J. "Health Care Economics: The High Cost of Getting Well." *Science*, May 26, 1978.

deVries, Herbert A. "Exercise Intensity Threshold for improvement of Cardiovascular-Respiratory Function in Older Men." *Geriatrics*, April 1971.

————. "Prescription of Exercise for Older Men from Telemetered Exercise Heart Rate Data." *Geriatrics*, April 1971.

————. and Adams, Gene M. "Comparison of Exercise Responses in Old and Young Men." *Journal of Gerontology*, Vol. 27, No. 3, 1972.

————. and Adams, Gene M. "Electromyographic Comparison of Single Doses of Exercise and Meprobamate as to Effects on Muscular Relaxation." *American Journal of Physical Medicine*, Vol. 51, No. 3, 1972.

Drinkwater, Barbara L., et. al. "Aerobic Power of Females, Ages 10 to 68." *Journal of Gerontology*, Vol. 30, No. 4, November 4, 1975.

Durnin, J.V.G.A., et. al. "Effects of Short Period of Training of Varying

Severity on Some Measurements of Physical Fitness." *Journal of Applied Physiology*, January 1960.

Edington, Dee W., et. al. "Exercise and Longevity: Evidence for a Threshold Age." *Journal of Gerontology*, Vol. 27, No. 3, 1972.

Elman, Robert. *The Hiker's Bible*. Garden City, N.Y.: Doubleday and Company, Inc., 1973.

Erdelyi, G.J. "Effects of Exercise on the Menstrual Cycle." *The Physician and Sportsmedicine*, March 1976.

Executive Health, ed. "On Walking . . . Nature's Own Amazing 'Anti-Age Anti-Biotic.' " *Executive Health*, Vol. 14, No. 10, July 1978.

Fanning, Tony and Fanning, Robbie. *Keep Running*. New York: Simon and Schuster, 1978.

Finley, John. "Traveling Afoot." In Mitchell, Edwin V., ed., *The Art of Walking*. New York: Loring and Mussey, 1934.

Fixx, James F. *The Complete Book of Running*. New York: Random House, Inc., 1977.

Flanagan, John T. *Profile of Vachel Lindsay*. Columbus, Ohio: Charles E. Merrill Publishing Company, 1970.

Fletcher, Colin. *The Man Who Walked through Time*. New York: Vintage Books, 1972.

———. *The New Complete Walker*. New York: Alfred A. Knopf, 1978.

Ford, Norman D. "The Wonderful World of Walking." *Retirement Living*, July 1974.

Frank, Charles W. "The Course of Coronary Heart Disease: Factors Relating to Prognosis." *Bulletin of the New York Academy of Medicine*, August 1968.

Friedman, Meyer and Rosenman, Ray H. *Type A Behavior and Your Heart*. New York: Alfred A. Knopf, 1974.

Galub, Jack. "Walking: The Most Obvious and Natural Sport." *Glamour*, June 1978.

Getchell, Leroy H. "Energy Cost of Playing Golf." *Archives of Physical Medicine and Rehabilitation*, January 1968.

Gilbert, Douglas and Kilby, Clyde S. *C.S. Lewis: Images of His World*. Grand Rapids, Mich.: William B. Eerdmans Publishing Company, 1973.

Glasser, William. *Positive Addiction*. New York: Harper and Row, 1976.

Graham, M.F. *Prescription for Life*. New York: David McKay, 1966.

Graham, Stephen. *In Quest of El Dorado*. New York: D. Appleton & Company, 1923.

Gross, Jane. "Blue-Collar Walker." *Sports Illustrated*, November 23, 1970.

Gsell, Daniela and Mayer, Jean. "Low Blood Cholesterol Associated with

High Calorie, High Saturated Fat Intakes in a Swiss Alpine Village Population." *American Journal of Clinical Nutrition*, June 1962.

Guild, Warren R. *How to Keep Fit and Enjoy It*. New York: Harper and Brothers, 1962.

Gwinup, Grant. "Effect of Exercise Alone on the Weight of Obese Women." *Archives of Internal Medicine*, May 1975.

———. "Walking: The One Exercise that Does Everything." *Harper's Bazaar*, May 1976.

Haddon, E.P. "Take the Whole Family on a Wilderness Escape." *Today's Health*, August 1970.

Hart, John. *Walking Softly in the Wilderness: The Sierra Club Guide to Backpacking*. San Francisco: Sierra Club Books, 1977.

Heinzelmann, Fred and Bagley, Richard W. "Response to Physical Activity Programs and Their Effects on Health Behavior." *Public Health Reports*, October 1970.

Higdon, Hal, ed. *The Complete Diet Guide for Runners and Other Athletes*. Mountain View, Calif.: World Publications, 1978.

———. "Creepers, Floaters and Squirmers." *Sports Illustrated*, April 27, 1970.

Hlavac, Harry F. *The Foot Book*. Mountain View, Calif.: World Publications, 1977.

Hoagland, Edward. *Red Wolves and Black Bears*. New York: Random House, Inc., 1972.

———. *Walking the Dead Diamond River*, New York: Warner Books, Inc., 1974.

Howorth, M. Beckett. "The Art and Technique of Walking." *Consumer Bulletin*, April 1973.

Huizinga, Johan. *Homo Ludens: A Study of the Play Element in Culture*. Boston: Beacon Press.

Human Behavior, ed. "The Telltale Walk." *Human Behavior*, May 1978.

Ingraham, Mike. "What Sort of Man Competes in the Olympics?"*Columbia Missourian*, June 25, 1972.

Jessup, Elon. *A Manual of Walking*. New York: E.P. Dutton and Company, Inc., 1936.

Johnson, Harry J. *Eat, Drink, Be Merry and Live Longer*. Garden City, N.Y.: Doubleday and Company, Inc., 1968.

———. and Bass, Ralph. *Creative Walking for Physical Fitness*. New York: Grosset and Dunlap, 1970.

Kahn, Fredrick H. and Visscher, Barbara R. "Water Disinfection in the Wilderness." *The Western Journal of Medicine*, May 1975.

Kasch, Fred W. "The Effects of Exercise on the Aging Process." *The Physician and Sportsmedicine,* June 1976.

Kazin, Alfred. *A Walker in the City.* New York: Harcourt, Brace & World, Inc., 1951.

Kjellstrom, Bjorn. *Be Expert with Map and Compass.* New York: Charles Scribner's Sons, 1976.

Koepke, Keith R. and Luria, Myron H. "Physical Conditioning in Medical Personnel." *Archives of Internal Medicine,* Vol. 130, September 1972.

Kowinski, William Severini. "The Malling of America." *New Times,* May 1, 1978.

Kraus, Hans. *Clinical Treatment of Back and Neck Pain.* New York: McGraw-Hill, 1970.

———. "Reconditioning Aging Muscles." *Geriatrics,* June 1978.

Kuntzleman, Charles T., et. al. *Rating the Exercises.* New York: William Morrow and Company, Inc., 1978.

Laird, Ron. *Competitive Race Walking.* Los Altos, Calif.: Tafnews Press, 1972.

Lamon, Ward Hill. *The Life of Abraham Lincoln: From His Birth to His Inauguration.* Boston: Osgood & Co., 1872.

Lathrop, Theodore G. *Hypothermia: Killer of the Unprepared.* Portland, Ore.: The Mazamas, 1975.

Leaf, Alexander. "On the Physical Fitness of Men Who Live to a Great Age." *Executive Health,* Vol. 13, No. 11, August 1977.

Lewis, C.S. *Out of the Silent Planet.* New York: The MacMillan Company, 1964.

Lindsay, Vachel. *Adventures While Preaching the Gospel of Beauty.* New York: Mitchell Kennerley, 1914.

Lindstrom, Aletha. "A Sport for All Seasons." *Parents Magazine,* August 1969.

Look, Dennis. *Joy of Backpacking: People's Guide to the Wilderness.* Sacramento, Calif.: Jalmar Press, Inc., 1976.

Luria, Myron H., and Koepke, Keith R. "The Physical Conditioning Effects of Walking." *Journal of Sports Medicine and Physical Fitness,* September 1975.

Mandel, Paul. "The Most Walkable City in the World." *Holiday,* March 1968.

Manning, Harvey. *Backpacking: One Step at a Time.* New York: Random House, 1973.

Mayer, Jean. *A Diet for Living.* New York: David McKay, 1975.

———. et. al. "Relation between Caloric Intake, Body Weight and Physical

Work." *The American Journal of Clinical Nutrition*, March-April 1956.

McDermott, Barry. "Going Through Life at a Walk." *Sports Illustrated*, May 8, 1978.

Michener, James A. *Sports in America*. New York: Random House, 1976.

Mitchell, Edwin Valentine, ed. *The Art of Walking*. New York: Loring and Mussey, 1934.

Morley, Christopher. *Essays*. New York: J.B. Lippincott Company.

————. *Travels in Philadelphia*. New York: David McKay.

Morris, J.N., et. al. "Coronary Heart Disease and Physical Activity of Work." *The Lancet*, November 21, 1953.

————. "Vigorous Exercise in Leisure Time and the Incidence of Coronary Heart Disease." *The Lancet*, February 17, 1973.

Muir, John. *John of the Mountains*. Boston: Houghton Mifflin Company, 1938.

————. *South of Yosemite: Selected Writings of John Muir*. Garden City, N.Y.: Natural History Press, 1968.

Mumford, Lewis. *The Highway and the City*. New York: Harcourt, Brace & World, 1963.

Myers, Clayton R. *The Official YMCA Physical Fitness Handbook*. New York: Popular Library, 1975.

Nabokov, Vladimir. *Speak, Memory*. New York: Putnam, 1966.

Napier, John. "The Antiquity of Human Walking." *Scientific American*, April 1967.

Naughton, James M. "Crowds Delighted as Carters Shun Limousine and Walk to New Home." *New York Times*, January 20, 1977.

Netherby, Steve. "The Way to the Top." *Field and Stream*, February 1976.

New York State Journal of Medicine, ed. "Cornell Conferences on Therapy." *New York State Journal of Medicine*, January 1, 1958.

Osler, Tom. *Serious Runner's Handook*. Mountain View, Calif.: World Publications, Inc., 1978.

Paffenberger, Ralph S., Jr., and Hale, Wayne E. "Work Activity and Coronary Heart Mortality." *The New England Journal of Medicine*, March 13, 1975.

Page, Louise and Raper, Nancy. *Food and Your Weight*. Washington, D.C.: U.S. Government Printing Office, 1977.

Parfit, Michael. "The Road Less Traveled." *New York Times Magazine*, July 27, 1976.

Passmore, R., and Durnin, J.V.G.A. "Human Energy Expenditure." *Physiological Reviews*, October 1955.

Peattie, Donald Culross. "The Joy of Walking." *New York Times Magazine*, April 5, 1942.

Physician and Sportsmedicine, ed. "Drivers and Joggers Collide Over Safety." *The Physician and Sportsmedicine*, May 1978.

————. "Exercise for Elderly Is Conference Topic." *The Physician and Sportsmedicine,* January 1978.

————. "Overcoming Overprotection of the Elderly." *The Physician and Sportsmedicine,* June 1976.

Pollock, Michael L., et. al. "Effects of Walking on Body Composition and Cardiovascular Function of Middle-Aged Men." *Journal of Applied Physiology,* January 1971.

————. "How Much Exercise Is Enough?" *The Physician and Sportsmedicine,* June 1978.

Powell, R.R. "Effects of Exercise on Mental Functioning." *Journal of Sports Medicine and Physical Fitness,* Vol. 15, 1975.

President's Council on Physical Fitness and Sports and the Administration on Aging, ed. *The Fitness Challenge . . . In the Later Years.* Washington, D.C.: U.S. Government Printing Office.

————. *Adult Physical Fitness.* Washington, D.C.: U.S. Government Printing Office.

Profant, Gene R. "Responses to Maximal Exercise in Healthy Middle-aged Women." *Journal of Applied Physiology,* November 1972.

Rossi, Frank. "Larry Young: A Man of a Different Mold." *Columbia Tribune,* September 2, 1978.

Rudow, Martin. *Race Walking.* Mountain View, Calif.: World Publications, 1975.

Ryan, Allan J. "Sports Medicine Today." *Science,* May 26, 1978.

Schwenke, Karl. "Loning It Is the Only Way." *Field and Stream,* July 1969.

Science Digest, ed. "City Pace vs. Country Stroll." *Science Digest,* June 1976.

————. "Mechanics of Hip Swinging." *Science Digest,* February 1970.

Sheehan, George A. *Dr. Sheehan on Running.* New York: Bantam Books, 1978.

Shephard, Roy J. *Alive Man: The Physiology of Physical Activity.* Springfield, Ill.: Charles C. Thomas, 1972.

————. and Kavanagh, Terence. "What Exercise to Prescribe for the Post-MI Patient." *The Physician and Sportsmedicine,* August 1975.

Shock, Nathan W. "The Physiology of Aging." *Scientific American,* January 1962.

Snider, Arthur J. "Step to Catastrophe." *Science Digest,* November 1967.

Starnes, Richard. "Trouble Afoot." *Field and Stream,* March 1971.

Stephen, Leslie. *Studies of a Biographer.* New York: G.P. Putnam's Sons.

Stoddard, Charles Coleman. *Shanks' Mare.* New York: George H. Doran Company, 1924.

Stoneback, Thomas. "Walk Like You're Wearing a Crown." *Prevention,* September 1978.

Sunset, ed. "Backpacking with Young Children?" *Sunset,* February 1971.

Sussman, Aaron and Goode, Ruth. *The Magic of Walking*. New York: Simon and Schuster, 1967.

Teale, Edwin Way. *The American Seasons*. New York: Dodd, Mead & Company, 1976.

———. *Autumn Across America*. New York: Dodd, Mead & Company, 1956.

———. *Circle of the Seasons*. New York: Dodd, Mead & Company, 1953.

———. *Days Without Time: Adventures of a Naturalist*. New York: Dodd, Mead & Company, 1948.

———. *Green Treasury*. New York: Dodd, Mead & Company, 1952.

———. *The Lost Woods*. New York: Dodd, Mead & Company, 1945.

Thoreau, Henry David. *Cape Cod*. New York: Thomas Y. Crowell, 1961.

———. *Excursions*. Gloucester, Mass.: Peter Smith.

Time, ed. "Anti-Hero's Welcome." *Time*, October 14, 1974.

———. "Hit the Road, Jack." *Time*, February 22, 1963.

Trent, George D., ed. *The Gentle Art of Walking: A Compilation from the New York Times*. New York: Arno Press/Random House, 1971.

Trevelyan, George Macauley. *Clio, a Muse and Other Essays Literary and Pedestrian*. Folcroft, Pa.: Folcroft Library Editions, 1973.

Truman, Harry S. *Mr. Citizen*. New York: Bernard Geis Associates, 1953.

Tuttle, Russell H. "Knuckle-Walking and the Problem of Human Origins." *Science*, Vol. 166, No. 3908, November 21, 1969.

Verschoth, Anita. "Long Day's Journey into Night." *Sports Illustrated*, October 18, 1978.

Vogt, Bill. *How to Build a Better Outdoors*. New York: David McKay Company, Inc., 1978.

Walker, David. "Mother Nature vs. Juvenile Delinquency." *Field and Stream*, March 1969.

Walsh, John. "Federal Health Spending Passes the $50 Billion Mark." *Science*, May 26, 1978.

Wojcik, Sig. "Back Packing for Pleasure—Think Light." *The Conservationist*, June-July 1970.

Wolfram, Gerry. *Walk into Winter*. New York: Charles Scribner's Sons, 1977.

Young, Elisabeth Larsh. *Family Afoot*. Ames, Iowa: Iowa State University Press, 1978.

Zelqzo, Philip R., et. al. "Walking in the Newborn." *Science*, April 21, 1972.

Zuti, W.B., and Golding, L.A. "Comparing Diet and Exercise as Weight Reduction Tools." *The Physician and Sportsmedicine*, January 1976.